Whatever Happened to
PLANNING?

Peter Ambrose

Methuen
London and New York

For Marilyn

First published in 1986 by
Methuen & Co. Ltd
11 New Fetter Lane, London EC4P 4EE

Published in the USA by
Methuen & Co.
in association with Methuen, Inc.
29 West 35th Street, New York NY 10001

Typeset by AKM Associates (UK) Ltd,
Ajmal House, Hayes Road, Southall, Greater London
Printed in Great Britain
at the University Press, Cambridge

British Library Cataloguing in Publication Data
Ambrose, Peter
    Whatever happened to planning?
    1. Land use – Great Britain – Planning
    I. Title
    333.73′0941   HD596

    ISBN 0 416 37100 0
         0 416 37110 8 Pbk

Library of Congress Cataloging in Publication Data
Ambrose, Peter J.
    Whatever happened to planning.
    Bibliography: p.
    Includes index.
    1. Land use – Government policy – Great Britain.   2. Real
    estate development – Government policy – Great Britain.
    3. Regional planning – Great Britain.   I. Title.
    HD596.A43   1986   333.73′17′0941   86-12415

    ISBN 0 416 37100 0
         0 416 37110 8 (pbk.)

Whatever

ontents

Preface

Why write another book about planning? Certainly not to add to the literature on the evolution of planning legislation in Britain. For this, refer to Ashworth (1954), Cherry (1974), Hall (1974), Cullingworth (1975) or Ratcliffe (1981). Nor to compare the move towards planning in Britain with the experience in similar advanced countries. For this, try Sutcliffe (1981). Nor to build on the critical theory developed by Lefebvre, Castells (1978) and Harvey (1982), among others, and usefully summarized by such as Kirk (1980) and extended by Cooke (1983). Nor to bring together the wisdom of a number of commentators in a set of readings. Dear and Scott (1981), Paris (1982) and Barrett and Healey (1985) do this very well. No, the main reason for writing is to assess how a set of basically generous and rational intentions, the product of a postwar period of collective idealism, is making out in an increasingly cynical and individualistic political climate. More specifically the intention is to see how the set of regulatory devices built into the 1947 planning system, which was devised in the context of the 1930s era of land development, is coping with the forces now at work in the development industry – an industry advanced in its use of management techniques and political lobbying and increasingly international in its structure, organization and access to funds.

The urge to fashion a better built environment and produce a more orderly relationship between houses, workplaces, services and recreational facilities grew as a direct response to the demonstrable horrors of the nineteenth-century industrial city. By the early twentieth century a loose consensus had grown up that some control should be exerted on the hitherto purely private sector business of land development. Uncontrolled growth had produced dangerously poor public health conditions affecting the capability of many of the lower orders to work and fight to defend the Empire. The overcrowded rookeries of London and the other large cities were likely seedbeds for radical dissent and destabilizing action. The visual monotony of much of the lower-quality housing and the threat to the countryside posed by chaotic urban sprawl alarmed those with a sensitivity to environmental aesthetics. In addition, in an age when public morality still counted for something, many were shocked at the existence of grinding poverty at the heart of the world's richest empire.

The consensus for some form of intervention, while based on a variety of motives, therefore included reformist politicians, captains of industry such as Cadbury and Lever, social visionaries such as Howard, academics such as Geddes and numerous churchmen. Those more politically aware or technically informed clearly saw that intervention to regulate the land development market would not be easily achieved since the interests who were likely to be offended enjoyed immense economic power and political influence. Nevertheless it was obvious by the outbreak of the First World War that some attempt should, and would, be made. In fact the first modest town planning act was passed in 1909. Its main purpose was to influence the process of suburbanization by which, it was expected, the ills of the congested city centres were to be cured (Ashworth, 1954). Given the crisis-ridden nature of the interwar period, the politics of Ramsay MacDonald and the growing preoccupation with the rise of fascism in Europe in the latter 1930s, it is not surprising that the emergence of mandatory legislation regulating land development was delayed until the advent of the 1945 Labour government. During the interwar decades the cities sprawled still further, the bypasses and arterial roads neutralized enormous areas of farmland and a large proportion of middle-income people became owner-occupiers – cosily co-opted into a system that produced a good environment for them, excellent profits for the volume housebuilders and continuing neglect of the festering inner cities. Whatever the mix of self-interest and altruism in the long line of reformers from Robert Owen to Patrick Abercrombie, the 1946–7 legislation covering new towns and planning looks, in retrospect, a generous and genuine attempt to cure some of the ills produced by a century of rapid urbanization and to ensure better living conditions for all.

The Guardian, 14.12.85

PM VETOES RATE HELP FOR POOREST PENSIONERS

By David Hencke, Social Services Correspondent

The Prime Minister has vetoed proposals to exempt two million of the poorest pensioners from paying 20 per cent of their rates bill under the social security changes.

The last-minute change to the white paper is a further blow to Mr Norman Fowler, the Social Services Secretary.

It is understood that the Cabinet, at Mrs Thatcher's insistence, threw out the extra concessions to pensioners in the draft white paper on the grounds that Mr Fowler had contradicted himself by putting them forward in the first place.

The rigid orthodoxies of the 'new right'

Now, forty years on, we live in different and meaner times. As the capitalist crisis has deepened since the early 1970s the Keynesian philosophy of a public sector led recovery has been supplanted by the rigid orthodoxies of the 'new right'. In Britain, under direct pressure from the IMF, the contraction in the finances, and therefore the power, of the public sector began in the mid-1970s. The move towards economic management by market forces rather than democratic agencies would probably have stayed somewhere within the expected range in British politics had it not been for the advent of brutalist politics in the shape of the Thatcher government, with its explicit commitment to deregulation and market-based solutions to virtually all problems. The effects have been grievously divisive. Unemployment, or the possibility of it, has affected the security of perhaps half the households in the country. Changes in the tax and social security systems have been geared to increasing the differences between rich and poor. The public sector, and especially those parts of it which grew up to achieve a progressive redistribution of health care, education and welfare, has been partially dismantled by a government whose members, overwhelmingly, use private sector agencies for their own needs. The cynicism that has encouraged massive pay rises for high-earners and denied, on the personal insistence of the Prime Minister, a minor rates concession to 2 million poor pensioners has produced unease in the minds of air marshals, judges and even captains of industry. It has registered also in the consciousness of residents in many inner city areas and blighted estates. They have taken to the streets in a score of well-publicized 'riots'. The response of government has been typically dishonest: public holier-than-thou statements about law and order but panic measures behind the scenes to restore some of the financial resources whose removal has led to the problems.

In the areas of policy dealt with in this book, events have taken a bizarre turn and the planning consensus has been seriously undermined (see Cooke 1983, chapter 4). The country is polarized, economically, socially and regionally, as never before since the 1930s, or perhaps since Disraeli wrote of the Two Englands more than a century ago. The housing problem is quite out of control. The planning of a large area of inner London docklands has been removed from local democratic accountability altogether. One result is that developments such as the massive £1.5 billion Canary Wharf scheme, which will amount to the largest finance/commercial complex in Europe, can apparently go ahead without any meaningful consultation with either the national architecture and conservation monitoring bodies or, more important, with local residents. Such a possibility finally buries the postwar understanding that there should be some form of local citizen participation in the regulation of development. But this government has no time for the 'equal citizen' concept; apparently the people who live in docklands are not their sort.

Before 1979, some of the unease about these matters would have surfaced in the gentlemanly and well-researched form of a Royal Commission or government committee report. The Thatcher government does not welcome such possible sources of implicit criticism and it has rejected calls for official inquiries wherever possible. Private 'Royal Commissions' have consequently been initiated by concerned members of the establishment. The Duke of Edinburgh chaired a review of housing policy instigated by the British Federation of Housing Societies, and the Archbishop of Canterbury's Commission on Urban Priority Areas produced a comprehensive analysis of the ways that government urban policy has consistently helped the rich at the expense of the poor. The response of members of the government to the latter report was predictable; some patronized it by implying the authors did not understand the 'real world' (there were actually some very worldly academics among them), some urged the churchmen to devote their time to filling their churches, while others branded the report as

The Guardian, 20.12.85

HOUSING PROBLEM OUT OF CONTROL

GEOFF ANDREWS ON THE HELPLESSNESS OF MANY LOCAL AUTHORITIES FACED WITH A PROGRESSIVELY DETERIORATING STOCK

The size of the Housing Investment Programme bids put in by some of the worst affected local authorities show that the problem in both the public and private sectors is now almost beyond solution in the short term.

Leicester has almost 5,000 unfit homes, more than 7,000 without inside toilets and baths, 33,000 others in need of repair, and 10,625 households on the waiting list, of whom 6,578 are in urgent housing need. The council claims that in real terms it can now only invest £3 for every £10 it spent on housing in 1979/80.

Manchester, with serious tower block problems, estimates that it would cost £600 million to get itself out of trouble, including a £90 million demolition programme, £150 million for dealing with known failures in low-rise blocks, and £100 million for replacing antiquated heating systems.

The city has 37,000 on the waiting list and nearly 5,000 homeless households. This year it received only £36 million from the programme.

The London borough of Camden, with one of the highest rates of homelessness in the country, was allocated £27 million last year, after bidding for £78 million.

In this year's bid it included the need to address a £34 million repairs bill on work already begun, and £8.8 million for repairs it is obliged to carry out by law. More than £200 million was needed for urgent structural repairs in council homes.

Mrs Sandy Wynn, chairwoman of Camden's housing development committee, said that the council owned land on which they wanted to build but the Government would not give them the cash to start.

The London borough of Haringey sought £65 million and got nearly £26 million last year. It needed well over £200 million for its public sector housing, while its investment had been cut by 50 per cent in real terms since 1979.

The cuts have led to longer waiting lists and more homelessness. In the private sector more than a third of houses are officially sub-standard. Last year only 28 council houses were started, an all-time low, with a further 116 from the private sector.

Housing requires massive new investment to put right rapidly worsening living conditions.

'Marxist'. The Duke of Edinburgh's report was received somewhat less critically due to protocol and Tory good breeding.

How, then, is the basically altruistic notion of planning surviving

Construction News, 5.12.85

DUKE ATTACKS HOUSING POLICY

The Duke of Edinburgh fiercely attacked the Government's housing policy in a private meeting involving senior industry and union figures at NEDO.

Using what seems like family terminology for abuse he described Government housing policy as a "carbuncle". He further criticised the Government's "knee-jerk response" to the inquiry into British housing which he chaired and which reported results earlier this year.

Specifically he argued that mortgage interest relief should be phased out over a 10-year period and that councils should be allowed to spend more of their capital receipts.

However, sources at the meeting say the Duke was irritated at what he felt was a "knee jerk political response" to the inquiry into housing.

He argued that there were major problems in housing which were being exacerbated by a "massive lack of investment" about which "we see no prospect for change".

Housing policy reviews have called for the phased removal of the owner-occupier subsidy – a government 'sacred cow'.

under a small-minded government to whom the whole idea of collective caring and shared social responsibility is anathema? This book seeks to provide some kind of an answer. The design is simple. Part I discusses the particular ways in which money is made under capitalist forms of land development, identifies the interests involved prior to 1939 and deals, in Chapter 2, with the emergence of the 1947 planning system. In Part II planning as a force is related to the other main forces at work in the 'development system' – that is to say the population at large (Chapter 3), financial institutions (Chapter 4), the state (Chapter 5) and the construction industry (Chapter 6). Part III consists of two chapters, each dealing with the development system in operation in a key 'arena': Chapter 7 deals with 'greenfield' areas on the periphery of major settlements, and Chapter 8 with London's docklands. Part IV attempts an overall evaluation of the effects of the 1947 planning system and identifies what might be some politically realistic ways forward.

The book is written from a viewpoint basically sympathetic to the notion of collective and democratically based regulation of land development and in this sense, in the context of Britain, it comes from somewhere left of centre. But hopefully it is not doctrinaire. We live in a largely capitalistic economy and it is pointless to write as if truly socialist solutions were possible. In fact one point of the book is to show that the retreat from the 1941–2 proposals to control land development occurred precisely because they were, more or less, socialist in nature. The offer of postwar regulation of the reconstruction process formed part of a loose 'contract' worked out at a time when offers needed to be placed on the table to boost morale and contain dissent. It was a question of national survival. Once Britain clearly *had* survived, there began a steady retraction of the offer under pressure from historic landed, and other develop-ment, interests. This began several years before the 1947 Town and Country Planning Act was even on the statute-book. Unfortunately there is plenty of evidence that in the general consciousness, and perhaps within the profession itself, the true balance of power in the land development process has not been grasped. Many people believe that planners actually command and allocate resources in some decisive way. Certainly, and in this case understandably, many applicants to read urban studies at my own university think so as they seek to enter a profession which, they hope, can help solve some of the grave problems facing Britain. It is for them as well as for planning committee members, community activists, students of disciplines related to urban development and concerned members of the public – in fact anyone with his or her ideals still reasonably intact – that this book is written.

Acknowledgements

During my years teaching Urban Studies at the University of Sussex I have been fortunate to be part of a large, friendly and very talented group of urban and regional analysts. I have taught with, listened to and discussed ideas with (in alphabetical order, which seems the only way) Jenny Backwell, James Barlow, Mark Bhatti, Alan Cawson, John Dearlove, Peter Dickens, Simon Duncan, Mick Dunford, Tony Fielding, Fred Gray, David Klausner, Kevin Morgan, Pete Saunders, Mike Savage, Andrew Sayer, Ian Winter, and others. None of them bears any direct responsibility for the contents, but there is something of each of them in the final product.

To venture into print requires also other forms of inspiration. In a marvellous book Maynard Solomon wrote:

> if we lose our awareness of the transcendent realms of play, beauty and brotherhood which are portrayed in the great affirmative works of our culture, if we lose the dream of the Ninth Symphony, there is nothing to counterpoise against the engulfing terrors of civilisation .... Masterpieces of art are instilled with a surplus of constantly renewable energy – an energy which provides a motive force for changes in the relations between human beings. (Solomon, 1980)

As sources of motivating energy and visions of a better social order, I owe most to two great commentators on the human condition, fellow Rhinelanders and radicals, L.v.B. and K.M.

The author and the publishers would like to thank the following for their kind permission to reproduce copyright material:

GLC Record Office and Library for Figure 1.1
Aerofilms Ltd for Figure 1.3
Jonathan Buckmaster for Figure 1.5
Humphrey Spender for Figures 2.1 and 2.2
Syndication International Ltd for Figure 2.4
Topham Picture Library for Figure 2.5
HMSO for Figure 2.6
East Sussex County Council for Figure 2.7
Blackfriars Photographic Project for Figure 3.1
Docklands Community Poster Project for Figure 3.2
Local Authorities' Property Fund for Figure 4.2
Royal Life for Figure 4.3
Birmingham Public Libraries for Figure 5.1
Lambeth Borough Public Relations Office for Figure 5.5
Legal and General Group PLC for Figure 5.6
Construction News for Figure 6.5
Department of Trade and Industry for Figure 6.8
The House Builders' Federation for Figure 7.3
The Guardian for Figure 8.6
Mike Mosedale for the cartoon on p. 252
Simon Duncan for Figure 9.3

PART I
The historical context

Land development and the state

Land development is as old as civilization itself. It involves raising money to bring together land, labour, materials and expertise so as to produce a building – which might be anything from a pyramid to a tower block. An initiator or promoter is required to get things moving. This person may or may not be the owner or user of the building, but will invariably have promoted the operation for a return of some kind either in terms of profit, personal utility or prestige. In principle the activity has changed very little in thousands of years – and the same applies to some of the production methods with which it is carried out. In fact it is perhaps the only industry where some products several thousand years old are as good as or better than those made today.

The development of land for profit is simply a special case of the general process by which entrepreneurs seek to accumulate wealth by involvement in a production cycle. This is shown as a simple chain of conversions:

$$M \longrightarrow C \longrightarrow C^1 \longrightarrow M^1$$

M	C	C^1	M^1
(an initial stock of money is committed)	*(commodities are purchased to carry out the production)*	*(a product results from the production process)*	*(the value of the product is realized on the market)*

For the operation to be justified, M^1 must be greater than M since the value $M^1 - M$ is the new capital accumulated (a negative value here clearly means a loss). The surplus or profit may be kept by the owner of M or ploughed back to start another production circle or paid to the state as tax – normally it is split between these three.

The precise way in which it is split, and the price paid by the entrepreneur for the various commodities C (which usually includes labour), more or less defines what much of domestic politics is about.

Accumulation by means of this production cycle proceeds most surely and effectively when the various elements in the chain have certain characteristics. It often helps, for example, if M is not all owned by the entrepreneur, but is to some extent borrowed. Interest must, of course, be paid but the size of the operation can be enlarged. It is advantageous also if the operation $C \longrightarrow C^1$ is complex and difficult for the general public to understand in any detail. This reduces the political risk which might otherwise arise should M^1 be generally seen to be 'unfairly' greater than M. As a related point, the less labour involved in the $C \longrightarrow C^1$ process (and the less well organized that labour), the less is the risk that industrial militancy will reduce the rate of accumulation. Perhaps most important of all, the long-term success of the accumulation process depends on the nature of C^1, the commodity produced and sold. If this commodity is required by everybody, and thus cannot be substituted by another, and if powerful interests such as governments are concerned for their own reasons that enough of C^1 is available, then the success of the enterprise is more assured because it will tend to be underwritten in some way by these interests.

There are three commodities which are, by their nature, non-substitutable: food, clothes and shelter. Our concern here is with the provision of shelter, in other words, the provision of new or renewed built environment. This always requires land and at some point involves the conversion of this land from one use to another. It is therefore worthwhile to relate the general capital accumulation process outlined above to the specific circumstances of land development. This will help to show why property has always been such a fruitful area for investment. We will therefore substitute 'new built environment' for C^1 in the chain.

The production of buildings, more than that of most commodities, requires considerable capital, or M, to be found at the outset of the operation. The realization of M^1 may then take, typically, either up to one year or perhaps fifty or more years depending upon the *mode* of accumulation, as we shall see later. This requirement for 'front end' capital has meant that long ago it became common practice to develop buildings using someone else's money. This process has been fostered by the device of offering the building itself as security for the loan. It is probably true to say that most buildings are, or have been, subject to a mortgage agreement. Thus the land development industry, perhaps more than any other, has operated very largely on borrowed money. In fact the history of property development is full of cases where millions have been made on only a few thousand pounds of own account capital (balanced, it is fair to say, by many spectacular crashes due to over-borrowing).

Another factor safeguarding the rate of capital accumulation via land development lies in the complexity of the $C \longrightarrow C^1$ transformation. Although when considering the production of, say, ballpoint pens or video recorders the details of production may remain a mystery, the general principles are clear enough. Materials, labour and finance are combined and profit results if the product's final selling price exceeds the total cost of the inputs. This general principle also applies to property, but with several important complications. There are often speculative profits to be made from one of the inputs (land) before ever the final combination of elements and sale of the product occurs. The products of land development are durable and continue to yield a profit in one of a number of forms even *after* the title has passed to the user. In addition to these special features, making profits from property requires very little labour or work space, but much ingenuity and capacity to take large-scale risk. The business is volatile in the short term. Vast empires can quickly be built up on paper but sudden changes in such uncontrollable factors as interest rates or government fiscal policies can wipe out the paper profits. Buildings themselves are solid enough (or should be) but their value can be truly tested only when they change hands. Any sudden concerted drive to sell them can itself cause their value to collapse.

All these complications are fully understood by only a tiny handful of people. Few of them are in political office; if so, they are usually there to defend property interests. Nearly all *users* of the built environment, the rest of us, also find the $C^1 \longrightarrow M^1$ conversion (with its valuation procedures, reverse yield gaps, reversionary interests, sale and leaseback arrangements, etc.) totally incomprehensible. The property industry is, in short, almost impossible to organize *against* both from outside (because of the technical complexities) and from inside (because so little permanently employed labour is involved in the $C \longrightarrow C^1$ transition). This point is germane to the events of 1940–7, to be discussed later. For the moment we need to consider the $C^1 \longrightarrow M^1$ stage and distinguish the two quite distinct forms of realization.

From the point of view of the user, payment for the use of a building (of whatever kind) can take one of two general forms. Either a lump sum is paid and the user acquires a freehold right of ownership and disposal as well as a right of use. Or periodic payments can be made for use only (probably with an agreement as to the length of the arrangement). Payments of either type can be made for almost any use. Thus, given sufficient resources, we can either rent or buy a house, a factory, a shop or an office, although it is, of course, true to say that in Britain most homes are purchased and most business premises are rented. But it is very important to later arguments in this book to turn the picture around and to understand land development profit-making *from the point of view of the private sector providers*, not the users. To these interests there are two possible routes to capital accumulation. The first involves buildings that are constructed or acquired for renting. These buildings constitute a continuing *investment*, similar in nature to an investment in stocks or commodities. Profit lies in ensuring that the total annual stream of income from such a building exceeds the total annual outgoings, including interest on the money tied up in its construction. This is true regardless of the use to which the building is put (it might, for example, be for residential, recreational or business use).

By contrast, a building that is constructed and then sold with freehold land to the user is not an investment – its disposal is a once-for-all operation. The profit lies in ensuring that the lump sum received exceeds the total cost of the production inputs. The gain, if it occurs, is a *production* gain. This is quite different from the *investment* gain which can be derived from a property let out to tenants. Since the dynamics of the two types of development, the mode of realization in the $C^1 \longrightarrow M^1$ transition and the *speed* of this realization are quite different, the two forms of development need to be analysed, and politically regulated, quite differently. But *the planning system does not do this*. In fact the very significant political point about the way in which land use planning evolved in Britain is precisely that all its categories, all its legislation and all its regulatory mechanisms are related to the *uses* to which land is put and not to the mode of value realization (investment vs production gain) that forms the mainspring of the development process. Formally it even fails to recognize that two different modes exist. We shall return later to some of the implications of this failure.

Two main forms of profit-making from land development have so far been identified: streams of revenue and production gains following a freehold sale. (It should, in passing, be noted that the latter type of gain can, and usually does, also occur on the sale of a building that had been held for revenue.) The third main form of profit occurs after the $C^1 \longrightarrow M^1$ value realization so it does not, strictly speaking, derive from land development. It lies in handling the *trade* in property of all kinds. Freehold houses change hands in Britain, on average, once every six or seven years. This means several million transactions per year. Each of these houses has to be surveyed, valued, marketed by estate agents and finally conveyed to a new owner by lawyers. All the same operations apply to changes of land ownership as development occurs. Lettings of investment properties are arranged and managed by property agents, valuations are required on a periodic basis and finance has to be raised for new developments on the security of existing properties.

Figure 1.1   *'Gentrification' proceeding in Islington, a London inner suburb with good access to the City. Low-income residents are 'squeezed out' by a variety of methods and the housing, which is of considerable architectural merit, is renovated for middle- to high-income people. Since the land use – residential – has not changed, planning has little control over the process.*

This third field of property trading is dominated by a relatively narrow set of interests who either have, or claim to have, 'professional status'. Profits are normally taken in the form of a percentage of the value of property turnover, which is an extremely high value annually. Significantly, these trading operations, and the large profits they generate, are not really within the field of vision, let alone the area of intervention, of the planning system. Planning is concerned only with the *use* to which buildings are put and the use categories are very crude and socially insensitive. Large-scale gentrification, which is really more of a trading than a development operation, can 'ease out' a low-income population from an area and replace it, within a decade, with high-income people. This may conflict with the planning authority's expressed Structure Plan intention to encourage more low-rental housing. But since the *use* (residential) has not changed, the matter is not strictly a planning issue. This part of the Structure Plan might just as well not have been written. What *does* result from such operations is a large-scale generation of income for the 'trading' group – surveyors, valuers, estate agents, tenant-'winklers', lawyers, and so on.

Apart from the specific interests which seek to accumulate capital by land development and trading, there is a broader capitalist interest in the evolution of the built environment since it is necessary for the reproduction and welfare of the labour force. Employers require an adequate supply of healthy labour. The level of this requirement varies from time to time depending upon the stage of the business cycle and the extent to which machinery has replaced labour in the production process. The 'marginalized' group who are *not* required at any point in time (currently these number between 3 and 4 million) may well suffer the indirect effects of their redundancy in the form of reduced social expenditure on the various programmes (housing, education, etc.) that are necessary for labour reproduction. Employers in all forms of enterprise also have an interest in fostering a configuration of homes, workplaces, transport facilities and services that is conducive to high rates of capital accumulation rather than the reverse. Clearly a land development pattern which produces average journey to work times of five minutes is more likely, other things being equal, to produce more profits in production than one involving sixty-minute journeys to work; the time spent at the workplace can be longer. This partly explains the actions of early 'philanthropic' industrialists and mineowners who clustered their workers' tenanted cottages around the factory or pit.

But such patterns can be counter-productive. The public health risks inherent in this close intermeshing of homes and factory chimneys led to lower levels of health in the workforce and pressures to separate out different uses into larger blocs of single uses. This separation of uses is one product of 'planning', and it is generally acceptable from the employers' point of view so long as the necessary investment in mass transit facilities to service the resultant increased movement is not fully charged to them. From their point of view such investment should either be a profitable activity for other entrepreneurs or the public sector should provide it (so long as the costs falling on enterprises via taxation are less than the value of benefit from the healthier workforce). This relationship can be shown by extending the original model slightly:

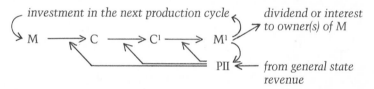

where PII = *public infrastructural investment, i.e. money partly abstracted from M_1 in taxation and spent on planning a more efficient physical infrastructure (roads, airports, zoning, etc.) and social infrastructure (education, health, etc.) so as to provide 'external benefits' for entrepreneurs.*

The element PII can be seen as a 'lubricant' for the three operations $M \longrightarrow C, C \longrightarrow C^1$ and $C^1 \longrightarrow M^1$. It enables each to proceed more smoothly and effectively by subsidizing transport facilities for goods and people, by helping to bring about accumulation-conducive, rather than accumulation-inhibitive configurations of uses and by aiding the reproduction of an ample supply of fit, suitably educated and compliant labour. In this way the increment $(M^1 - M)$ can be greater, both for individual enterprises and in aggregate, than it would otherwise have been. Thus capital's long-term interest is to ensure that the resultant *increase* in the value $M^1 - M$ is greater than the element PII which is abstracted from M^1 to help bring it about. If this is so, a net long-term gain for capital has occurred. The overall effects of land use planning should, in other words, be assessed not only in aesthetic or environmental terms. It is at least equally important to try and assess whether, for any particular time period, the ratio

$$\frac{\text{increase in } (M^1 - M)}{\text{PII (from } M^1)}$$

is greater or less than unity. If it is greater than unity, it is likely that land use planning and other publicly funded programmes have helped to enhance the conditions for capitalist accumulation (see Chapter 8 on London's docklands).

There are two final points to note when buildings are the final product (C^1) in a production cycle. A number of factors combine to safeguard the long-term level of demand. Buildings are non-substitutable – working, eating, playing and sleeping under a roof of some kind is unlikely to go out of fashion in most climates. Changes in methods of production and distribution, and in recreational activities, produce demands for new or adapted buildings even if the overall *level* of population and economic activity remains static. Buildings decay and have to be renewed or replaced. Governments have, from time to time, an electoral interest in new construction drives. If of a Keynesian persuasion, they may even use increased investment in the building industry as a means of regenerating the economy. Therefore, while total demand for new built environment may vary quite considerably in the short term, it never dries up in the long term. A slump in activity must be followed, sooner or later, by a boom. It follows that much depends upon the strategies adopted by property entrepreneurs to survive the slumps.

The second point is that *self*-provision of something as expensive and complex as a building, even a single house, is something that few would now embark upon. This situation, is historically, quite new. Before the urban-industrial revolution in Britain, and for some time after in rural areas, buildings were either constructed by their users or else produced by local jobbing builders, probably on the initiative of the local landed gentry. Now in Britain (although not elsewhere in Europe) most buildings are constructed by medium- to large-scale corporations – often operating on a transnational basis. Within two centuries the autonomy of the individual has been, in a very important respect, expropriated. We can no longer, in most cases, provide buildings for ourselves or, equally important, can no longer understand from local observation just *how* the provision is being arranged and the cost to the user arrived at. Consumer power in terms of the amount and standard of built environment one gets for one's money is now virtually negligible. This has become in Britain, almost exclusively a matter for the providers to determine.

It is to these that we now turn in order to identify as clearly as possible the specific *types* of enterprise and capital involved in the process of capital accumulation via land development in the decade or so prior to the 1947 intervention. This is necessary partly out of general interest. More specifically, given that the government was drawn or driven to attempt measures which most thought would reduce the $(M^1 - M)$ increment, we need to see what sort of capitalist interests were likely to be most affected by a seemingly draconian move of this kind. Were they small scale, atomized, less than coherent or marginal to 'the establishment' in some way? Or were they powerful, concerted and accustomed to exerting political influence at the highest level? The answer to these questions should help to illuminate the nature and effectiveness of the *resistance* to the government's intentions in 1940–7. This, in turn, facilitates a better understanding of the postwar evolution of land use planning and the reasons why the 'long retreat' from planning has occurred.

What form did capital take in pre-1947 land development?

So far the word 'capital' has been used as if its meaning were self-evident. In fact, despite the total tonnage of writing on the subject, its meaning is still hotly contested and the very use of the word has value connotations – although Harvey (1982), if anyone, has helped to clarify matters. For present purposes the word is *not* used to denote the counterpart, or antithesis, of 'labour' since such a scheme of analysis is dangerously over-simple and misleading. Capital, in this book, is a 'shorthand' term to denote privately owned money available for fresh investment in commercial ventures. The individuals and institutions who have the power to invest it – whether they happen to be the legal owners of it or not – are referred to as 'capitalists'.

Before outlining the specific nature of the capital and capitalists prominent in land development in the decades prior to the 1947 intervention, it helps to note the key 'entry conditions' to activity in this field. There are perhaps two necessary requirements for entry on any significant scale. Land development requires land, and it requires relatively long-term financing. The first requirement is self-evident but often not easy to satisfy – land, as many commentators have noted, is something they've stopped making. The second requirement, for long-term finance, arises because money has to be committed to a development (whether for investment or sale) at the *beginning* of its life. The payback period may be one year or so if the property is sold, or ten to twenty years if it is held as an investment. Taken together, the requirement of access both to land (or to the use of it for a number of years) and to finance of this type inhibits entry to the field. As a further condition, entrepreneurs who would operate in property must have the foresight and capacity to guard against certain external risks such as changes in fiscal policies or in the cost of money. If not, they may go under comparatively quickly.

To consider land first, it has been shown by Flemming and Little (1975) that of all forms of private wealth, this is the form most concentrated in the ownership of the better-off. The more wealthy the individual, the more likely that a large part of this wealth will take the form of landholding. As a logical corollary, it is the form of wealth held least by the worst off. Massey and Catalano (1978) have examined the British land ownership pattern and have distinguished three main groups of owners: those with inherited holdings, industrial entrepreneurs and financial institutions. For present purposes it is necessary to separate out the ownership of purely agricultural or forestry holdings from land that is currently or potentially available for building development. When seeking to do this, one rapidly runs up against insuperable difficulties of non-access to data. Official statistics are notoriously silent on questions of land ownership and they do not categorize different forms of capital in the ways required for critical analysis (neither of which is surprising). So when trying to assess retrospectively what kinds of capitalist interests became involved in the large-scale land conversions of the interwar years, one is driven back largely into case-study, or even anecdotal, evidence.

The need for long-term finance also limits the kinds of capitalist who can become involved in land development. Broadly speaking, it is likely in 'normal' circumstances that three groups will have the most ready access to such finance: those who have inherited wealth, those with assets (perhaps mainly land and existing buildings) against which long-term finance can be borrowed and those who have already accumulated capital in some other branch of production or trade. Various case studies and empirical accounts of land development between the wars make it clear that all three groups were involved. But there was a fourth group who achieved striking success in land development and dealing during the rather abnormal circumstances of the 1920s, 1930s and 1940s. These were the opportunistic, ingenious and hardworking set of men, often from humble backgrounds, who achieved fame (or notoriety) and fortune mostly in the field of investment-type development. We will consider this field first.

Development for investment, 1919-39

In Britain in this period (although this is not true of other places and times) the development of buildings for the stream of rentals to be derived from them was almost exclusively an urban phenomenon, taking place typically on city centre or 'suburban shopping centre' land. The demand for new forms of built space arose as more and more of the growing workforce came to be employed in shops and offices rather than in factories or on the land. Simultaneously the growth in disposable incomes, and the changes in retailing structures and technology, led to a massive demand for new shop premises by the rapidly expanding multiple chain stores. There were 81 Woolworth stores in Britain in 1919. By 1939 there were 768. In all, the total number of multiple store branches increased from under 25,000 in 1920 to over 44,000 in 1939 (see Jefferys, 1954).

Much of this development took place on land which had previously formed part of the urban estates of the landed aristocracy. Cannadine (1980) has discussed the declining role of the old aristocratic families in the new surge of interwar development. The threats to this group went back into the latter decades of the nineteenth century. Death duties acquired much more bite and forced the sale of many inheritances. Lloyd George's 1909 budget introduced no fewer than four duties on land: a duty on increases in site value, a reversion duty payable by the lessor when a lease ended, an annual duty on undeveloped land and a duty on mineral royalties. Although the first three were repealed in 1920, the general direction of government thinking was apparent. The recurring discussion about leasehold reform which would have reduced the rights of freeholders, the passing of the 1909 Housing, Town Planning, etc. Act, which enabled local authorities to prepare 'schemes' and the Liberals' very warlike noises about land taxation all combined to alarm the aristocratic landowners.

Many of them, in Cannadine's words, took a 'conscious decision to restructure and rationalise their assets' (ibid., p.424). Before and after the First World War there was a rash of urban land sales by the gentry (although this is not to underestimate the enormously valuable urban estates they retain to this day). In 1913 the Duke of Bedford took the decision to sell the Covent Garden estate. After the war, much of the Duke of Westminster's Mayfair estates were sold – similarly the Berkeley Estate including the famous square. The pattern was the same all over the country – in Folkestone, Bournemouth, Huddersfield, Sheffield and many other towns. In addition to the estates, many aristocratic town houses were sold, mostly on sites that proved ideal for residential flat developments undertaken between the wars as an investment. The aristocracy, then, made a partial, but only a partial, move out from what subsequently became an enormously lucrative arena of development. Who moved in? The interwar investment property scene has been chronicled by Marriott (1967), Jenkins (1975) and Rose (1985), among others. (See Figure 1.2.)

Figure 1.2   *Much of the interwar property investment was in new suburban shopping parades.*

Typically, much of this investment development was of new shopping parades. The enormously rapid expansion of the suburbs, especially around London and Birmingham, led to a lively market in road frontage land, preferably close to an underground station or bus terminal, on which a parade of shops could be built. If one of the growing multiples (such as Boots or Sainsbury's) could be secured as a first tenant, the success of the scheme was probably assured. An equally brisk market for such developments existed in established high street locations as the 'corner shop' pattern of retailing inherited from the previous century became increasingly outdated. The retailer–freeholder in his little Victorian shop gave way to the multiple chains leasing units in newly redeveloped parades. A large volume of retail sales meant large-scale purchasing and this, in turn, led to the need for newly designed and developed single-storey warehouse premises preferably near rail links. This constituted a further field for property investment and development. (Many of these older multistorey warehouses, often on inner urban land, survived to experience transformation into valuable office premises in one of the postwar property booms.)

A large market share of this activity was gained by a group of estate agents including Hillier, Parker, May & Rowden, and Healey & Baker. Increasingly, as they became more expert at assessing the potential retail trade in every town in Britain, the advice they gave to their clients about which premises to acquire and how much to offer became more and more valuable. Naturally enough, they did not remain content to take only an agent's percentage share of the profit. The obvious step was to enter the market in shop development and trading as principals. This pattern was followed not only by the emerging giants of real estate, but also by many middle- or small-size estate agents. Their information network and fieldwork enabled them to identify promising sites and to turn this knowledge into private profit.

The other main prerequisite, long-term finance, was becoming increasingly available as the life insurance business mushroomed, new premiums flooded in and the life houses needed to find avenues of investment that were both adequately secured and gave a prospect of long-term gain. The Prudential, the Eagle Star, the Royal Liver and many others found that it made sound sense to invest in retail developments and build up their property portfolios. According to figures quoted by Marriott (1967), the total real property investments of British insurance companies rose from around £57 million in 1927 to over £148 million in 1947. This level of involvement by the life insurance companies has political significance. Government has a clear interest in the long-term liquidity of such institutions since the alternative to private life insurance payments on retirement and death can only be increased public expenditure on pensions and death benefits. This means higher taxation. We shall return to this point later.

Office development was not a particularly lucrative activity between the wars. Various big schemes were carried out, notably in Holborn and the City, but the largest company involved, the City of London Real Property Company, faced wide fluctuations in rental income and there was nothing like the long-term growth in rent levels evident in retailing. There was however, in marked contrast to the present day, a booming market in the development of rented flats for the growing group of urban white-collar workers. In particular, the Bell Property Trust, founded and run by a minor businessman and the son of a farmworker, built large blocks of flats at Marble Arch, Putney, Ealing, Chiswick and Streatham. Further details of such developments are given by Marriott (1967) and Jenkins (1975). The present purpose is not to pile up empirical detail, but to identify the nature of the capitalists and capital involved so as to gauge what kind of resistance might be mobilized to any regulatory intervention by the state. We shall return to this point after reviewing interwar activity in the other main area of land development, speculative housebuilding for sale.

Housebuilding activity: 1919-39

The growth of real incomes for those in work, the fall in building costs, the political and fiscal support for the building societies, the drastic reduction in public sector housing programmes and the opening up of new suburban land by mass transit systems were among the factors that combined to produce the speculative urban fringe housebuilding boom of the interwar years. This has been well described by Jackson (1973), Burnett (1978), Boddy (1980), Ball (1983) and others, all from their particular perspectives. Speculative housebuilders showed in their advertisements that they were selling not only a house, but also 'the persistent myth of a rural tranquillity somewhere beyond the edge of the big cities and

Figure 1.3 *The speculative housebuilding boom of the interwar and immediately postwar years*

industrial towns in which most people were forced to live', as Ball (1983, p.38) puts it. In fact much of the growth was self-destructive of this myth. The new estates simply spread outwards from the urban fringe in a rather uninspiring way, focusing on underground or railway stations and making heavy use of 'bypass variegated' or 'Tudor-bethan' architecture. There was no planning in the post-1947 sense. As Bevan later remarked, 'the speculative housebuilder, by his very nature, is not a plannable instrument' (Foot, 1975, p.71). Who were these housebuilders? How did they operate? And what resistance could they mount to the attempts government were soon to make to 'plan' their activities? (See Figure 1.3.)

The boom got off to a slow start in the early 1920s, despite the subsidies offered by government for each speculative house completed and the Housing, etc. Act 1923, which gave local authorities power to guarantee payments to building societies by house purchasers. Building costs remained high throughout most of the 1920s, due partly to the action of building material suppliers in keeping their prices high in the face of weak opposition from the then highly fragmented housebuilding industry. But the long-term factors were moving in favour of suburban owner-occupancy and housing development on greenfield sites. The total number of private vehicles in use rose from around 229,000 in 1918 to 3,149,000 in 1939. Electric tramway and motorbus services were expanding rapidly and around London the underground spread its network far out into the countryside. Uncertainties in other areas of investment, especially following the 1929 crash on Wall Street, led many depositors to favour the building societies. Money for home loans was readily available as a result. Interest rates on these loans, and on money borrowed to finance buildings, fell after 1932. Labour costs remained stable or fell as unemployed workers flooded to the growth areas looking for any jobs with little regard to the wages that went with them.

All these factors favouring the speculative building boom were complemented by the activities of the underground and railway companies and their collaboration with housebuilders and investors in land development. Jackson (1973) gives details of builders who either gave land for stations to be built, contributed towards construction costs or bought shares in the relevant railway company. Later the railway companies themselves invested in improvements in many suburban stations designed to increase the passenger and freight throughput and often developed a parade of shops for leasing out on Station Approach. The Underground Railway Company also had a view on the desirable density of housing development. Jackson (ibid.) records the arguments of Lord Ashfield, chairman of the company. A development density of twelve houses per acre gave only 24,000 people within a half-mile radius of a station and this translated to about 3 million passengers per year. On financial grounds at least another million was desirable, and this implied higher building densities. No doubt, this argument was not lost on the speculative builders who had their own reasons for trying to achieve higher development densities in order to save land and other costs per house built.

As the 1930s progressed many of the smaller housebuilders overreached themselves, or tried to build in areas where they had little first-hand knowledge of the market. It was the builders who avoided these dangers and worked to a well thought out formula that survived to become household names. For example, Wates were founded in 1901, but operated on a fairly modest scale until after the First World War. By confining their activities largely to an area they knew (south London) and always building within easy walking distance of a Southern Electric railway station, they became one of the volume builders and completed over 30,000 houses between the wars. To quote one of the directors, Wates sought to build for the bus driver, the postman and the policeman earning £3–£4 per week. By 1934 they could produce a two-bedroom terraced house selling for £295. This could be secured for a £5 deposit and a mortgage could be arranged over twenty-one years with repayments of about 37½p per week. Three-bedroom houses were sold for about £400. Wates avoided casual labour and used workers who lived within cycling distance of the site. They aimed to make a profit of £30 per house, roughly the cost of the plot itself. As volume built up more advertising was used, and the turnover of capital became very rapid. Low selling prices squeezed out smaller competitors, whose often jerry-built products represented much poorer value for money. Similar building programmes, using slightly different formulae, were carried out by the other large-scale builders such as Costain, Crouch, Davis, Laing, Wimpey and the largest of them all, New Ideal Homesteads. Few of these firms were very important before the First World War and some actually started from nothing in the interwar years.

Towards the other end of the size scale, the process can be typified on the outskirts of Brighton (Mead, 1983). George Ferguson, a Scot who started work as a housepainter and who accumulated capital by developments in London and Sussex in the 1920s, purchased some farmland in 1931 at Patcham, some way north of the built-up fringe of the town. The vendor was keen to sell since his type of farming (sheep–corn) was even more depressed than most others. Brochures were produced which stressed that the development was being carried out by a man who had a social, rather than a financial, object in mind ('for the good of the homeseeking community'). The houses were to be brick-built with cavity walls (an advanced feature for the period), they were to be all-electric ('The supply of electricity from the Brighton Corporation is almost the cheapest in England') and fitted with damp-courses and weatherproof window-frames. The estate was to be laid out on 'garden city lines' with gently curving avenues lined with fruit trees. For the housewife there would be a local shopping centre, and for the breadwinner a new nearby rail station and bypass road for easy access to work (the latter was finally approved in 1984!). The electricity supply and the transport improvements demonstrate the significance of the PII element in the model on p.7 to Mr Ferguson's rate of capital accumulation (although at this time most of the necessary infrastructural investment was private rather than, as today, mostly public).

Between 1933 and 1936 Mr Ferguson's company had built and sold about 1300 houses, partly on a subsequent land purchase. The architecture progressed from a rather austere vernacular style, through houses with Dutch and Spanish 'effects', and the 'country retreat' look to several pure Le Corbusier copies. Prices ranged from under £500 for bungalows to £550–£650 for houses (with a few more expensive properties). Most were complete with turfed gardens and 'sunburst' gates. (See Figure 1.4.) The building societies stood by with funds, the estate sales staff were ready to meet any potential purchaser by car at Brighton Station and any property could be secured on paying a £5 deposit. The houses and bungalows sold well, most of the purchasers were apparently well satisfied (despite the non-arrival of the proposed new station and bypass) and a good proportion live there today, fifty years later. There is no reason to believe that Mr Ferguson's development was different in any essential characteristic from speculative suburban

£550 Freehold Semi-detached Houses.

Brief specification :—Eleven-inch cavity walls, Sussex stock facings. Bitumen damp course—storm-proof windows, steel and wood. Varied rough-cast and cement finishes. Coloured roof tiles in the following shades :—reds, browns, greys, greens and blacks. These variations in colour finish are not to Purchaser's choice.

How to Purchase :—

Deposit, £55. Building Society advance, £495. Total costs, £5.

Repayments, 16s. per week,
  over 20 years.
Rates, 2s. 11d. per week.
Annual Assessment, £21
  (7/- in the £).
Water rate, 9d. in the £.

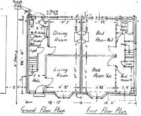

7

Figure 1.4 *New properties on the Ladies' Mile Estate, Brighton in the early 1930s.*

developments all over the country.

How, then, should the capital and capitalists involved in interwar land development be characterized? The question is significant because there was an apparent intention by the state between 1941 and 1947 to make a significant intervention in land development activity. Most, if not all, entrepreneurs must have regarded this intention as a potential threat, a factor of unknown strength that would inhibit the capital accumulation process. They would naturally line up against it. What was the strength of the line up? What factors were working for, and against, them in their resistance to any significant interventionary moves by the state?

There are two key points to make, relating, firstly, to the actual people involved in development, and secondly, to the political, social and economic functions they were carrying out. The people, on the whole, were *not* those who have traditionally sipped their brandies in dignified leather-upholstered calm in the Athenaeum or rubbed shoulders with ministers and peers at Westminster. The landed gentry, well versed in these activities, had made a partial withdrawal from urban land development around the time of the First World War. The estate agents and property dealers who moved into the partly vacated space were often quite non-establishment in their backgrounds. There were tradesmen who, by hard work, had built up construction firms. There were farmers' sons, ex-soldiers from the First World War who used their service gratuities to accumulate capital in war surplus materials deals, and émigrés from various European countries, often Jewish, who had flair and the capacity to see an opening that spelled success in this field. It is difficult to believe that, collectively, people with such backgrounds could easily achieve any ready degree of access to the all-important informal networks of influence in Whitehall and Westminster or be regarded with any natural warmth by the key governmental advisers, with their good family/public school/Oxbridge backgrounds. Judged purely in terms of the personalities likely to be most affected as at 1939, it seems that effective state action to limit land development profits would be more likely to emerge than measures, say, to end grouse shooting.

But the issue transcended personalities and family backgrounds. By 1939 the land developers had carried out important functions for the continuance of the social and political status quo. In the aftermath of the First World War, up to the failure of the General

Strike in 1926, the danger of large-scale social upheavals haunted the minds of men of affairs. The necessity for more property ownership as 'a bulwark against bolshevism' (Bellman, 1928) was accepted by rational political analysts, not just by paranoid alarmists. By 1939 nearly a third of the population had achieved home ownership (and the debt-encumbrance that went with it) and millions more aspired to it. For most of these, thrift (necessarily), loyalty to 'the system', prudence and the avoidance of any industrial militancy that might lose them their job became elevated in the scale of virtues. The social formation as a whole survived the trauma of massive unemployment throughout the 1930s with surprisingly little in the way of effective protest. The rapid growth of owner-occupancy was arguably a contributory factor in explaining this comparative absence of dissent. The speculative house-builders must have been regarded by those in power as allies of the state in its larger role as guardian of the long-term status quo.

Simultaneously in the investment land arena the new consumer durables, those ensurers of the good and labour-saving life, were being marketed in newly developed shopping parades and multiple stores. An increasing proportion of the finance for this kind of development was coming from the 'enforced savings' of middle- and upper-income employees, channelled by the rapidly growing pension funds and insurance companies. These institutions, too, were generally regarded as embodiments of personal and corporate security, as symbols of the ultimate stability of the British financial system. No government, without very good reason, could allow them to get into serious trouble by changing the rules in one of their most lucrative areas of investment – property development.

In the years immediately preceding the Second World War, therefore, there existed a balance of forces for and against any fundamental intervention by government in the land development process. The capital accumulating group was not, in general, one to which those in political power would feel any natural or historical affinity. Yet the functions they were carrying out were system-stabilizing rather than system-disruptive. There was no lack of demands for 'planning', mostly in physical and environmental terms. For example, 'ribbon development' was generally acknowledged to be an unfortunate feature that needed control of some kind and there were fears, as the war approached, that too many of the national eggs were in the vast and difficult-to-defend basket of

London. But there is no reason to believe that anything short of a severe external shock to the system would provoke any fundamental move by the state to reduce the power of private capital or otherwise change the rules of the game in the land development process. There was, in the interwar years, no imperative strong enough to produce such a move. The social upheavals of the Second World War, and the widespread destruction of British cities, were to change all that.

What is 'the state'?

Land use planning, whatever its effects might be, is an attempt at regulating free market land development processes. It is carried out by the state at the national and local level. What, therefore, *is* 'the state'? How can its functions best be characterized in a predominantly capitalist system? As Clark and Dear have pointed out, 'The role of the state in urban and regional spatial processes has been curiously neglected' (Clark and Dear, 1981, p.45). This is not completely correct. There is a mass of literature on the nuts and bolts of regional policy and the legislative mechanisms of land use control. But it has mostly been too bland and uncritical. Too little attention has been given to any theoretical consideration of how the 'democratic' agencies of government actually interact with powerful private interests bent on maximizing the accumulation of capital. This gap in understanding is now being filled (see, for example, Cooke, 1983) and key questions are being addressed. To what extent, and by what means, do government and the local authorities, as representatives of 'the public interest', actually affect the behaviour of capitalist institutions and entrepreneurs? What, in the end, sets the limits to these regulatory attempts? In what ways are 'capital' and 'the state' still separate autonomous entities anyway? If in practice the distinction between them has been blurred and shifting, both in terms of function and personnel, then the task of analysing any large-scale interventionary attempt (such as the 1947 Act) becomes that much more difficult.

During the 1970s there was a considerable growth of writing on the role of the state, and the nature of state intervention, in mature capitalist systems. O'Connor reviewed, and further stimulated, this work. He drew attention to a basic contradiction in capitalist economies in 'the fact that production is social whereas the means of production are owned privately'. This leads to the premise that:

> the capitalist state must try to fulfil two basic and often mutually contradictory functions – *accumulation* and *legitimization*. . . This means that the state must try to maintain or create the conditions in which profitable capital accumulation is possible. However the state also must try to maintain or create the conditions for social harmony. A capitalist state that openly uses its coercive forces to help one class accumulate capital at the expense of other classes loses its legitimacy and hence undermines the basis of its loyalty and support. But a state that ignores the necessity of assisting the process of capital accumulation risks drying up the source of its own power, the economy's surplus production capacity and the taxes drawn from this surplus (and other forms of capital). (O'Connor, 1973, p.6)

The significance of this passage to the analysis of the postwar planning intervention cannot be overemphasized. The British state enacted in 1947 regulatory mechanisms which, had they been as powerful in reality as they were on paper, would have severely inhibited the rate of capital accumulation via land development. As we shall see, the intervention was necessary partly on grounds of legitimization. The political dangers of *not* intervening were judged to be too great, both by the wartime coalition and by the postwar Labour government. For a brief period the protection of the capital *accumulation* function lost out to the *legitimization* function – to draw on O'Connor's analysis. But quite rapidly, by the late 1950s, the balance of the two functions had been reversed, or perhaps more accurately had reverted almost to the prewar norm in Britain.

It is relevant to note at this point that the 'coercive forces' referred to by O'Connor are, in the British case, much more firmly rooted in ideology and the control of ideas than in force and the physical control of actions. The protection of the highly inegalitarian status quo (Atkinson, 1974) owes more to the rigid management of the agenda of public broadcasting (Glasgow University Media Group, 1982), the narrowly based ownership of the national press and the ideologically self-reproductive nature of the formal educational curriculum than it does to the agencies of 'law and order'. These latter are still not even armed in normal circumstances, although there has been a marked increase in saturation policing and new crowd-control weaponry in the 1980s to contain the increasingly militant dissent in the poorer urban areas. The issue of ideology is raised here because the way in which land use control is widely *believed* to operate is itself part of the dominant set of legitimizing ideas. The process of capital accumulation via, say, a city centre commercial development that disrupts the lives of thousands of existing residents in the area is protected if the partial fiction can be maintained that it was 'the council' or 'the planners' or simply 'progress' that brought about the scheme.

In addition to O'Connor's work, which has been vigorously supplemented by Gough (1979), a range of related theories have been advanced since the late 1960s to help clarify the essential nature of the state's role in mature capitalist economies (which of course includes its role in 'planning'). All of them call seriously into question, or even totally dismiss, the 'liberal democratic' view that we all elect a government via the ballot-box, that the government (in Cabinet) makes the key decisions and that these are then implemented by the executive (the civil service). Even when a pluralist dimension is added to this simple model, by admitting the effects of specially formed interest groups on decision-making *between* elections, this interpretation of events has gaping holes. Where is account taken of the powerful financial interests and institutions known as 'the City'? What of the relatively autonomous power of the vast multinationals, and where is allowance made for the loss of national sovereignty to other governments (especially those powerful in Nato, the EEC or the IMF)? Yet, remarkably, the liberal democratic or pluralist models of the workings of the state are usually the only ones available even to the small minority who reach the stage of an A level in Politics. In the field of land use planning many of the books produced in the last decade or so are based on the liberal democratic or pluralist position – if they embody any explicit political theory at all.

Miliband (1973) produced a much more penetrating analysis. He argued that decision-making processes which were tacitly held to be 'democratic' were in fact powerfully affected by pressures emanating from narrowly based interest groups in the private sector of the economy. In Britain, and similar mature capitalist economies, private sector corporations had become so powerful that their interests could not adequately be served by the liberal democratic procedure of casting votes every four or five years.

These interests required much more direct access to the seat of decision-making, whether this seat be Parliament, the Cabinet, Whitehall, the Athenaeum or elsewhere. Thus a 'corporatist' theory of the state began to emerge (Cawson, 1982) with the dominant trilogy of 'the state', 'capital' and 'labour' using and extending a complex but constitutionally informal network of communication. Along this network there is a constant traffic of representation, information, specific requests, favours, decisions, 'deals', and so on. The clear implication is that this network, and the myriad interactions that daily pass along it, works to bypass the electoral process, thus partially disenfranchising the majority of the population.

Miliband held that this functional integration of the interests of 'capital' (the owners and/or managers of the means of production), 'labour' (the unions, etc.) and 'the state' (definition much more problematic) was reinforced by the constant interchange of personnel between the so-called public and private sectors. This, in turn, had further blurred the liberal democratic distinction between 'public' and 'private' interests. Thus, argues Miliband:

> state intervention in economic life entails a constant relation-ship between businessmen and civil servants, not as antagonists or even as representatives of different and divergent interests, but as partners in the service of 'the national interest' which civil servants, like politicians, are most likely to define in terms congruent with the long term interests of private capitalism. (ibid., p.112)

Miliband's analysis has been both highly contested and highly provocative of later work. It is 'instrumentalist', in that it sees the state largely in terms of a set of decision-making individuals who have been recruited from a narrow range of backgrounds and socialized into a particular way of thinking so as to serve, in effect, as instruments of capitalist interests. This interpretation has been too individualistic for some, notably Poulantzas (1973), who in the words of Saunders (1979), 'makes it clear that ... such individuals are merely the bearers of objective structural relations between the state and the various classes in the social formation'. Poulantzas argues that there are underlying 'structural relationships' in any capitalistic production system which are necessary for the achievement of the system's 'objective requirements'. These requirements include the need continually to reproduce not only the *mode* of production (with the ownership and/or control of the means of production retained by a relatively small group), but also the *social relations* of production that flow from this narrowness in the ownership/control base. Thus the state is not really an independent entity working in the interests of one group rather than another. It is rather the visual manifestation of the balance of group interests at any particular time. By its actions it serves as a kind of 'cement' that holds the system together by reinforcing the underlying relationships required to keep it operational.

In other words, the state *has* to be primarily capitalistic in nature if the dominant mode of production is to remain capitalistic. Any other behaviour pattern on the part of the state simply could not work in the long term, although some deviations may occur from time to time as a response to short-term crises or unusual configurations of circumstances. If this perspective is adopted, it follows that interpretations which portray the 1947 planning system as a partial victory for socialism, as a significant shift in capital – state relations or as an expression of 'community power' are at best debatable and at worst quite unsound.

There has been much subsequent theorizing about the nature of the state and particular state interventions in mature capitalist systems (see, for example, the literature reviewed, in Held, 1983, and Cooke, 1983, chapter 8) and the issue remains hotly contested. It would be premature to assert that any particular theory is correct and the rest wrong. Equally it would be worse than foolish to offer an analysis of land use planning that did not start from some reasonably explicit theoretical position. This particular analysis, then, starts from the position that the 'liberal democratic' and 'pluralist' interpretations of the state are altogether too naïve and uncritical. The work of Miliband, Poulantzas and others who advocate that the state can only properly be understood in the context of capitalist 'laws of motion' seems to offer a much more promising line of advance into the heartland of understanding. Nothing happens in the field of land development without the investment of money. If the money is privately owned and/or controlled, as most of it is, no investment will occur unless there is the clear prospect of further gain – *the drive for further capital accumulation is thus the main imperative and dynamic.* Successive British governments have been seen to influence, or react to, changes in the conditions in which this imperative operates; sometimes seeking to regulate and at others acquiescing; sometimes apparently gaining in control, at others apparently in retreat; sometimes seemingly sensitive to the electorate and concerned with legitimation; and sometimes blatantly encouraging increased capital accumulation. The history of the 1947 planning system needs to be interpreted in the light of this general theoretical understanding.

Where and why might the state intervene?

As a postscript to this brief discussion of the nature of the state in predominantly capitalistic systems, and as an introduction to Chapter 2, some thought should be given to identifying the kinds of circumstances in which important interventionary moves by the state are most likely. The most coherent, if perhaps not the most comprehensible, discussion of this point occurs in Habermas (1976, in translation). Habermas, in common with many in the Frankfurt School of critical social theorists, wrote much on the inherent crisis tendencies in mature capitalist systems. Crises, in this context, are seen as 'persistent disturbances of *system integration*': 'crises arise when the structure of a social system allows fewer possibilities for problem solving than are necessary to the continued existence of the system.' In other words, a 'control-overload' occurs, due not to accidental events but to structurally inherent weaknesses of the system itself when confronted with tests of a particular kind.

In these difficult situations the forces operating for the status quo will exhibit various responses. In order to maintain as much of the necessary mass loyalty and social consensus as possible the evident weaknesses of the system when faced with crisis will be interpreted as a lapse in the efficiency of the *functioning* of the system, not as an inherent structural defect. In other words, questions of the *ultimate validity* of the system are interpreted, and presented in public pronouncements, as questions of *temporary poor performance or behaviour*. In this way the crisis can be depoliticized since the latter questions are clearly less threatening than the former.

'Crisis', argues Habermas, can mean something as fundamental as a disturbance in the local or world ecological balance resulting from insensitive exploitation of natural resources. It can mean dangerous disturbances in the international balance of power, perhaps partly due to the same reasons, and made increasingly hazardous by the spread of potentially world-destroying weapons. It can mean long-term difficulties for the capitalist economic system stemming from any number of causes such as anarchic and wasteful patterns of investment and commodity production, a systematic fall in the rate of profit or growing competition from developing countries. Or it can be manifested as deep political unease, leading to social disturbance, when the level of mass loyalty to the system is tested to destruction by political regimes whose fundamental perspectives are felt to be alien to the nature and wishes of a majority of the population (see Figure 1.5). For example: 'A rationality deficit in public administration means that the state apparatus cannot, under given boundary conditions, adequately steer the economic system' (ibid., p.47).

To be more specific, Habermas argues that advanced capitalist societies are in danger from at least one of the following possible crisis tendencies:

the economic system does not produce the requisite quantity of consumable values, or:
the administrative system does not produce the requisite quantity of rational decisions, or:
the legitimation system does not provide the requisite quantity of generalized motivations, or:
the socio-cultural system does not generate the requisite quantity of action-motivating meaning., (ibid., p.49)

In Chapter 2 we shall consider events in Britain in the period 1940–7, especially as they bear on the emergence of land use planning, with these four possible tendencies in mind. At least the last three were in evidence in that period (although it could be argued that Churchill temporarily solved the problems raised by the last two).

To return to the theoretical argument, Habermas argues that a number of responses are possible by the capitalist state. Clearly some action must be taken to safeguard the existing mode of production and the continuance of capital accumulation by the minority in market-dominated conditions, while at the same time maintaining the necessary level of mass loyalty to the system. The form of the action can vary. Steps can be taken to protect the market

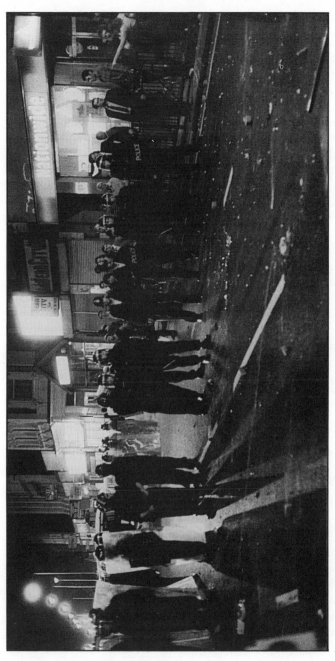

Figure 1.5   The state's response to a failure of 'mass loyalty'. There is evidently a rapid turnover of business property in the area. Possibly the building society branch here is geared more to attracting deposits in than to financing increased owner-occupancy.

system from overproduction or destructive side-effects. Changes in the legal, fiscal or business-regulating legislation can be introduced to bolster capital accumulation. The government can itself become a customer for profitable but ultimately wasteful commodities (such as weapons of destruction). There can be an ideological or propaganda offensive calculated to defend the system. A reformist 'contract' can be agreed between capital and the labour movement. Or publicly funded agencies can be set up to ensure the adequate delivery of services necessary for labour reproduction – in particular, education, health care and housing for low-income people. Expenditure on such items, or on fundamental research or exploration for minerals, does not usually lead to a short-term profit for private investors yet it is absolutely necessary for the long-term continuance of the capital-accumulation process.

The emergence of land use planning needs to be seen in the light of these theoretical arguments since it can be related to them at many points. The crisis that beset Britain in 1939, coming after the widespread deprivation and unrest of the 1930s, was perhaps the most serious of any since the Civil War. A battery of responses by the state was inevitable. The promise of a planning system which would ensure a better built environment and thus satisfy the aspirations of all the people was precisely one of these responses.

The emergence of planning: 1940–7

Every thought must be referred back to the historical situation in which it arose, to the real context of interests behind it.
(Horkheimer, *Zeitschrift* essays).

Harold Nicolson was one of the best-liked and best-informed 'men of affairs' during the 1939–45 war years. He worked hard, wrote voluminously (diaries, reports, books, letters, etc.) and socialized widely:

22nd July 1943
Dine with Sibyl [Colefax]. She had managed to get hold of the Wavells, and had chosen a careful party. The Duchess of Devonshire, T.S. Eliot, Oliver Lyttelton, Stephen Spender. She had also invited Dicky Mountbatten and Edwina, but they were summoned to dine at the Palace. (Nicolson, 1967)

Thoroughly gregarious, he was just as likely to be dining with politicians, diplomats, visiting foreign ministers or even General de Gaulle. He served as junior minister at the Ministry of Information under Churchill from May 1940 to July 1941 but lost his office largely as a result of the necessary party share-out of offices under the wartime coalition – and perhaps because he was not, in his own view, 'formidable' as a politician. In his free time, if not engaged on firewatching duties at the House or taking a turn in a munitions factory, he escaped to Sissinghurst in Kent. There he joined his wife Vita Sackville-West, to whom he had a remarkable and devoted marriage (Nicolson, 1973), and together they created one of the finest gardens in the country.

Nicolson can safely be said to have had his finger on one, at least, of the pulses of British life throughout the war. He recorded the feelings of the time meticulously in his diary (Nicolson, 1967). He noted the view held by Clement Attlee (the Labour leader in the coalition – as expressed by his parliamentary private secretary) that whereas the Germans were fighting a revolutionary war for definite objectives, the British were fighting a conservative war to retain a status quo (*Diary*, 3 July 1940). Britain too, urged Attlee's PPS, should be fighting for a new order and admit that the old one had collapsed. This led Nicolson, after discussion with advisers, to draft some ideas on war aims, despite Churchill's frequently expressed insistence that the unconditional surrender of the enemy should be the only war aim. Nicolson's draft advocated a possible federal structure for postwar Europe and increasingly socialist measures at home. He rashly talked to the Fabians about these ideas, they published the talk and an American journal reprinted it as did the *Manchester Guardian* (3 February 1941). Churchill 'absolutely blew up . . .' (*Diary*, 11 February 1941). The episode gives some support to the view that Churchill's approach to the war was indeed pragmatic, tactical and conservative – in no way was it, in his view, a war to achieve any specific set of economic or social objectives. The job in hand was simply to defeat fascism.

But even Nicolson, who was not that closely in touch with the feelings of 'the masses', picked up some of the generally felt bitterness and disillusion in the early years of the war. When recording that the king and queen had recently been booed while visiting the bomb-damaged areas of the East End of London (*Diary*, 17 September 1940), he notes the view of a Liberal colleague that: 'if only the Germans had had the sense not to bomb west of London Bridge there might have been a revolution in this country. As it is they have smashed about Bond Street and Park Lane and readjusted the balance.' This thought was expressed very early in the blitz. As the devastation spread in the poorer areas of London and the other major cities it was perhaps as well from the point of view of 'mass loyalty' that Buckingham Palace was also hit (13 and 15 September 1940). Had it not been, it might have been necessary, to preserve the notion that 'we are all in this together', to pretend that it had.

While Nicolson, from his viewpoint as a well-connected junior minister, was recording the reactions of those in authority, popular feeling was often very different. If indeed we were 'all in this together', it was reasonable to expect that we should all get something out of it. The range of popular reactions by ordinary people to the war has been fully discussed by Calder (1971). His work draws heavily on the findings of the Mass Observation team which had begun its work in the mid-1930s. These paragraphs, in turn, draw on Calder. The conscripts and volunteers to the forces 'were determined not to be fooled as their fathers had been. Everyone knew the story; Lloyd George had promised "Homes for Heroes", and when the heroes had come back, there had not even been jobs for them' (ibid., p.61).

Dunkirk was the first of the great collective traumas. Orwell (1941) argued that the crushing defeat in France could be one of the 'great turning points' in English history: 'In that spectacular disaster the working class, the middle class and even a section of the business community could see the utter rottenness of private capitalism' (ibid., pp.68-9). Lehmann saw the survivors of Dunkirk similarly: 'A more effective army of revolutionary agitators, penetrating to the furthest villages, could not be imagined – could not have been organised by the cleverest political party' ('Cato', 1940, p.15).

They had fought with Bren-guns against bombers, bayonets against machine-guns. The 'old gang' (Baldwin, MacDonald, Chamberlain, Hoare, Simon, etc.) had betrayed them. Despite mass unemployment in the 1930s, the economic system had failed to produce the arms to stave off a devastating and costly defeat. Even *The Times* (1 July 1940) thundered about the need for a fairer society and for an attack on privilege of all sorts. Clearly neither the subsequent slow change in the fortunes of war over the next five years, nor the genuine love for Churchill as an inspirational leader, nor the massive propaganda designed to drum up patriotism and support for the established order were sufficient to assuage this deep-seated bitterness. In a sense the result of the 1945 general election was already preordained by the early summer of 1940.

The second great trauma was the blitz, and it led to the emergence of land use planning as part of the postwar 'offer' in a number of direct ways. The German air force began the serious bombardment of British cities in the late summer of 1940. London suffered first followed by a succession of other cities – Coventry, Birmingham, Southampton, Glasgow, Plymouth and most other centres of equivalent size. Again, despite the heroic tone of contemporary newsreels, there was much bitterness at the lack of adequate preparation for the onslaught, which had after all been long expected. Fire brigades were still equipped largely for peacetime emergencies and firemen were badly paid. Clydeside, as in 1914–18 an area of industrial militancy, was poorly provided with air-raid shelters yet the town of Clydebank was so heavily bombed that 35,000 of the 47,000 residents were made homeless. As many as 50,000 people left Plymouth following repeated raids in April 1941. Some slept in barns, churches, tunnels and even on Dartmoor. The dockside areas of Merseyside suffered a week of bombing in May 1941 while bureaucracy argued about whether to amalgamate the separate fire brigades of Bootle and Liverpool. The Mass Observation report on Liverpool (no. 706, 22 May 1941) revealed the fury felt by many local people at the ineptitude of the city leaders and of the government. There were even rumours that martial law was in force. As Calder remarks, 'This was municipal trauma on a bigger scale than Stepney's' (1971, p.246). The onslaught continued until Germany attacked Russia in midsummer 1941 and a large proportion of the *Luftwaffe* moved east. Only then did a breathing space occur.

Reports from all over the country showed that by now morale was shattered, feelings were running very high and loyalty to 'the system' was in severe jeopardy. Nicolson recorded the deep worries of the War Cabinet (e.g. *Diary*, 7 May 1941). There is much evidence of the depth of this concern. Churchill made sure that the true reason for the arrival by air of Rudolf Hess (Hitler's deputy) in Scotland was not made public. The flight seemed to be some kind of a peace offer, even though apparently not sanctioned by Hitler, but this was judged by the Cabinet to be too tempting a possibility to be made widely known to the people of the blitzed cities. The mass bombing of the civilian population, as well as of legitimate targets, was not militarily decisive; neither was the far heavier saturation bombing of Cologne and Dresden by the Allies later in the war. But the *political* pressures it produced were judged to be potentially explosive. Something clearly had to be placed on the table to prop up morale and provide a vision of what people were suffering for (Backwell and Dickens, 1978). Postwar aims, of some kind, had to be enunciated, despite Churchill's obvious reluctance on the grounds that the fragile political consensus of the Coalition government might be undermined.

Some steps in the direction of greater equality had already been taken because they were necessary for the war effort. Wholesale food prices had risen by 50 per cent between 1939 and 1941 partly due to the forced reduction of imports. Yet a large proportion of the poorer population was expected to do heavy work on munitions production for long hours. Food rationing was the obvious answer and while there was much complaint about matters of detail the general principle was almost universally accepted as fair and correct. In fact Lord Woolton, the Minister of Food, rapidly became one of the most popular figures in the government. The Beveridge Committee, set up in June 1941 following promptings by the TUC, finally reported in December 1942 (Cmd 6404). Queues formed outside His Majesty's Stationery Office and sales of the report, and the brief official summary, topped 635,000. Nine out of ten people surveyed believed its proposals for a systematic social security system should be adopted (Calder, 1971, p.609). Churchill, in all his voluminous writings, scarcely mentioned the report or the massive discussion it engendered.

But it was clear that no matter what limits may have been imposed on discussion in Parliament, the debate about the nature of the postwar society was a lively one. In the depths of the London blitz the widely read weekly *Picture Post* published an edition (4 January 1941) entirely given over to this question. It dealt with ten topics including 'Work for all' (Thomas Balogh), 'Health for all' (Julian Huxley) and 'When work is over' (J.B. Priestley). The ideas put forward included state control of the banks, a national economic plan, a minimum wage, the redistribution of farmland to farmworkers, education for all up to 18, an end to private education, a healthy diet and proper free health services for all. The edition was graphically illustrated; photographs of the 'bad old days' of the 1930s were contrasted with newly planned hospitals, housing and factories. In fact the key concept was 'planning' – for employment, investment, land, welfare, education and health. There seems little doubt that *Picture Post* was voicing what millions were feeling. Today such demands would be regarded, collectively, as so far to the left that few Labour politicians could safely endorse them in public. But in 1941 they would have won a landslide election victory. Such has been the move to the right in British politics, and in dominant ideologies, in the past forty years.

Attitudes to the vision of a rationally planned, more egalitarian brave new postwar world were naturally dependent to some extent on the complex and changing 'official' attitude to the most obvious available model of such a society – Soviet Russia. At the outbreak of the war, just after the signing of the Nazi–Soviet non-aggression pact and especially after the Russian invasion of Finland, official British opinion towards Russia could hardly have been more hostile. Yet public opinion was curiously friendly to the soviet state (see Calder, 1971, p.87). When Germany attacked Russia in June 1941, some conflicts of loyalty might have been expected to show in the public stance of Churchill and his predominantly Conservative War Cabinet. Not at all; the official line changed overnight to one of support and admiration for Mother Russia and her heroic Red Army. Within weeks supplies were flowing to the new ally via the Arctic sea-route. 'Tanks for Russia' weeks were organized, labour relations in numerous factories improved when the product was known to be for 'Uncle Joe', old ladies knitted socks for Russian soldiers and as a final seal of approval the Russian ambassador, Maisky, was elected to the Athenaeum. By the time the battle for Stalingrad, the decisive battle of the war, had been won, there were no limits to the admiration for the strength, courage and single-mindedness of the Russian people. Packed audiences in civic halls sang the 'Internationale' at meetings to celebrate the twenty-fifth anniversary of the Russian revolution and politicians proclaimed the solidarity of Anglo-Soviet relations. Millions compared in their minds the impressive performance of the Russian generals and army with the disasters experienced by the British Forces both before and after Dunkirk. If military victories on this scale could be achieved in a country where, apparently, women had equal rights, the workers ran the factories, and the economy was centrally planned, what conclusions could one draw about the sorry story of capitalist Britain in the 1930s? Macmillan (and other enlightened younger Tories) had no doubts; socialism, in his view, was the inevitable postwar route for Britain (see Nicolson, 1967: *Diary*, 23 October 1942).

The environmental legacy of the 1930s

By 1939, following ten years of economic depression and nearly as many of complacent leadership by a rightist government, there was a large number of planning problems evident in Britain. These can be grouped under three general headings: social, aesthetic and functional. The housing conditions and general social circumstances of the poor have been extensively documented (see, for example, Mowat, 1955). For millions the decade was one of demoralization and indignity, of the 'means test', the slum and the 'dole'. (See Figures 2.1 and 2.2.) Yet as Priestley (1934) pointed out, there were at least two other Englands both relatively prosperous: one was the green and pleasant land of rural Old England and the other the new glossy world of petrol stations, bypasses, Woolworth's, dance halls and, one might add, the new estates such as Patcham. For those in secure work – as has been pointed out many times – the 1930s was a period of prosperity, falling living costs and the acquisition of all-electric domestic comforts.

These three disparate worlds were brought into mutual confrontation by an unprecedented social phenomenon: the evacuation of several million people, mostly children, from 'evacuation' zones to 'reception' zones in order to avoid the risk of aerial bombardment. Vast numbers of children were transported from the poorer urban areas and billeted by some quasi-voluntary or even compulsory process on middle- and upper-income families in numerous small towns and villages. The culture shock was traumatic; one half of the population at last found out how the other half had been living. The shockwaves were transmitted to the level of political and official decision-making via formal reports by Medical Officers of Health and others and by the 1700 reports by local Women's Institutes to their National Federation (National Federation of Women's Institutes, 1940). Informal reports were also influential. Vera Brittain, whose pen was sufficiently powerful to penetrate to official levels, described the effect of an influx of evacuees on the good, though upper-crusty, ladies of the Oxford Women's Voluntary Service (Brittain, 1981). A large number of mothers and children were temporarily housed in a cinema where they slept on mattresses and cushions. The smell was 'overpowering', apple cores, orange peel and soiled newspapers were disposed of in the simplest way (on the floor). The canteen staff were frantically engaged in trying to produce tea of the required strength and colour while the doctors and nurses responsible were engaged in some fairly elementary health education. Vera Brittain was a sympathetic observer and reflected that the evacuation had at least produced some improvement in health standards for a section of the urban poor. But,

Figures 2.1 and 2.2 *Some urban environments in the 1930s.*

What remains to be done is harder and cannot be achieved in a day, nor a month, nor a year; it is nothing less than the elimination of those too long tolerated differences of standards which evacuation schemes have revealed throughout the country. The apple cores and the soiled newspapers will not disappear until the West End really knows and cares how the East End lives. (ibid., p.170)

The elimination of such inequality, it was understandably felt by the committed observers of the day, could be achieved by 'planning'. The *Picture Post* referred to earlier contained an article by Maxwell Fry, an architect with extensive local authority experience. He broadened out the critique to include aesthetic and functional considerations as well as purely social issues. The rapidly growing urban areas had sprawled out in the 1920s and 1930s, wasting farmland by an unplanned use of space, despoiling the rural environment with linear 'ribbon development', yet failing to achieve the easy communication and the production efficiencies that were the main rationale for heavy investment in new roads and factories. Because the patterning of different uses had just grown in a completely unplanned way, much of the investment, whether public or private, had been self-defeating. There were still heavy traffic-congestion costs, poor sanitation and health standards (for lack of proper provision of public utilities and usable open space), and consequently poor economic performance and labour productivity (for a recent discussion of these issues see Hardy and Ward, 1984).

Fry had no doubts about the way forward. Postwar housing reconstruction, the extension of the trunk road and port systems, and industrial/economic development must proceed in accordance with a national plan that would co-ordinate investment, land use and the efficient deployment of human and material resources. Jerry-built housing, cramped and dingy schools, narrow crooked roads and out-of-date riverside wharves were to be swept away (the latter an ironic point in the present context of fierce dispute about the redevelopment of docklands, see Chapter 8). Non-compatible uses such as housing and industry were to be separated out, high-rise flats, schools and health centres were to stand in parkland and the rivers were to be lined with amenity space. The planning was to be comprehensive. It could not be done in the context of private land ownership and speculative development processes:

Picture Post, 4.1.41

THE NEW BRITAIN MUST BE PLANNED

BY MAXWELL FRY

AUTHOR IS AN ARCHITECT AND TOWN PLANNER, ONE OF THE LEADING YOUNGER ARCHITECTS IN THIS COUNTRY. HE HAS BUILT WORKING-CLASS FLATS, HOSTELS AND SCHOOLS IN LONDON AND THE COUNTRY.

The ordinary Englishman makes himself comfortable almost anywhere; and he doesn't bother much about the town he lives in, so long as his own kitchen and parlour are all right. That some of our bigger towns are inefficient and untidy to a degree which no woman would tolerate in her kitchen and no man in his workshop, may be news to many — and may not seem to matter much. But bad towns are an invisible burden on every citizen — damaging his health, his pocket, his enjoyment of life. And bad towns are unnecessary. It is a question of thought — of *planning*.

Given the will to plan, we could, in a quarter of a century or less, substantially transform our worst towns. Where they are black with soot, they could be at least partly green with trees and grass. We could bring the country into the town in great swathes of parkland never more than a step round the corner from the homes of the people. We could, by reorganisation, shorten the weary long journeys to work, and at the same time make the workplace itself more cheerful. We could replan and reconstruct many of our outworn public services, to stop the drain of money to no purpose.

WHAT WE WANT

- **Everybody to live in cheerful, healthy conditions, which only proper planning can ensure.**
- **An attack on the slums to begin immediately after the war.**
- **A bold building plan to civilise our industrial towns in twenty years — or less.**
- **Plans for industry, housing, schools, hospitals, and transport.**
- **A plan to get the best out of town and country: to bring green grass to the towns, and town amenities to the village.**

Figure 2.3   Picture Post, *read by millions, called for reforms in the dark days of the 'blitz' – partly perhaps as a boost to morale.*

There is no use blinking the fact that unless land resources are pooled by one system or another, town planning will come to a dead end and we shall lose our chances of recovery, if not our will to survive. (*Picture Post*, 4 January 1941, p.19)

This passage is interesting, in that it proposes a very considerable change in the structure of resource ownership, with consequent implications for private capital accumulation, in the interests of equity, efficiency *and* mass loyalty (see Figure 2.3). Clearly the vast

Figure 2.4   Picture Post's *vision of the future.*
Source: Picture Post, *4 January 1941*

majority of readers – ordinary people risking their lives in the armed forces or working exhausting hours on war production – went along with the overall aims. Few of them would have realized the political strength of the property lobby, or the economic power of the building industry and the financial interests behind it. Few, therefore, could have grasped the enormous complexity of the issues and the difficulty of translating a morale-raising set of general statements about the future into the body of legislation, necessarily damaging to capitalist interests, that would be required in order to bring about the New Jerusalem. (See Figure 2.4.)

The promises and the committees

The task of attempting this translation fell initially upon Sir John Reith. Reith was an upright and moralistic Scot, a respected man of affairs who could however be difficult to deal with. His name is inextricably linked with the origin and growth of broadcasting in Britain and in many ways he *was* the BBC from its birth at the end of 1922 until his resignation as Director-General in late 1937. His influence remains in the continued adherence to the concept of 'public service broadcasting' and in the oft-repeated but naïve claim that the BBC is apolitical, or politically neutral, because of the fine balance of its presentation. Critics, for example Hartley (1982), tend to see the BBC as about as apolitical as the monarchy or the Established Church. The point is often made that mass loyalty seems most secure, and jingoistic sentiments are most pervasive, when all three of these hallowed institutions come together at royal weddings, coronations and state funerals.

Reith went on to be chairman of Imperial Airways. Soon after the outbreak of war, Chamberlain appointed him (in an interview where Chamberlain surprisingly confessed himself to be 'really a Liberal': Reith, 1949, p.352) as Minister of Information. In May 1940 Churchill (to Reith's disgust) made him Minister of Transport. In October of the same year, as part of a ministerial re-shuffle, he was appointed to the newly formed Ministry of Works with responsibility for both current building and some aspects of postwar reconstruction. The job became more onerous as enemy bombing became heavier. Reith was responsible for organizing materials supply, so that the construction industry could be rapidly redeployed to undertake essential repairs in furtherance of the war effort. This task was obviously his top day-to-day priority.

But there was also the longer term to think of. The massive scale of the destruction was raising important technical and political issues about the way postwar reconstruction should proceed. Already the sharper estate agents were actively prospecting for bomb-damaged buildings that might be acquired for an immediate offer which was well below the potential postwar site value (Marriott, 1967, p.60) This opportunism was in striking contrast to the great wave of public feeling in favour of a more egalitarian and collectively ordered postwar world. Reith, although by no means technically equipped by his background, attacked the issue

Figure 2.5 *Citizens of Coventry pick their way over rubble in the aftermath of the raid on 14 November 1940. Within weeks a high-powered civic delegation was confronting ministers with the question 'On what basis will postwar reconstruction be carried out?'*

of postwar reconstruction with his customary vigour. By late 1940 he had prepared a memorandum urging controlled redevelopment, rational land utilization, limitation of suburban growth and inner urban redevelopment. Churchill approved it in vague terms, probably without having the time to think through the deeper implications. At this juncture, very early in 1941, new pressures for action arose in the shape of a deputation of seven civic leaders from Coventry, led by the mayor. Their city had been savagely bombed (see Figure 2.5). What was to be done for them? On what basis was the rebuilding to be carried out? Reith answered with more heart than prudence:

> I did not know what authority I had or was going to have, but I would not allow this high-powered civic deputation to return to their battered city with a tale of Whitehall gruntings and

wafflings, telling their wives it was all a waste of time and that they had gotten nowhere. These poor men were perplexed and dismayed; had thought that it was to me they should come for advice. They would get advice. For this occasion anyhow the credit of the Government rested with me. Coventry would be a test case – not for me and my authority – but for the Government and for England.

So I told them that if I were in their position I would plan boldly and comprehensively; and that I would not at this stage worry about finance or local boundaries. They had not expected such advice, so quickly and so categorically; not by a long way. But it was what they wanted and needed; it put new heart into them. The mayor thus 'I've been coming on deputations to Whitehall for twenty years, but I've never had such treatment as this'. I took them all to lunch in a private room at Claridges; when they returned to Coventry they were each carrying two or three daffodils from the lunch table. (Reith, 1949, p.424)

This passage contains minor ambiguities (where did daffodils come from so early in the year?) but the central assurance given by a minister of state to a group of civic leaders was clear and surprising. It was an official promise that postwar reconstruction would not be inhibited by lack either of finance or local authority powers. The promise was taken at face value in Coventry (Richardson, 1972) and elsewhere. Reith by his own account (Reith, 1949, p.428) gave 'the same emphatic advice' to the leaders of at least five other cities. Something substantial would have to be delivered to back up the promises.

The first stage of the delivery process was to consider the linked problems of *compensation* and *betterment*. If the postwar planning was to be as comprehensive and as socially directed as was promised, the power to allow and to prohibit development would need to be transferred from individual land owners and vested with some form of public planning agency. The only effective alternative to the public acquisition of this power would be the public acquisition of all development land itself. As will be seen, this possibility was very much on the agenda but it clearly raised such large political issues that it was really a strategy of last resort. But if the power to allow or prevent development was to be taken from the site owner, he or she would reasonably claim that subsequent development profits would be lost unless and until an official consent to develop were granted. Even then the consent might be for a smaller, and therefore less lucrative, development than the owner would have carried out had no development control been in operation. It was therefore necessary for consideration to be given to the nature and scale of compensation to be paid for lost development rights. It was also necessary to consider the reverse situation where the value of a site was materially *increased* by some publicly determined action. This increase in value could result either from the granting of a consent to develop land for some more lucrative use (such as building houses on existing farmland) or it could result from public investment in, for example, a main road which increased the accessibility, and thus the value, of the site. Clearly if the state was proposing to offer compensation for lost development rights, it was both fair and expedient that the betterment conferred to owners should be taxed in some way. It would thus, in an ideal world, be possible for the state to break even following its new intervention in the land development market.

The issues to be faced were both technically complex and politically contentious. There was general acceptance of the need for some kind of central body to administer the future acquisition, planning and development of land, but should this be a commission or a whole new ministry? Should 'development' land be distinguished from 'non-development' land and treated differently – and could this in practice be done? How would any new central body relate to the established hierarchy of local authorities? How could the land speculation already taking place be prevented? What pattern of regional development was desirable and how could it be implemented? What scale of compensation payments and betterment levies should apply and what would be the net cost to the Exchequer (nobody anticipated a net surplus)? How would the Treasury, a traditional opponent of planning, react to the cost? Should existing cities and towns simply be allowed to expand by suburban growth or should new 'satellite towns' be envisaged – and if so, by what agencies could they be planned and built?

This general set of problems was referred to the War Cabinet Committee on Reconstruction Problems headed by Arthur Greenwood (see Cullingworth, 1975). The division of responsibility between Greenwood's committee (on which Reith sat) and Reith's office was by no means clear to either of them, and the administrative confusion itself seems to constitute evidence of the low priority accorded in Parliament – as distinct from in government propaganda – to the issue of postwar reconstruction. After more discussion, Reith was given specific responsibility for devising ways of preventing the current spate of speculation in land and, for the longer term, making workable proposals in the complex field of compensation and betterment.

In January 1941 he approached Augustus Uthwatt, a King's Counsel, to head what was necessarily to be an expert group. Uthwatt was joined by two experienced chartered surveyors, Gerald Eve and James Barr, and another lawyer, Raymond Evershed – hardly a group to advocate the socialist millennium. An Interim Report was produced in less than four months (Uthwatt, 1941), dealing mainly with the shorter-term problem of preventing actions that would prejudice the task of postwar reconstruction. On the strength of his group's ongoing work, Reith made a forceful statement in the House of Lords (to which Churchill had elevated him on appointment) making it clear that 'planning', on a national, regional and local scale as appropriate, was to be part of the postwar world in Britain (Reith, 1949, p.426). He subsequently outlined some of the main ideas in the Interim Report: that land compulsorily taken into public ownership should be acquired, in principle, at 31 March 1939 values, that there should be a 75 per cent levy on all urban site value increases as determined by quinquennial valuations, that all building activity should be licensed by a national agency so as not to prejudice postwar reconstruction and that devastated areas eventually should be comprehensively rebuilt in large-scale schemes, (see Parker, 1985, for an excellent short discussion of the report). In May 1941 the Greenwood Committee on Reconstruction Problems, and the government, accepted these ideas in general terms, although it was by no means convinced that the time was right to proceed with another of Reith's important policy proposals – the setting up of a central authority to oversee future development planning. Reith himself was dismayed by this reluctance and thus could not subscribe to the committee's statement accepting the document.

By October 1941 the government's approval of the Interim Report had apparently been firmed up, but it was noticeable that the postwar aims now being enunciated by the Greenwood Committee were becoming rather more 'all things to all men' (see

Cullingworth, 1975, pp.65–6). The hard, specific proposals made by Uthwatt, such as public acquisition of land required for postwar reconstruction at values ruling in March 1939, were now somewhat diluted by general statements about land utilization: 'to the maximum social and economic advantage of the community.' The government would, when the time was right, ensure the speedy provision of housing, clear slums, end overcrowding and provide 'all necessary public services'. These few months in mid-1941 were perhaps the crucial ones for the future evolution of planning in Britain. The hard language of the expert technicians had started to become the soothing noises of the coalition politicians. A definite something was on the table. It was clear that this something was intensely political, in that it was a clear threat to capital-accumulation processes. In terms of the model in Chapter 1, there was a threat to the M^1 – M increment in relation to the past, present and future investment of M in land. No doubt much speculative investment had already occurred in bomb-damaged land. To pin the future value of this land to its prewar value would lead to the diminution, if not the total cancellation, of the anticipated gain. Apart from this the collectivization, or nationalization, of the right to develop would change the rules of the land development game in fundamental and unpredictable ways. Powerful interests became alerted to the danger. It can be assumed that property capital as a whole agreed with the National Federation of Property Owners in the point it made to the Uthwatt committee that the state acquisition of the right to develop 'would mean, in effect, the nationalisation of a part of the owner's interest in the land, and thus strike at the very root of the principle of private enterprise in property' (*Estates Gazette*, 31 May 1941, p. 582).

The land and property lobby is historically – and still – a very significant element in British politics. It believed (in error, as events have turned out) that development control meant the end of development profits. This was not within the range of what it judged to be acceptable in the context of British capitalism. Even in the darkest days of the war, the voice of property capital was raised in anguished protest. But the dark days were soon to become lighter. In June 1941 Hitler rashly attacked Russia and the balance point of the war moved to the Eastern Front. Some of the pressure was lifted from Britain. The long-term prospects suddenly looked more promising. The historic balance of power in Britain between those with substantial capital (in this case property capital) and the rest of the population could begin to reassert itself. The long retreat from the dangerous and uncharted territory into which Reith and Uthwatt had dared to enter could now begin.

The start of the long retreat

The retreat was indeed long. It has been going on (with brief counterattacks and short-lived advances) down to the present day. In fact it could be argued that the 1979–85 period has seen almost a final collapse of planning as an effective force. But only the passage of time will show whether this is a reasonable assessment. The issue must be seen in context. During the early years of the war other key committees reported on matters relevant to postwar planning. During the 1930s there had been chaotic and politically dangerous imbalances in the pattern of industrial development. Mass unemployment in the depressed areas had led to chronic and destabilizing industrial action and hunger marches. There was also growing official concern at the large proportion of industrial plant in areas that, as early as 1934, the Air Council had designated as either 'unsafe' or 'dangerous' from the point of view of aerial bombardment (i.e. the Midlands and the south-east). In 1937 Neville Chamberlain, as Prime Minister, set up the Barlow Commission to consider all aspects of the distribution of employment and population in Britain. The committee reported at length early in 1940 (Barlow, 1940). The report has generally been regarded as good in terms of analysis and data but timid (so far as the Majority Report goes) in terms of hard implementable policy proposals. It is, however, noteworthy that the Barlow Commission gave an estimate of £500 million as the total development and redevelopment value of all land undeveloped as at 1937. This estimate, although based on a vast set of shaky assumptions, lodged itself in the collective mind of officialdom for future reference.

The Scott Report on Land Utilization in Rural Areas (Scott, 1942), while 'a remarkable hotch-potch of innumerable reflections and over a hundred separate recommendations on a mixture of subjects more or less connected with rural life' (Cullingworth, 1975, p.41), to quote the remarkably dismissive view of the official historian of British planning, shared at least something with the more technical work of Uthwatt – its central aims could not possibly be achieved without a new land use control machinery. Thus there were pressures from two other bodies, Barlow and Scott, for a definite move forward towards a more democratically planned postwar world.

But these various 'offers' to a population engaged in a life and death struggle to defend the system were at different levels of specificity in the threat they posed to capital. Barlow and Scott, the latter especially, were about vaguely defined reforms. They dealt with matters so vast, for example the future distribution of the population, that few could disagree with the grand principles they set out. In fact many industrialists (such as Sir Malcolm Stewart and W.L. Hitchens) publicly agreed with the concept of better planning of the distribution of industry. Hitchens made the point, in evidence to the Barlow Commission, that 'a comprehensive planning system ... would in the long run prove of the greatest assistance and help industrialists to find the sites best suited to their requirements' (Minutes of Evidence, Barlow, 1940, p.871). This was a very early recognition by a representative of industrial capital that a land use planning system, by centralizing information and preventing self-destructive and economically inefficient patterns of development, could materially aid the process of capital accumulation. But Uthwatt was different; it was about real money, not about vague blueprints for the future. It would, if implemented, actually affect the value of investments already made and perhaps drastically reduce the range of possibilities for future capital accumulation via land development. It needed to be rolled back.

The gradual change in the tide of war was a vital background to the rolling back process. In the early summer of 1940, when invasion seemed a near-certainty, owners of land and other real estate were naturally very ready to convert their assets into something more liquid such as money or gold. Such assets could be transported, if feasible, should invasion occur. The more certain did victory become, the more surely did the historic premium attached to real estate begin to reassert itself. The tide had effectively turned by the end of 1941. Once both Soviet Russia and the United States had entered the war, there could be only one eventual outcome. This slowly growing confidence in final victory led not only to the gradual return of landed interests to their established place in the historic pattern of power relationships, it also reduced the political pressure on the Coalition government to produce morale-boosting visions of the new postwar order. Possibly, too, once the United States had joined in the war, there was no longer the same need to convince the American people and President (a committed 'New Dealer') that Britain was also aiming to achieve a 'new deal' after the war.

In any event, Reith's various initiatives were producing much political resistance. Powerful figures in the Cabinet (such as the Chancellor of the Exchequer, Sir Kingsley Wood) objected on every possible ground to the notion of a central planning agency. Nevertheless, much committee work went on during late 1941 and early 1942 aimed at clarifying the complex relationships between various ministerial areas of responsibility. Reith worked on these difficult tasks with characteristic energy and enthusiasm. But they were clearly low on Churchill's list of priorities. This was perhaps understandable. February 1942 brought various military disasters such as the fall of Singapore. Churchill was harassed and depressed and had to face a vote of confidence as his stock fell to its lowest point in the House. A large-scale ministerial re-shuffle was one of his responses. In this rearrangement of responsibilities both Reith and Greenwood were curtly dismissed. Reith felt that his sacking was partly due to his intractability on some issues and partly to his lack of any party organization to support him (he was not a member of a party and described his own politics as 'vague'). But primarily he felt that a group of Conservatives connected with the building industry and working through the Government Chief Whip had demanded his expulsion and replacement by 'a good Tory'. He was raising problems – 'Moving too fast, too much planning all round... even fear of land nationalisation perhaps' (Reith, 1949, pp. 445–6).

Reith was probably correct in this interpretation although he appeared to be politically naïve enough to be surprised at the power and reaction of the interests ranged against his proposals. As Cullingworth remarks at the beginning of his excellent official history. 'The essence [of planning] is political even when issues are defined in technical terms' (Cullingworth, 1975, p. xi). It seems possible that Reith never fully grasped this essential truth.

Greenwood's successor was Sir William Jowitt. The post was downgraded, in that he was not given a place in the War Cabinet. On going to see him, Reith was informed that the Bill in preparation based on the Uthwatt Report was to be postponed and that planning was to be restricted to bomb-damaged areas only. On

contacting his own successor, Lord Portal, Reith formed the view
that he was little interested in postwar planning. As for Reith, he
turned down Churchill's offer of the post of Lord High Commissioner
at the General Assembly of the Church of Scotland and instead
joined the navy as a lowly lieutenant-commander (although this did
not prevent him from dealing with admirals on fairly equal terms).

The Final Report of the Uthwatt Committee (Uthwatt, 1942) was
produced in August 1942 (see Figure 2.6). Its most urgent proposal
concerned the prohibition of development on undeveloped land
except for publicly approved schemes. For the longer term it
proposed that land outside urban areas that was required for future
development should be compulsorily acquired by a Central Planning
Authority at existing use value and leased out for any new use at
full market value, thus leaving the state with the betterment. Land
within already built-up areas was to remain largely in the province
of the private market, although development was to be in accord
with approved planning schemes. Betterment was to be collected by
means of a 75 per cent levy, or something similar, charged on
quinquennial increases in land value. Finally, central government
grants were to be made available for city centre reconstruction
schemes.

There was enough here to offend virtually every private interest
connected with land development. The issues raised were of
ferocious technical, constitutional and financial complexity. As
the report began its progress through a bevy of committees, starting
with the Committee on Reconstruction Problems, it was obvious
that interminable delays would probably ensue before any Bill
could be produced. This was all the more evident now that the
abrasive energy of Reith was directed elsewhere. Early in 1943 an
Act was passed to set up the Ministry of Town and Country
Planning and W.S. Morrison, a Tory, became the first minister. He
was subjected to continuous parliamentary pressure concerning
rebuilding which was already proceeding, although judged by some
to be prejudicial to postwar reconstruction. He was also pressed for
information about when the Uthwatt proposals might be implemented. Following some rather uncharacteristic interest by
Churchill (Cullingworth, 1975, p.84), an Act was passed in July 1943
which prohibited any change of use without the consent of the
relevant planning authority. This at least extended the principle of
development control (established as a power that local authorities

Figure 2.6 *The 1942 Final Report of the Uthwatt Committee – still one of the clearest discussions of 'betterment'.*

Uthwatt Report 1942 Cmd 6386

Floating Value

23. Potential development value is by nature speculative. The hoped-for building may take place on the particular piece of land in question, or it may take place elsewhere; it may come within five years, or it may be twenty-five years or more before the turn of the particular piece of land to be built upon arrives. The present value at any time of the potential value of a piece of land is obtained by estimating whether and when development is likely to take place, including an estimate of the risk that other competing land may secure prior turn. If we assume a town gradually spreading outwards, where the fringe land on the north, south, east and west is all equally available for development, each of the owners of such fringe land to the north, south, east and west will claim equally that the next development will "settle" on his land. Yet the average annual rate of development demand of past years may show that the *quantum* of demand is only enough to absorb the area of one side within such a period of the future as commands a present value.

24. Potential value is necessarily a "floating value," and it is impossible to predict with certainty where the "float" will settle as sites are actually required for purposes of development. When a piece of undeveloped land is compulsorily acquired, or development upon it is prohibited, the owner receives compensation for the loss of the value of a probability of the floating demand settling upon his piece of land. The probability is not capable of arithmetical quantification. In practice where this process is repeated indefinitely over a large area the sum of the probabilities as estimated greatly exceeds the actual possibilities, because the "float," limited as it is to actually occurring demands, can only settle on a proportion of the whole area.

could voluntarily acquire by the 1932 Act) to all land. But clearly much more was needed.

The White Paper and Bill which Reith had promised in 1941–2 did not finally emerge until June 1944, more than two years after his dismissal. By this time the Allies were evidently going to win the war and many property interests were licking their lips at the prospect of an enormous postwar reconstruction bonanza (Marriott, 1967, pp. 58–61). Clearly Uthwatt-type thinking had no place in their preferred scenario. The White Paper (*The Control of Land Use*, 1944) was intensively discussed (see Cullingworth, 1975, chapter 6). Most of its key proposals were challenged, and some rejected, by the Reconstruction Committee which included the Chancellor of the Exchequer, now Sir John Anderson. What emerged was a Bill designed primarily to strengthen the compulsory powers of local authorities to acquire blitzed and blighted land.

While this was fairly uncontentious in principle, many interests in the property world were unhappy at the compensation levels. By contrast, the more radical commentators predictably found it all too timid. Lewis Silkin, one of its main supporters, called it 'a very short step and a very poor step' although, in retrospect, Cherry has called it 'a fundamental breakthrough in planning' (Cherry, 1974, p. 124). In addition to the lack of legislative bite, the Treasury grants to local authorities to implement the measure were set such that they would need to lease out much of the newly acquired land for high-income (commercial) rather than low-income (housing) use in order partly to recover their capital expenditure. (Thus was established a principle which has operated in numerous 'partnership' schemes ever since.) Few cities, other than Birmingham, made much use of the Act. It was clear to many contemporary observers that the ultimate aim of this measure was to disturb as little as possible the existing pattern of power relationships and to avoid encroaching on the postwar paths to redevelopment profits. As the Labour Research Department (1944) pointed out at the time, 'for the Government the major consideration is how best to protect vested interests'.

Little else of significance to the future of land use planning occurred in the remaining year of wartime Coalition government. The Labour leaders in the coalition, Attlee, Bevin and Herbert Morrison, were prepared to defer expression of their political differences with the Tories in order to finish the task in hand. But they were aware that the Coalition government was unlikely to outlast the war by many months and they had their own views on the likely outcome of the general election and the path forward that they wished to tread. Radical action by the wartime coalition on these social issues might well undermine the distinctive electoral appeal of the Labour Party in the coming postwar election.

In assessing the extent of the retreat from the days of 1941-2 to the end of the wartime Coalition government we need to see planning in the context of other social policy proposals. We have already noted the great public enthusiasm that greeted the Beveridge Report. Even the highly technical Uthwatt Report attracted much attention. Cherry (1974, pp. 136-7) reports a story that some anti-aircraft gunners had been overheard in Hyde Park at two in the morning discussing the relative merits of the Uthwatt and the 1944 White Paper proposals on the issue of compensation. (What Sir William Holford, who overheard the conversation, may not have known was that one of Britain's most successful young developers was, at the time, serving with an anti-aircraft battery in one of the London Parks.) Churchill's reluctance to countenance discussion of possible postwar social advances has already been noted. It must, of course, be conceded that he of all politicians was best placed to assess the economic difficulties that would face Britain after the war and the political conditions that might be attached to the aid that would undoubtedly be required from, for example, the United States. In January 1943 he wrote a note to his Cabinet on the subject of promises about postwar conditions. It included the following passage:

A dangerous optimism is growing up about the conditions it will be possible to establish here after the war [he then listed various proposed social reforms]. The question steals across the mind whether we are not committing our forty five million people to tasks beyond their compass ... Ministers should, in my view, be careful not to raise false hopes, as was done last time by speeches about 'homes for heroes' etc. The broad masses of the people ... are liable to get very angry if they feel they have been gulled or cheated. It is because I do not wish to deceive the people by false hopes and airy visions of Utopia and Eldorado that I have refrained from making promises about the future. (Churchill, 1951, p. 861)

Churchill was both constitutionally correct and politically prudent in seeking not to commit a future Prime Minister to any particular set of postwar policies. In the event, a Labour government was elected to office in July 1945 with a massive overall majority.

The 1947 Town and Country Planning Act

On taking office, the Labour government began to work seriously on the urgent question of postwar planning and on the delivery, so far as was possible, of the various social benefits that had been promised in the set of wartime reports. After all, it was their stronger programme on these issues which had won them a landslide victory. Lewis Silkin was the new Minister of Town and Country Planning and there is no doubt of the strength of his commitment to a more rational and socially accountable system of land development. There had been no shortage of expert reports and focused discussion during the war. There was also evident mass support for the implementation of land development procedures which had the general aim of producing a better urban and rural environment, less congestion and a more efficient and rational configuration of land uses. But as Uthwatt had clearly shown, the achievement of these aims was dependent either on collectivizing the *ownership* of all development land (rejected by most sides as a financially and politically unworkable solution) or on collectivizing the *right to develop* such land (generally regarded as perfectly feasible). This, though, inevitably meant that the right to determine how any piece of land should be developed, and thus the right to determine its future value, must pass from the owner to some public authority. The problem, therefore, of compensation and betterment simply could not be escaped. It struck at the heart of the capital-accumulation process and was bound to affect the way that wealth was distributed. All the years of wartime discussion had, predictably, failed to achieve any consensus on this essentially political point. A land owner with developable land might agree entirely with broad statements about the need for a better, cleaner and more efficient environment. But if this meant, in concrete terms, a compensation offer of £10,000 for lost development rights which he judged to be worth half a million, the altruistic sentiments might evaporate.

Postwar planning legislation by the Labour government included measures to facilitate the containment of urban areas by 'green belts', to implement the policy of new 'satellite' towns for London and other major cities and to create National Parks. These are all important measures but they have been fully discussed elsewhere (for example, Cullingworth, 1975, 1982; Cherry, 1974). The key piece of legislation underpinning all postwar planning was the large and complicated 1947 Town and Country Planning Act. The process by which this Act reached the statute-book, and the work of the Whiskard Committee set up to advise Parliament on various complex and contentious issues, have been admirably set out by Cullingworth (1975). The task now is to review its main provisions.

The Act effectively collectivized the right to develop or redevelop any piece of land. This right was to be conferred or not, as the case might be, by the newly empowered local planning authorities (the counties). If the matter were to be disputed, decision-making power was to rest with the minister. If consent to develop was refused, no compensation was payable except to those who could show that their land had some unrealized development value on the day the Act was to come into force. (A total sum of £300 million was allocated to the Central Land Board to cover such claims and the total of claims finally made amounted to £380 million.) The logic of this refusal to compensate for the loss of future development rights in all other cases rested on the argument that values over and above existing use values are created by the community at large, and not by the owner. This was held to be so because the increased value flowed basically from society's increased need to use the land in some way. It did not matter whether this increased need was expressed in the form of a particular planning scheme (thus producing consents to develop) or whether it derived from a more general increase of activity, population and public expenditure in the area. In all these cases the increase in value was created by society at large and it should not be privately appropriated. Thus there should be no recompense for the land owner's loss of these future increases in value.

Similarly, where a consent to develop was granted, the increased land value that resulted (the 'development value') should rest not with the particular owner, but with society at large. To achieve this aim a tax called a development charge should be levied on the increase in value. There had been much discussion (as there has been since) on the rate at which this tax should be levied. There were some arguments for flexibility in setting the rate. This would allow a lower rate to be charged in areas where development (e.g. of factories to reduce unemployment) was especially desirable. But the idea of flexibility was dropped, partly on account of the administrative problems it would produce, and a flat-rate 100 per cent levy on betterment was to be paid to the Central Land Board. It further followed from this logic that where land was to be compulsorily acquired by a public authority to carry out some socially required development, the private vendor (who would probably be an unwilling vendor) was to be paid a value based on the *existing* use of the land. No allowance was to be made in the price for any 'hope value', that is value deriving from the anticipation of future development on the land.

The 1947 Act contained a mass of provisions apart from these financial ones. A complete administrative structure for plan-making and development control was set up, involving counties (including the LCC) and county boroughs as planning authorities. By conferring powers only on these larger bodies the number of authorities responsible for planning was reduced from 1441 to 145 (Cherry, 1974, p. 145). Development Plans were to be produced by each authority setting out its planning objectives. These Plans were to include a Report of Survey (giving the statistical and other background), a 'written statement' and a 'town map' to indicate detailed development intentions. These statutory requirements involved an immense increase in the workload of planning departments and a consequent rapid growth in the town planning profession which was, understandably, delighted. In fact the Town Planning Institute's Parliamentary Committee sent a memorandum to the ministry expressing its 'warm thanks' for the introduction of the legislation (*Journal of the Town Planning Institute*, vol. XXXIII, no. 3, p.81, 1947). However, the point here is not to evaluate the number of new jobs created or to accept at face value the notion that henceforth land development in Britain would be 'planned'. Rather the intention is to make a preliminary assessment of the impact of the new system on the profitability of capital accumulation by means of land development.

In the accumulation process $M \longrightarrow C \longrightarrow C^1 \longrightarrow M^1$, as applied to land development, the element C (the inputs to production) includes development land, labour and construction materials. The product C^1 had, before the war, been selected in the light of market conditions with the sole aim of maximizing the $M^1 - M$ increment, that is the profit. In fact, as we have seen, C^1 had typically been shopping developments and speculative housing for sale. The 1947 Act 'changed the rules' in several important ways. As noted earlier, some of the profit from land development in free market conditions stems from realizing increases in land values by speculative trading in land *prior* to its development. The 1947 Act produced a new and frustrating set of constraints. The sites to receive future development value were now to be identified by a statutory plan which set out the officially prescribed and democratically sanctioned pattern of future growth. So the total quantity of future development value was no longer 'floating' – the official plan would attach it to specific sites by identifying them as locations for development. And if land owners built instead of trading, the 100 per cent betterment charge would absorb all the increase in value resulting from the scheme. If the local authority itself carried out the development, the land would be acquired by them at existing use values, thus once again cancelling out any gain. The process of producing an $M^1 - M$ surplus either by land trading or developing would be drastically affected. The profit would be confined to what could be made by paying labour to turn a set of materials acquired at one total price into a product to be sold (with luck) at a somewhat higher one. One might just as well invest the capital in making saucepans.

These were not the only constraints imposed in the postwar reconstruction period. The actual choice of product (C^1) was largely determined by the building licensing system which had been set up during the war. Building work was divided between essential and non-essential, between factories, shops and offices, and between reconstruction and new development. Licences had to be obtained for any work above a minimal limit. Even local authority developments were subject to tight control. The Borough Engineer of Bridgewater complained that thirty-seven forms had to be completed before he could initiate any building work at all (Marriott, 1967, p.61). The strictness of the control led to a considerable black market in licences and to various illicit operations with pickaxes which transformed war-damaged buildings from the 'safe' to the 'dangerous' category – thus facilitating the granting of a licence to redevelop. While the tight control of building activity clearly stimulated the ingenuity of property entrepreneurs, it was not, in the long run, a situation they would wish to tolerate.

The overall effect of these measures was largely to stultify the land development process. The public sector, by and large, was not sufficiently funded to carry out the amount of new development and redevelopment that had been hoped for. This resulted partly from general economic difficulties and partly from the more specific fiscal severities necessarily accepted in order to obtain aid from the United States under the Marshall Plan in 1947-8 (Cooke, 1957, chapter 26). Landed interests, who often take a long-term view of events, tended to hold land off the market or else sold it, if they could, at a price that represented full development value. Those withholding land clearly anticipated a change of government in the foreseeable future. Development interests, often seeing little to attract them in construction contracts, turned increasingly to acquiring portfolios of land and existing properties in the confident expectation of a considerable property boom following the relaxation of controls. Both sets of interests anticipated well.

The retreat continues: 1951-85

The Conservatives returned to office in 1951. By this time the attempt to forge an economic recovery based on central control, austerity and the careful deployment of resources had wearied the electorate. In the field of land use planning the administrative machinery was clearly working too slowly anyway; only 22 of the 145 planning authorities had obtained ministerial approval for their plans by this date. The Conservatives were naturally committed to a return to free enterprise in land development. They took the view that the development charge would always, by some means or other, be added to the price at which land was sold for development. Thus it must increase development costs and, in the end, be paid by the ultimate *users* of the development (a chain of logic which is difficult to fault). As a result, the development charge was abolished by the 1953 Town and Country Planning Act and the collection of a tax on betterment was left to the general taxation system, in which bewildering jungle property company accountants and the Inland Revenue have stalked each other ever since. The subsequent 1954 Town and Country Planning Act drastically limited the circumstances in which compensation would be paid for the refusal of an application to develop. The glaring ambiguity left by these two Acts was that whereas land sold privately could achieve a 'free market' price, land subject to compulsory purchase by local authorities was acquired at existing use value only. This dual market in the sale of development land was abolished by the 1959 Town and Country Planning Act which effectively returned all development land to a free market and restored 'fair market price' as the basis for acquisitions by local authorities. This Act left an even greater ambiguity, still not effectively resolved. The right to develop land is still granted by the state but the resultant land value increases can be privately appropriated by the vendors of development land.

The return of a Labour government in 1964 led to further attempts by the state to grapple with this ambiguity. Following a White Paper in 1965 which made the same points about the iniquities of the land market as had been made by critical commentators going back to the 1780s (Ambrose, 1976, p.30), two new steps were taken. The 1967 Finance Act introduced a capital gains tax which affected, among other items, gains made by means of land value increases within the current use. The 1967 Land Commission Act introduced a new betterment levy (initially set at 40 per cent of the gain) and set up a Land Commission whose task would be to ensure that land required for the implementation of 'national, regional and local' plans could more readily be acquired should the 1947–53 experience of some vendors holding land off the market be repeated. The Land Commission's powers were to be stronger than normal local authority compulsory purchase powers because a reserve procedure was to be added (it was never actually put into operation) by which the commission could acquire land by 'a simplified procedure', that is without the appeal rights of unwilling vendors which had hitherto been available.

The Land Commission, as a new central body, was given the impossible task of working in harmony with the complex, and politically varied, existing structure of local planning authorities. Its progress was inevitably slow and by the time the Conservatives returned to power in 1970 fewer than 4000 acres had been purchased. The Tory government was pledged to abolish the Land Commission and promptly did so on the grounds that it had 'no place in a free society'. According to Ratcliffe (1976, pp.44–5), the Land Commission had in any event been attacking the wrong problem. Development, he argued, was being held up more by the slowness of planning authorities to zone land than by vendors refusing to sell. This was probably a valid conclusion to draw from empirical observation at a pragmatic level. More fundamentally, however, the land problem cannot simply be defined in terms of the *rate* of development in any given period. The essential issue (as Ratcliffe sees elsewhere with admirable clarity) concerns the division of the gain in land value resulting from current or future development. How much should go to the vendor and how much to the public purse?

The 1968 Town and Country Planning Act (1969 for Scotland), the consolidating legislation of 1971 and 1972, and the 1974 reorganization of local government which produced a complex two-tier structure of planning powers can be regarded, in the last analysis, as cosmetic steps. The notion of drawing up broad-brush (or broad felt-tip) Structure Plans at the higher level and then seeking to implement them by detailed land allocations in 'local plans' at the lower level may be theoretically sound. In practice, however, the Plans are often little more than a set of well-intentioned statements about, for example, the need for more low-cost housing, more public transport and more semi-skilled employment (see Figure 2.7). The point is that the processes which produce, or fail to produce, such outcomes are not remotely amenable to control by planning departments. In practice also, the Structure Plan may take so long to produce, and to update, that much actual development on the ground is carried out following *ad hoc* planning decisions taken in the absence of any statutory local plan. Ratcliffe argues that although considerable resources have been devoted to the task of structure planning, the result has often been to provide 'a refinement in inexactitude' (1976, p.75).

More radically, Pickvance (and many others) has seen the entire post-1968 apparatus as 'trend planning' – as a complicated way of incorporating in plans a pattern of land development that would have occurred in much the same way anyway. This criticism will be examined more closely later (as indeed Pickvance himself does in a later footnote). Structure planning, in essence, seems to be about local authority procedures, about computer-based techniques, even about career advancement. It does not seem to be about intervening in the land development process in any way that either produces more socially sensitive development patterns or effectively reduces the very large element of unproductive speculative gain in the

A.9 Services and Facilities

To guide the provision of sufficient facilities in phase with residential development and in appropriate locations for health, welfare, cultural, educational, recreational and utility services.

Operational Aims

A.10 Function of the Structure Plan

To set out the County Council's general planning policies, within which major development decisions can be made, investment programmes can be drawn up, and detailed local plans can be prepared.

A.11 National and Regional Policy

To relate planning within the County properly to the planning of the region and nation.

A.12 Local Planning

To integrate local planning objectives and policies with those for the County as a whole, and to provide an adequate basis for the preparation of Local Plans.

A.13 Social and Community

To provide a framework within which the social needs and aspirations of local communities can be expressed and realised.

A.14 Feasibility

To ensure that policies and proposals are economically, socially, and technically feasible.

A.15 Implementation

To ensure measures are available to put policies into operation, and carry out proposals, using both public and private agencies.

A.16 Flexibility

To ensure that long-term policies and proposals are sufficiently adaptable to enable them to be modified, having regard to social, economic, and technological changes, or to changes in objectives.

A.17 Monitoring

To ensure continuous monitoring of the performance of policy in the light of changing circumstances.

Objectives

2.3 Listed below in no order of priority are the initial OBJECTIVES relating to the main subjects with which the first County Structure Plan is concerned. Further objectives will be added when the policies omitted from this Plan are being prepared.

Housing

H.1 To make provision in terms of land and services, to meet the housing needs of predicted future increases in the number of households (Aim A.4).

H.2 To make provision in terms of land and services for the elimination of shared dwellings from the existing housing stock (Aims A.4, A.5).

H.3 To create the circumstances within which the redevelopment or improvement of sub-standard housing can take place (Aims A.4, A.5).

H.4 To encourage the provision of low price housing with wider choice of

M^1 – M increment. The Uthwatt Committee – and many others before and since – saw quite clearly that these two aims were virtually identical, or rather could both be achieved by a single set of interventionary measures. The structure planning of the last decade or so has simply lost sight of the wood for the bureaucratic, career development, 'participatory', 'info-tech' trees.

The long retreat from Uthwatt continued with a foolhardy and ill-thought-out advance that rapidly turned into a rout – the 1975 Community Land Act. The origins, operation and demise of the Community Land Scheme have been exhaustively discussed else-where (see, for example, Barrett *et al.*, 1978; and Boddy, in Paris, 1982). The scheme attempted to impose a betterment tax and to give planning authorities the kind of powers that had been given to the long defunct 1967 Land Commission (Cox, 1980). It aimed to give structure planning authorities the right to acquire develop-ment land in order to facilitate the implementation of preferred developments. In this it went little beyond existing compulsory purchase powers. But the *price* at which sites could be acquired was to be market value less the Development Land Tax (DLT) which the vendor would have paid to the Inland Revenue in respect of the sale. This was a newly devised tax relating specifically to profits on land dealing. If set at 100 per cent, the theoretical effect would be to enable a local authority to purchase at whatever price the vendor originally paid for the land. The authority could then retain the freehold and seek to attract developers on a leasehold basis or it could sell at full market value and retain in the public purse what might, in loose terms, be called the betterment.

The theory is reasonably sound, but in practice the scheme was a disaster. Local authority treasurers were deluged with a mass of highly technical directives about how to implement the scheme and often had to turn to expensive private consultants for advice. Endless discussions ensued between district councils (as zoning authorities) and county or metropolitan councils (as the originators of strategic plans) about which sites should be acquired under the scheme – a discussion not made any easier by the often antagonistic

Figure 2.7 *Extract from a typical Structure Plan – the operational aims, objectives and goals, etc. are worthy but largely non-implementable by the planning agency.*

Source: *Extract from the East Sussex Structure Plan, 1975 and subsequent years*

politics of the upper- and lower-tier authorities. Meanwhile land owners whose interests were threatened by the danger of a compulsory sale at a 'net of tax' price engaged in some long-winded and creative accountancy to show that there was in fact no gain being made on the site in question, consequently no DLT liability and thus no reduction to be made from full market value. If given the task of designing a scheme that had the theoretical aim of recouping betterment, but which could not possibly work in practice, the result might look rather like the 1975 Community Land Scheme. The scheme was well on the way to being both 'bent into shape' by the development industry (Ambrose, 1976) and of dying of neglect (Boddy, 1978) long before its statutory death on the election of the Thatcher government in 1979.

The demise of planning has been hastened by a rash of measures since that date. Land use control has effectively been removed in the many Enterprise Zones set up under the legislation of the early 1980s. The related ideas of Simplified Planning Zones and Flexible Planning Permissions are well on the way to implementation. The most recent policy move is the so-called Reform of the Use Classes Order which will make it unnecessary to seek planning permission for most changes of use in existing buildings. Inner urban areas with attractive architecture, for example the Georgian areas near the centre of many provincial cities, are likely to become a speculative arena wherever there is the possibility of converting residential buildings into small suites of offices with a higher rental potential. The free play of the market will overcome 'public interest' considerations such as extra traffic generation, environmental aesthetics and housing loss – all matters which are currently taken into account by the development control system.

Thus the post-Uthwatt retreat from a strong state interventionary role in land development, a retreat interrupted by brief advances in 1946–8, 1965–70 and 1974–7 has now by the mid-1980s become a rout. In Chapters 3–6 we examine the current structure and operation of the land development system under an administration that is, paradoxically, the most centrally controlled since the war and probably the most rightist since the coming of universal suffrage earlier this century.

PART II
The development system

This part of the book outlines the system which currently produces additions to, and renewals of, the built environment. It will be followed, in Part III, by two case studies of the system at work. A system means a set of elements which are connected up together by a pattern of linkages. This arrangement does not 'work', or produce any outcome, until it is 'energized' by flows along the linkages (just as the wiring system of a house does not produce light or heat until switched on). In the system which produces buildings, shown overleaf as a diagram, there are fifteen numbered elements. The linkages between certain pairs of these elements carry flows of money, political influence or some other form of interaction. The relationships producing the flows, which are often clearly stronger in one direction than the other, may be statutory, contractual or informal.

The model incorporates the shortcomings common to all such attempts to simplify a very complex reality. The elements are by no means as separate or neatly differentiated in real life as the diagram would imply. In addition, the set of connecting linkages shown could be made much more complex since some kind of relationship, however tenuous, probably exists between most pairs of elements in the system. In fact the theoretical maximum number of links in such a system is $\frac{1}{2}[n\,(n-1)]$, where n is the number of elements. In this system, where $n = 15$, this means 105 possible connections between pairs of elements. The particular connections shown represent a trade-off between the competing claims of completeness of coverage and the intelligibility of the diagram.

Two other preliminary points should be made. First, the model

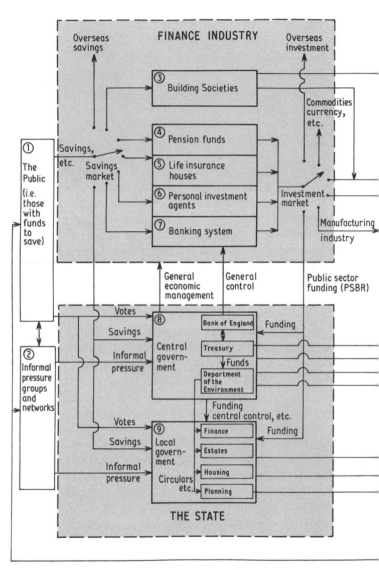

The development system in the UK.
(© Peter Ambrose 1984)

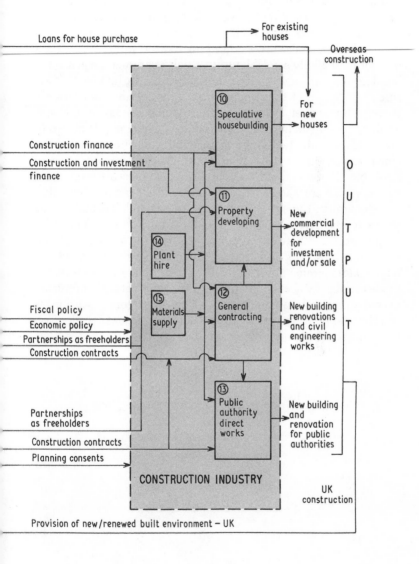

Loans for house purchase

For existing houses

Overseas construction

⑩ Speculative housebuilding

For new houses

Construction finance

Construction and investment finance

O

U

T

⑪ Property developing

New commercial development for investment and/or sale

P

⑭ Plant hire

U

T

⑮ Materials supply

⑫ General contracting

New building renovations and civil engineering works

Fiscal policy

Economic policy

Partnerships as freeholders

Construction contracts

⑬ Public authority direct works

New building and renovation for public authorities

Partnerships as freeholders

Construction contracts

Planning consents

CONSTRUCTION INDUSTRY

UK construction

Provision of new/renewed built environment − UK

really identifies separate *functions* rather than mutually exclusive sets of people or organizations. We all play a number of roles in the system. For example, individuals in a local government planning department are also members of the general public. They probably invest their savings in the finance industry. Some of them may even be members of a pressure group trying to exert influence on their own (or more likely a neighbouring) local government department. Similarly, certain large construction companies are involved in two, three or even all of the construction activities shown. Certainly some of the largest are also very active in the finance industry. Secondly, the model is drawn such that each element is placed in one of three main 'fields': the finance industry, the state, and the construction industry. Most elements fall clearly into one of these fields but the general public (1) and informal pressure groups and networks (2) are shown as outside all three fields. One other sub-element in the system, the Bank of England, has ambiguous status. It was nationalized in 1946 so it is, in theory, democratically accountable and part of the public sector. Its general stance and behaviour, however, is hardly distinguishable from that of the large-scale capitalist interests that together dominate the rest of the finance industry. The issue of the partial fogging of the theoretically clear distinction between private and public sector institutions is one that has attracted much critical debate in recent decades (see, for example, Miliband, 1973) and the matter is simply noted here.

3
People

The general public (1 in the diagram on pp.68–9) links up with the development system in three main ways: as a user of the product (new or renovated buildings), as a political force seeking to influence the system and as a source of capital (M). The first of these is straightforward. Most human activities require specially designed built space – buildings in which to live, work, exchange money for goods and services, be educated, be cared for when ill, and enjoy recreational and cultural experiences. Since all buildings decay at some rate, the task of renewing some of the total stock is continuous. But the general public's requirement of the development system is more complex than this. People need an appropriate *mix* of the various forms of built space within easy access of their home, unless they deliberately choose to live in places where such a requirement is unreasonable. This appropriate mix of workspace, playspace, shopping space, etc. is a necessary condition for comfortable living. It is not, however, a sufficient condition. For example, the work buildings (e.g. factories and offices) may exist but the operation of the local economy may cause them to be filled with jobs unsuitable for the local population, or may cause the jobs to be lost altogether by plant closures.

There is thus an important distinction (not always evident in planning deliberations between the local pattern of *buildings* and the pattern of economic and social activity being carried on *in* those buildings. The former may look perfectly adequate in terms of some accepted way of relating a given level of population to their workspace, shopping space and recreational space needs as expressed in units such as square metres. But as a result of the workings of political and economic forces, these buildings may be inaccessible

to some local people because, in simple terms, the access requirements are beyond their means. As an example, there may be a large
number of houses on the market within easy reach of an inner
urban area of housing stress. But if they cost £50,000 each and the
average local wage is £100 per week, they are not available to all
local people. Similarly, a newly developed covered shopping mall,
full of relatively expensive supermarkets and trendy boutiques and
aimed at car-borne shoppers, is almost equally unhelpful for a local
population with a low car-ownership level who may desperately
need more local dispensing chemists to have prescriptions made up.
This distinction between an apparently sufficient provision of local
buildings and the degree of user *access* to these buildings will be
discussed more fully in Chapter 8. It has become clear that
'planning' can do something to bring about the buildings but it has
very little power to ensure equitable access.

The second form of linkage between people at large and the
system is political. Since the behaviour and output of the system is
of some significance to literally everyone, it is to be expected that
the general public will seek to influence the way it works. In terms
of the 'liberal democratic' view (see Chapter 1) the 'public interest' is
safeguarded by the formal arrangements of central and local
democracy. Both levels of government are elected, and periodically
re-elected, by a democratic process based on almost universal
suffrage (although it should be noted that turn-out rates in local
elections typically vary between 35 and 50 per cent). Between
elections public influence can be exerted in a number of ways.
Structure Plans, before they are officially adopted, are subject to
Examination in Public. Individual planning applications can, if the
Secretary of State is convinced of the need, be 'called in' and
subjected to a Public Inquiry. In both these cases evidence and
opinion can be brought forward, in theory, by any member of the
public or any group. By these and related means the public is invited
to 'participate' in the 'planning process'.

The quotation marks have been used above because for a number
of reasons it would be naïve to believe that these arrangements
produce any really significant degree of power-sharing. The issue
will be more closely examined in Part III but for the moment a
number of general points can be made. As the development system
becomes more complex, powerful and internationalized, so it
becomes more difficult for people not directly connected with it

either to comprehend its workings or, as a logical consequence, to affect them. As the issues become defined more in terms of professional jargon, technical models and computerized data, and less in terms of plain English, so the politics of choosing between options becomes obscured and the issue is made to appear more as a matter for the planning 'expert', rather than ordinary people, to decide. As the timespan lengthens between the origin point of a big development (for example, a motorway, airport or large-scale shopping precinct) and the point when its likely effects 'surface' in the media and general consciousness, so it becomes more difficult for members of the public to predict the implications of the scheme *for them*. By the time these implications are generally evident the scheme is probably almost at the concrete-pouring stage – several years too late for any protest to be effective. 'Public participation', it has frequently been argued, is an almost meaningless phrase, or one

Figure 3.1 *The 1979 Coin Street Public Inquiry in session. Coin Street, near the south bank of the Thames, was a classic 'homes versus offices' issue. The inquiry lasted nearly a year and produced over 800 documents. The Inspector and two Assessors preside on the left. Visible among the mass of papers are highly paid QCs, local politicians and a prominent MP in the gallery. Following strong arguments by the Coin Street Action Group that the proceedings had been taken over by jargon-toting lawyers, the inquiry was halted for a week while a 'Social Assessor' was appointed.*

with misleading connotations. For all the legislative provisions, and the attempts of many planning officers to engender debate about local issues, the consultation procedures often seem to have the effect of absorbing, rather than transmitting, local opinion about developments. (See Figure 3.1.)

The third form of linkage between people at large and the development system stems from the need felt by virtually everyone to set aside some proportion of current income against their own, or their dependents', future needs – principally against needs resulting from illness, accident, retirement and death. The growth of private sector systems of provision, from the locally based 'benefit societies' of Victorian times to the massive financial corporations of today, is well enough known. The parallel advance of the state into the insurance and pensions field, marked by sudden steps forward such as the Beveridge Report in 1942 has occurred as expectations about social security have risen and as demographic trends have lengthened the average timespan between retirement (or redundancy) and death. Private capitalists, as employers, have in broad terms welcomed and supported the state's intervention in the field of welfare provision. Clearly, for them, it is advantageous if the cost of maintaining the health and educational level of the working population, and thus ensuring an adequate supply of usable labour, is met out of general taxation and individual contribution ₁ather than paid for by the employer. But the advance of state provision in these fields came to a halt in Britain sometime in the 1950s or early 1960s (see, for example, Kincaid, 1973). Although the state social security schemes have continued, their significance relative to private sector schemes has declined. The vast majority of the British population are now linked into private savings, insurance and retirement schemes. This means that the total amount of money deducted from current income and invested via the private sector to provide for future needs, that is the 'deferred income' of the great majority of working-age people, is extremely large. It is also growing in real terms as the insurance industry works out ever more comprehensive schemes of cover and as the post-retirement lifespan slowly lengthens.

Most of this provision that millions of people make for their future needs, plus the short-term saving of temporarily surplus funds, is invested on their behalf by one of the five types of institution shown as 3 to 7 in the diagram on pp.68–9. A significant proportion of it is allocated, via the investment market 'distributor', to provide the energizing power (or M) for housebuilding and property development. Thus most members of the public are themselves the ultimate providers of much of the money which flows through various paths in the diagram and produces, in the end, additions to the built environment. But in parting with their money people are acting as atomized units. They do not acquire commensurate and collective power to condition the output of the system. In theory, their collective wishes are transmitted via central and local government (8 and 9) supplemented by informal pressure groups and networks (2). But to the extent that there is unrest about the pattern of output, for example, about the amount, price and quality of housing produced, so to that extent can elements 8 and 9 be seen as working imperfectly. In this situation feelings may increasingly be channelled through element 2.

Informal pressure groups and networks

Much of the recent literature referred to in Chapter 1 on the nature of the state in capitalist systems has been concerned with the extent to which a five-yearly visit to the ballot-box can be regarded as a meaningful exercise in participatory democracy. The range of issues on which people are asked to vote, the clear mass media and press imbalance in favour of status quo attitudes and solutions, the technical complexity and information management that makes well-informed decision-making on some issues (for example, the preferred pattern of housing subsidies) impossible, and the insensitivity of governments to expressions of public concern *between* elections, all combine to reduce the effectiveness of quinquennial voting as a means of effective power-sharing. One response to this situation is to seek other means of representation by lobbying in some informal group (2). Almost any group that expresses a collective view on some matter can be regarded as a pressure group although the size, strength, effectiveness and permanence of such groups vary enormously. At one extreme the 'roads lobby', an amalgam of international oil, construction and vehicle-manufacturing interests (Hamer, 1975), has worked successfully to shift the balance of freight and people's movement from rail to road (and from public transport to private). At the other extreme a small group of local residents may come together temporarily, and usually too late, to try to modify some development scheme that affects their interests.

In the context of the diagram on pp.68–9, element 2 represents groups which have their roots in the general public and which seek to influence the behaviour of the development system either by exerting pressure on the national or local state or by direct negotiation with property developing institutions or possibly, as a final consciousness-raising gesture, by direct action on a building site. Even within this more narrowly defined set of pressure groups, considerable differences exist. Some groups, for example Shelter (the National Campaign for the Homeless), have a corporate status and a public aura that is both a strength and a weakness. In Shelter's case the strength derives from its (presumed) permanence, its capacity to research and publicize important information that government would rather conceal and from the goodwill it enjoys across a broad political spectrum. Its weakness lies in the constraints imposed by the methods of funding on which its existence depends (grants, bequests, charity status, proceeds of church bazaars, etc.). Full-time workers in organizations such as Shelter are well able to comprehend the inevitable relationship between, on the one hand, a largely capitalist market in land and housing and, on the other, a shortfall of provision for those with least economic power to compete in that market. But their critique of events, and their public pronouncements, must fall some way short of criticism at this structural level.

Citizens' groups that form spontaneously around local development issues have a converse set of characteristics (see Figure 3.2). They lack permanence, often coming together (like the Brighton Marina Action Campaign) in response to a specific threat to what they regard as important and then often dissolving when the issue is resolved against them or (more rarely) partly in their favour. This dissolution is not inevitable, and there are various examples of groups which formed over one issue and have lived on to contest others. The funding of such groups is haphazard, and professionals who require some level of payment for their services (such as lawyers) sometimes show declining levels of interest when their fees cannot be met. Citizens' groups usually depend heavily upon the commitment, analytical ability and organizing drive of a limited number of people. These people can get tired. If they do, and no obvious successors come forward, there is no formal structure,

Figure 3.2 *Citizens' action groups at work, organized in this case around several important issues in London's docklands, notably housing and Stolport (see Chapter 8).*

source of finance or constitutional basis to ensure the continuance of the work. In many cases the hard-won information and carefully thought out arguments are lost for lack of a permanent secretariat and sometimes another group needs to start almost from scratch when the same contentious issue, having lain dormant for ten years, surfaces again. Informal citizens' groups are also vulnerable to the question (usually from elected politicians), 'Who elected you?' The question obviously has some force. 'Public opinion' is a very slippery concept and it is often a moot point whether a citizens' group (self-appointed and politically aroused on this particular issue) or members of the local council (elected by others and in some kind of touch with constituents on a broad range of issues) are more closely attuned to the complex set of feelings held on any contentious local issue.

The main strength of citizens' groups lies in their strong feelings about the fairness or otherwise of particular possible outcomes. Politics is nothing without emotion. Most action groups exhibit deep feeling to which is harnessed, very often, a well-documented

Figure 3.3   *Southwark people express their opinion of a high-price private housing development on the south bank of the Thames. Strong defences and surveillance equipment is apparently necessary for security. The riverside walk is barred to non-residents. Luxury converted warehouses are visible across the river. (© Peter Ambrose 1986)*

and penetrating analysis of the local issue plus (which is crucial) the connections between this particular issue and the general workings of the development system. There is now a considerable under-standing, which it would be wrong to devalue with the adjective 'theoretical', of the way higher-revenue uses drive out lower-revenue uses in most urban rebuilding situations. The new development schemes which are often foisted on lower-income inner city residents almost invariably reflect a drive for increased capital accumulation by investors, not a concern for the needs of the area and its people. This motivation is predictable and its manifestation in different areas has surface variations only. The outcomes, in terms of the new distribution of costs and benefits for local people and others, are also predictable – the poorest and politically weakest usually come off worst.

Many citizens' groups are better able to understand and confront this linkage between general forces in capitalist development and their local manifestation far better than are the general run of locally elected politicians and the officers that serve them (who are often uncomfortable if drawn into public debate on the matter). In the end, the arguments presented by action groups based on material produced on a shoestring budget are usually more penetrating, more accurate and show a much sharper perception of the forces at work than does the mass of neatly printed official material produced for the consumption of councillors, ministers, public inquiry inspectors and the press. The value of this judgement can be assessed later by reference to the case studies in Part III.

Finance

The finance industry is not an industry in the generally understood sense. It does not bring together raw materials, labour power, capital, etc. and convert them into a finished product for sale. Instead it deals in one commodity – money. Principally it borrows money in the form of deposits, savings or pensions and insurance contributions, and then lends or invests it again. It gains an $M^1 - M$ increment (see Chapter 1) by paying a certain percentage to the owner for the use of the money, or promising to pay back a larger sum at some future date, and then re-using the money in ways which produce a percentage or return in excess of this. One could at once ask why the original owner does not invest the money directly into the activities that produce the higher return. A small minority do, principally by placing their funds at risk in initiating some entrepreneurial activity of their own. But the uncertainties of this course of action make it unattractive to the majority. To minimize the risk expertise is required, and often investment on a scale that very few individuals could contemplate.

Large financial institutions have therefore grown up, over several centuries, to carry out the function of channelling the flow of surplus private funds available for investment, so that they reach the hands of entrepreneurs requiring further capital. Because they offer expertise and are capable of collecting and processing information on a wide variety of possible markets for the money, these institutions have gained immensely both in their throughput of business and their political influence. In Britain they now collectively constitute what is called 'The City' (Coakley and Harris, 1983). This is not, of course, to say that the activities of the British finance industry are confined to London. As foreign currency dealing and investment overseas have gradually become more important the trade in money has become literally worldwide, aided by the weightless nature of the commodity. Virtually all trans-actions, apart from the occasional shipment of gold, are book entries and a deposit, loan or currency exchange can be carried out instantaneously in any centre in the world assuming the presence of state-of-the-art information technology. This growing inter-nationalization of the trade in money is itself an important element in the changing commercial environment in which the develop-ment system functions. In this necessarily selective chapter we look at five different forms of institution in the finance industry: building societies, pension funds, life insurance houses, personal investment agents and banks. Together they form an immensely powerful force in the British economy and thus exert powerful political pressures on government.

Building societies

The main contemporary function of building societies is to invite deposits from the public at large, using an ever increasing number of high street collecting points. The resultant funds are lent out, primarily to house-purchasers and almost invariably on the security of the property being purchased. This has not always been the prime function of the societies, which have existed in one form or another for over 200 years. More information on their history and changing role can be gained by reference to Boddy (1980).

The building society movement has had considerable success in attracting an ever increasing share of private savings over the past sixty years (see Figure 4.1). Nearly all this money has been re-lent to finance house purchase and this has been the facilitating mechanism behind the striking growth of owner-occupancy over this period (from approximately 10 per cent of households in 1920 to over 60 per cent now). This growth obviously cannot continue indefinitely since there must be some saturation point beyond which owner-occupancy cannot be increased. So the building society movement has been active in exploring other ways in which to expand. Some societies are interested in financing housing production, trading in development land or expanding their role in conveyancing, insurance and estate agency; others favour the possibilities of developing their banking role and extending their

Figure 4.1   *The building society movement has largely financed the immense expansion of owner-occupancy since 1919. This advertisement dates from the 1930s and emphasizes the considerable debt (in more ways than one) that grateful purchasers owed to societies such as the Worthing Permanent.*

range of lending. Some legislative changes will be required to permit significant moves in these directions since the current state of the law makes it difficult for building societies (which are formally Friendly Societies) to engage in most of these potentially profitable activities.

In the diagram on pp. 68–9 the building societies (3) are shown as separate from those parts of the construction industry with which they are most closely connected – namely speculative house-building (10) and property developing (11). But this could be misleading. In practice there is often, at the local and national level, a strong presence of construction industry interests (landowners, land dealers, constructors, engineers, surveyors, estate agents, etc.) on building society boards. This is not surprising since the building societies have become, in a sense, the hire-purchase system for the housebuilding industry. The producers of housing and the credit providers have an almost identical interest in ensuring that house values (which in aggregate represent most of the assets of the building societies) rise at least as fast as inflation. Equally the house-purchase loans translate directly into the capital sums received by the housebuilders for their product. Thus the greater the throughput of funds, the faster the growth of both building society business and the market for new houses. This close congruence of interests is both significant and unusual. Few, if any, comparable countries have a system where so large a proportion of purchase finance (typically 85 per cent or so) is provided by lending institutions which have this business as their main function. The possibilities for oligopolistic management of the housing market, and especially house price levels, seem to be even stronger here than in comparable capitalist countries.

The effects of the building societies on the output of the development system are very significant and pervasive, although they are not declared in any obvious way; for example, it would be very unusual for building society interests to be prominent at Structure Plan Examinations in Public or at planning inquiries. Since the building society/house construction complex has a strong interest in promoting house sales, it is equally keen to help promote the social conditions conducive to this aim. Such social conditions include growth in real incomes, political stability, property-oriented consumerism, 'regular' lifestyles, thrifty long-term attitudes and the avoidance of destabilizing industrial militancy or any other remotely radical thoughts or actions.

These aims, it can be readily seen, are generally congruent with those of all Conservative and, so far, most Labour governments. As a result, the building society movement is a highly influential element in British politics, although as is the case with most really powerful lobbies, this influence is neither generally very visible nor easily measurable. One tangible result, evident for many decades now, has been for governments to make a very costly tax concession to house-buyers (interest on house-purchase loans is tax deductible). This inducement to purchase has been complemented in the past decade or so by a steady move to close down the other main housing system – publicly developed housing for rent. The amount of public subsidy per housing unit in the public sector has been drastically reduced over recent years and it is now only a small proportion of that granted per unit in the owner-occupied sector. The enormous increase in the cost to the Exchequer which has resulted from the expansion of owner-occupancy, and the tax concessions offered to support it, is an indication both of the political power of the building society/housebuilding lobby and of the often explicit view held by successive administrations that increased home ownership fosters a more stable and governable society.

Certain specific situations arise in which the lending policies of building societies affect development outcomes. Societies in a particular area may take the view, which often appears to be collectively held, that no loans for house purchase should be made in certain defined, or 'red-lined' zones – typically in inner urban areas. This may be because there is an evident risk of public land acquisition for roadbuilding or some other purpose. Or possibly such zones have an obvious potential for high-revenue commercial redevelopment. Fostering a higher level of owner-occupancy would not make sense in either situation. Large road schemes are likely to reduce house values (which reduces the security for the loans) and lucrative commercial redevelopments may be complicated if the area is peppered with new owner-occupiers. When local building societies make these judgements, they are acting as powerful reinforcing agents accelerating the rate of physical decay in these zones. Conversely, if they lend freely in other inner city zones, this is both an indication and a reinforcement of social 'upgrading' tendencies in these areas since an increasing proportion of owner-occupiers is usually believed to mean better preservation of the housing fabric, more powerful citizen pressures for environmental improvements, better schools and, in extreme cases, an inducement to private capital to invest in the area (see Chapter 8 on docklands).

These expectations, and the lending policies based on them, are culturally determined and clearly contestable. The point is not whether they are true, but rather that they are *believed* to be true by most private and public decision-makers who have power to condition the nature of housing investment in the areas in question. On current trends more and more of these decision-makers are likely to be working in the building society movement rather than in public sector authorities. It follows that the views collectively held within the movement, whether about the desirability of a general move towards more private home owner-ship or in relation to preferred outcomes for specific sites, are likely to play an increasingly important role in influencing the output of the development system. These views are often likely to be reinforced, in the current ideological climate, by many outside the movement who aspire to home ownership in the belief that it is the surest way to increase their personal financial assets – by no means always a correct assessment.

Pension funds

Reference was made in Chapter 3 to the widely felt need for some systematic and reliable mechanism for deducting a proportion of working-age income and investing it in order to provide a post-retirement income. Pension funds (4, in the diagram on pp.68–9) ful-fil this function. The degree of post-retirement comfort will depend upon whether or not the fund which produces this 'deferred income' can invest in such a way as to beat inflation and thus to increase the real value of the money put in. Some funds are privately owned and managed (either by the employer or some specialist agency) and some are owned and run by state corporations (such as the Post Office). The former basis is bound to produce a 'limited responsibility' pattern of investment since the fund managers, as trustees, need to have regard only to the interests of their specific contributors (and/or the employer). They will therefore invest for maximum profitability, consistent with safety, with this in mind. The latter basis should incorporate, in theory, a broader degree of social responsibility since public corporations are formally a part of the state, the government of which is ultimately answerable to the whole electorate. In practice, there is no discernible difference between the investment behaviour of the two types of fund.

There are also two possible *bases* on which post-retirement provision can be arranged. The *current transfer system* requires that in any given year (or other appropriate period) those in work contribute sufficient money from their pay to support the current cohort of retired people. The state exchequer collects and distributes the money on a publicly accountable 'pay as you go' basis and no investment, or 'storage' of funds is necessary. This is more or less the basis on which *state* pensions are currently administered in Britain. Alternatively, each working individual can be a member of some contributory scheme run by the employer (or the employer's advisors) under which the contributions are invested primarily as private venture capital and the size of the eventual pension depends, to a large extent, on the success or otherwise of the particular set of investments selected by the fund managers. No account need be taken by the managers of such questions as 'general societal needs' in framing their investment policies. Because of the duty to the contributors, all investment decisions must take account *only* of the achievement of the maximum possible growth of the fund consistent with generally acceptable levels of safety. It is on this basis that virtually all non-state pension schemes are run.

From the point of view of the investment market, especially in relation to property, the pension funds are one of the main sources of capital (see Minns, 1980). In normal circumstances finding the money for a big property scheme is one of the easiest aspects to arrange. The funds (together with the insurance companies) have more than £50 million of new money available to invest *per day*. The recent pattern of this investment will be outlined after the next section, but it is important to note that considerable changes have occurred in recent decades in the strategies adopted. Traditionally the funds would make a long-term, fixed-interest loan to carry out a particular property development with the debt secured by a mortgage on the property in question. This simple strategy has evolved to something much more complex with the funds typically acquiring the freehold of land ripe for commercial development as an investment or buying the development on completion and leasing it back to the developer for him to rent out or acquiring a stake in the share capital of the development company or by entering an agreement by which the fund benefits from a proportion of the rental growth of the building. These do not exhaust the possible strategies and often a fund will provide the capital for a property scheme using some complex combination of these, and other, means of maximizing the return. Whatever the specific arrangements, they will tend to reflect the *long-term* nature of the fund's interest. Property schemes may not 'mature' financially for several decades, but once the current revenue flow begins to exceed the costs (some of which are historically fixed), it will probably continue to do so by an increasing margin until the time is ripe for a potential 'step up' in revenues following the redevelopment of the site after perhaps fifty years or more. For this reason, and because of their own long-term investment 'horizon', pension funds are generally interested in the flexibility which results from acquiring the *freehold* of a development site, or failing that, a lease of sufficient length (120 years or more) to ensure that at least one future redevelopment can be carried out on the site. (See Figure 4.2.)

Since the opening up of the debate about the political role of pension funds in the last decade or so, there has grown up an uneasy relationship between the funds, as essentially capitalist institutions, and the labour movement. This is an especially difficult interface for union officials who may serve as representatives of their members on the board of a company or even as part of the company's pension fund management team. Trade unionists in these positions are deeply co-opted into a system which has the pursuit of profit in the heartland of capitalism as its sole objective and conflicts of loyalty very often arise. For example, it may seem to make commercial sense to invest in a redevelopment which provides new space for high-technology, high-skill, capital-intensive manufacturing activity. As a result, the number of jobs may be reduced to a half or less of those formerly on the site – and the new jobs may not suit the employment needs of local people, some of whom may be members of the labour representative's own union.

Similarly, at times when a rightist government is selling off national assets at well below their market value (e.g. the British National Oil Corporation and British Telecom), it might make commercial sense to acquire shares. But this is tacitly to approve a process of privatization that usually leads to 'rationalization' and the shedding of labour. As another example, the logic of the capitalist market may induce managers to invest in some way that most people would probably regard as anti-social as when the pension fund of British Rail (nominally a public service organization) invested heavily via Sotheby's, in the 1970s, in important

The Local Authorities' Property Fund

Property Portfolio

Offices

Property	Description	Tenure	Tenant	Terms of Lease
EDINBURGH 47 Melville Street, and, 1 Melville Crescent	Offices of 8,000 sq. ft. on five floors	Freehold	Abacus Developments Limited	25 years from 23/10/81. 5 year rent reviews
ENFIELD Tower Point, Sydney Road	Offices totalling 128,650 sq. ft. with parking for 254 cars	Freehold	Eastern Gas Board	35 years from 17.12.69. 7 year rent reviews
GLASGOW 97-99 West Regent Street	Offices of 6,029 sq. ft. on basement, ground and two upper floors	Freehold	Lambert Smith and Partners (Scotland) Ltd	25 years from 8.3.82. 5 year rent reviews.
LONDON EC2 14-17 Dominion Street	Offices of 27,845 sq. ft. on basement, ground and seven upper floors	Freehold	Simmons and Simmons (Solicitors)	25 years from 19.9.75. 5 year rent reviews
LONDON, EC4 St. Paul's House, Warwick Lane	Offices of 27,000 sq. ft. on basement, ground and five upper floors with ground floor covered car park	Freehold	Moore Stephens and Company (Chartered Accountants)	25 years from 1.4.76. 5 year rent reviews

Figure 4.2   *The investment behaviour of public sector pension funds does not differ from those in the private sector. The Local Authorities' Property Fund specializes in commercial and industrial property and helps to place new investment for over sixty local authority superannuation funds. In the last few years the most favoured form of property has been prime retail developments.*
Source: *Extract from Annual Report and Accounts 1982/3 of the Local Authorities' Property Fund*

works of art. This was to deny public access to these works and to treat them purely as financial objects. Potentially this action is extremely significant to the already highly artificial art market since this fund alone was a more powerful buyer than the National

Gallery and the Tate combined. In practice pension funds, both individually and collectively, are free to adopt a virtually autonomous investment policy. It can easily be argued that the policies they do adopt are often in conflict with the long-term interests of many sections of the labour movement. But trade unionists who are theoretically in a position to advocate the channelling of investment into labour-intensive activities in inner city locations, or local authority schemes designed to serve lower-income residents, always face the compelling argument that such investment would be commercially uncompetitive and that the contributors they have a duty to protect would ultimately suffer lower pensions. There is no way around this impasse since it reflects one of the fundamental contradictions of capitalist organization.

The state, as well as organized labour, is closely interested in the development of the funds. Postwar governments have nearly all been active in securing an increasing share of pension provision for the capitalist investment market. Labour governments, and especially the Wilson administration of the late 1960s have been no exception (see Kincaid, 1973). The formation and growth of private pension schemes have been powerfully fostered by fiscal concessions both to individuals (whose contributions are tax deductible) and to the funds themselves (exemption from tax on various forms of profit). In aggregate the cost of these concessions is extremely large. It would no doubt be more equitable to abolish the concessions and to feed the extra revenue annually into the state pension scheme. This could then pay a more standardized pension which would mean that post-retirement incomes were more evenly distributed and were not, as at present, an exaggerated version of pre-retirement income inequalities. But such a reform has not, since the mid-1970s, been a prominent part of the Labour Party's electoral platform.

Although successive governments have, in effect, legislated the pension funds into a position of ever greater financial strength, there have been no noticeable moves to devise means of influencing or directing the way they use their enormous investment power. There would be an obvious electoral risk, in that the rightist response to any such moves would be along the lines 'state grabs your pension'. Unless the issues are thoroughly debated and understood, and pensions as an issue rarely commands much interest at election time, this could well be a telling electoral point.

In a cautious note of dissent in the final report of the Wilson Committee on the workings of the City (Wilson, 1980), there was endorsement for a TUC proposal that 10 per cent of the annual flow of money through the funds should be invested in *potentially* productive enterprises, preferably with a high job-generating capacity, rather than on narrowly commercial criteria. Such a proposal, timid as it was, could hardly have fallen upon less fertile ground than the Thatcher government. In any case, the dangers inherent in investing in high-risk enterprises (although presumably not in the way the TUC would have advocated) were graphically illustrated by the experience of several funds in the Brighton Marina fiasco where millions of pounds were literally sunk in building a breakwater to enclose land for a grandiose property scheme which has not, so far, happened.

In summary, the pension funds (together with the insurance houses) are currently a vital element in the development system. Highly self-effacing, carefully advised by merchant banks or 'in house' teams of experts, partially exempt from the information disclosure requirements that enable the public to assess the behaviour of other types of financial institution and heavily favoured by the tax laws, the funds are a most striking example of power without democratic responsibility. This is all the more ironic because most of the largest funds are those of the major nationalized industries (the Post Office, British Rail, British Coal, etc.) In terms of the diagram on pp.68–9 some of the largest pension funds should therefore be shown in the state sector. But in terms of their investment behaviour and general financial conduct they lie very near the heart of the finance industry. This ambiguity serves as a warning that such diagrams should be used with caution and that terms such as 'public' and 'private' which are often used as if they were self-defining are actually nothing of the sort.

Life insurance houses

The big life insurance companies (5 in the diagram on pp.68–9) have grown up mostly in the past hundred years. They serve purposes which overlap, but are not identical to, those served by the pension funds. There is no way of avoiding death, but one can at least put money aside to provide for dependants. Given that death normally comes after retirement, the life insurance houses often have an even longer period to use policy-holders' money than do the pension funds. As a result of rising real incomes and the slowly advancing average age of death, the flow of money channelled through the insurance sector and available for investment has increased dramatically in recent decades. This has been further enlarged by considerable state subsidy in the form of tax relief on the premium payments for annuities and life policies – a subsidy not available to those whose low income precludes their partici-pation in private insurance schemes. This increasing flow of funds had led to an expansion in the *range* of life insurance business. In particular, the growth of home ownership has provided new markets first for mortgage protection policies and more recently for mortgage endowment policies. Under these schemes a life policy is taken out which is geared to provide a sum at maturity which will repay the loan made to the house-purchaser by the building society (leaving the purchaser to make only the interest payments during the lifetime of the loan). Very often such policies are written such that the maturity value, including 'bonuses', is well in excess of the sum owed to the building society and the arrangement then becomes a concealed form of overinsurance.

This enormous increase in premium income has given the insurance companies (together with the pension funds) such an investment capability that together they have now become the largest shareholders in many, if not most, public companies of significant size. They are thus able, if they choose, to affect the trading and investment policies of these companies via the directors who, typically, sit in many boardrooms as their nominees. One striking example was the consciously visible part played in 1972 by Legal and General in seeking to persuade Distillers Company – in which they had substantial shareholdings – to make a more generous settlement with the families of the children affected by thalidomide. This attempt came only after threatened boycotts of Distillers' products and a consequent fall in share values (see Counter Information Services, 1973).

The attitude and actions of the financial institutions condition not only the behaviour of individual companies, but also the workings of the stock market as a whole. The success of a big new share issue, or the relative strength of stock in various areas of the market, depends to a large extent on the view taken by the institutions and on their week-to-week behaviour as large-scale

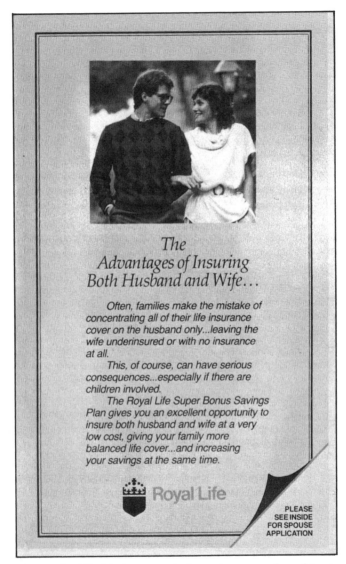

Figure 4.3 *The life insurance industry is constantly seeking to expand the range of its business. In this mailing to existing policy holders the 'target group' is uninsured spouses. A free cheque book wallet and calculator were on offer to those responding promptly. In an average year about 20 per cent of premium income is invested in property development.*

buyers or sellers. As holders, in total, of one-half or more of all the shares available on the market they are in a powerful position to bid up, or force down, the value of any particular share or to stabilize – or even to produce panic in – the market as a whole. Moreover, the growing proportion of shares held by a relatively small number of institutions facilitates the process of company takeover by means of a 'dawn raid' (Minns, 1982). A stockbroker acting for one company wishing to take over another can instruct, say, thirty of his staff to make three phone calls each to a total of ninety institutions to bid for the shares in question. Within a few minutes a sizeable proporton of the shares can be acquired by means of this technique.

In the field of property the institutions have achieved an enormous significance. This has stemmed from three key characteristics of property development as a form of business; the need for money at the 'front end' of a scheme, the excellent long-term prospects, and the great volatility in short-term returns that may be experienced on the way to eventual profit. Initially, back to the nineteenth century, insurance companies tended to make long-term, fixed-interest loans to fund a particular property scheme and accepted, as security, a mortgage on the scheme. Such a strategy became less attractive as sharp fluctuations occurred in interest rates (which successive governments used, after the Second World War, as devices to regulate the economy and protect sterling). Partly as a response, insurance companies, led notably by Eagle Star and Norwich Union, began to take a more active role in property development by acquiring shareholdings in property companies or by requiring an interest in the rental and capital growth of a scheme as a condition of the funding agreement. As the institutions became more deeply involved as creditors, and as the cyclical fluctuations in the fortunes of property companies became more marked (notably in the post-boom years from 1973 onward), numerous involuntary takeovers occurred as property companies got into serious default with loan repayments to their creditor institutions. As a result of these processes, the neat theoretical distinction between the finance industry and the construction industry shown in the diagram on pp.68–9 has been blurred and a number of large-scale finance/property conglomerates have emerged (see, for example, Cadman and Austin-Crowe, 1978, p.188). It would now be extremely difficult for finance institutions to disengage on any substantial scale from the property field, even if they wanted to, since few investors exist (apart from those with oil revenues to spend) with the necessary buying power to acquire their accumulated holdings in property.

The issue of social accountability needs to be considered. The life insurance houses have a clear responsibility to a limited number of people (their policy-holders) for whom they are effectively acting as trustees. Their task is to maximize the value of the premiums entrusted to them by playing a market dealing in various forms of shares (manufacturing, property, overseas companies, etc.). Their investment managers, almost all with a highly technical actuarial training, are not paid to consider the relative social utility, or even the longer-term economic implications, of any particular form of investment. All that matters is the medium-term safety and rate of return. If, for example, the electricity supply industry were privatized and shares in a new nuclear power station were on offer, little account would be taken of the longer-term evironmental dangers of nuclear power generators if the shorter-term share prospects looked good. An investment manager could not *afford* to allow general long-term risks to society at large to enter into consideration. He or she might lose out on a good short-term gain.

This might not be a cause for public debate if the institutions were investing *their own*, or their shareholders', risk capital. But the institutions are now acting on behalf of most of the population, in one way or another, as investment managers. They are all the time carrying out a pattern of investment which they cannot realistically refer back for approval to those who actually own the money. In other words, they have over a relatively short timespan, stepped in as intermediaries or brokers between millions of people with money to store, on the one hand, and thousands of enterprises seeking capital, on the other. The particular ways in which they carry out this task may or may not be acceptable to the majority of the population but at least their role should be clearly understood and perhaps more frequently debated.

The net investments of both pension funds and life assurance companies for a selection of recent years, and their respective total asset holdings as at 1983, are given in Table 4.1. Several points are worth noting. The combined asset value of the institutions is very nearly £200 billion. This position is the current product of a historic process of investment. British industry represents the

Table 4.1 Investment patterns by financial institutions, 1979–83

Form of investment	Net investment for year (in £m.)												Assets at end of 1983 (in £m.)			
	Life insurance companies						Pension funds						Life insurance companies		Pension funds	
	1979		1981		1983		1979		1981		1983					
	£m.	%	£m.	%	£m.	%	£m.	%	£m.	%	£m.	%	£m.	%	£m.	%
British government	2,541	60	2,207	40	2,092	32	2,295	45	1,873	29	2,565	42	25,794	28	21,757	21
UK local authorities	93	2	79	1	–19	–	4	–	–4	–	5	–	836	1	174	–
UK companies	759	18	1,176	21	1,907	29	1,527	30	1,916	29	1,687	28	35,126	38	48,158	47
Overseas companies	107	2	709	13	919	14	455	9	1,566	24	1,253	20	7,711	8	15,199	15
Overseas governments	–14	–	92	2	461	7	4	–	42	1	–28	–	1,148	1	507	–
Mortgages and loans	161	4	218	4	288	5	5	–	37	–	8	–	3,968	4	326	–
UK land and property	576	14	974	18	799	12	615	12	861	13	539	9	17,169	19	13,050	13
Other	15	–	54	1	56	1	196	4	266	4	90	1	495	1	3,585	4
Total	4,238	100	5,509	100	6,503	100	5,101	100	6,557	100	6,119	100	92,247	100	102,756	100

Source: British Business, 7 September 1984.

largest category of asset for both sets of institutions (38 per cent for life houses and 47 per cent for pension funds) but investment in British industry in recent years has been strikingly below the historic 'norm' both for the life funds and the pension funds (only 29 and 28 per cent of net investment respectively in 1983). Investment in British government securities has been uniformly above historic levels since the war. This is not surprising in view of the increasing part played by public expenditure in the economy in postwar decades. But the proportion of new investment committed to the public sector, especially by the insurance companies, has fallen sharply (from 62 to 32 per cent) since the advent of Mrs Thatcher's government – a considerable move towards the privatization of new investment.

Some of the shortfall in home investment in industry and government has been counterbalanced by a sharp increase in overseas investment following the abolition of exchange control in 1979 (from 6 per cent of combined investment at that date to 21 per cent in 1983). The effect on British industry and employment of this rapid switch in preference to overseas investment is too large a matter to be considered here, but the net total of £2605 million in new investment in overseas companies and governments in 1983 when many branches of British industry require massive modernization can hardly be a politically insignificant matter. In fact, of a combined total of £5766 million investment in home and overseas companies, over 38 per cent went overseas. Unfortunately, under present arrangements, there is no obvious way of inviting the real owners of the money (the UK contributors – many of whom may be unemployed) to comment on the matter.

The data most relevant to the development system concern the institutions' holdings in property. In 1983 over 15 per cent of combined assets were in the form of UK land and property (and a considerable further sum, no doubt, in overseas property). In the past few years annual investment in property has been slightly below this historic norm (except for the life funds in 1981) but over the past decade as a whole it has tended to conform to the norm and to vary between 10 and 20 per cent of total new investment. This year-by-year variation reflects the institutions' evaluation of the prospects for the type of property in which they have most interest – prime commercial and retail properties, leisure facilities, and so on.

It would be wrong to envisage the institutions as simply

responding to market trends in property development and rent levels. They are in fact in a position to *influence* these trends both in particular locations and in general. The rate and pattern of new development depends to a significant degree on the commercial judgements made by the institutions and on their actions as providers or withholders of finance. Many local activist groups when their areas have been threatened with large-scale commercial redevelopment proposals have painstakingly drawn up 'alternative' plans (such as the *People's Plan for Docklands*) incorporating smaller-scale mixed uses – community facilities, crèches, labour-intensive workshops, etc. The clinching argument against such schemes has usually been that they cannot possibly provide a competitive return on investment and, therefore, would be of no interest to any private sector funding institution. Given the savage cutbacks in public sector funding over the past decade, there is slight chance of money from this source. As a result, there is a very little hope for the kind of schemes that many local people clearly want.

Personal investment agents

These intermediaries (6 in the diagram on pp.68–9) between the savings market and the investment market are less significant than the previous two. Many higher-income individuals, as well as investing via contributory pension schemes and life insurance, also have funds left over to invest more directly via a lawyer, financial adviser or stockbroker. Such funds usually have to be in thousands rather than hundreds or the agent's fees for each transaction tend to negate the profit. A proportion of this money finds its way into the property sector either by the direct purchase of a property company's shares, by buying property bonds or by investment in a 'managed fund' specializing in property stock. Some of these agents, notably solicitors, may invest their own (and possibly other people's) money in particular property ventures but these are usually small-scale and residential rather than commercial in nature. There are no reliable figures to indicate the total volume of this activity, but it is probable that the flow of funds is too small, and too atomized, for the many agents who handle it to constitute any coherent manipulative force in the property market. They are, therefore, of no particular interest when analysing the political economy of the development system.

The banking system

Several useful books have been produced on the banking system (7 in the diagram on pp.68–9) in recent years. In their informative study McRae and Cairncross (1973) distinguish between 'branch banking' carried on for the population at large by the 'big four' and others, and 'money market banking' which incorporates a mass of specialist funding functions carried out mostly by the merchant banks. The 'mass market' banks accumulate capital basically by accepting the deposits of millions of small savers at one rate of interest (or no interest at all in the case of balances on current account) and then lending the money out at a higher rate using techniques of risk assessment built up over the centuries. The higher interest rates go, and the more they fluctuate, the more this activity begins to look like a licence to print money. Merchant banks and other 'money market' banks, on the other hand, carry out a complex and ever broadening range of functions. These include handling negotiations between companies setting up consortia to carry out specific projects, raising loans on international money markets, dealing in foreign currencies or stock, charging fees for financial advice and handling transactions in new or existing share issues. Banking has become more and more international in scope and in the co-ordination of its activities and the powerful political role now played by the leading banks in the major 'developed' countries has been very readably discussed by Sampson (1982).

In relation to property development the banks play a variety of roles. They are among the main providers of working capital for speculative housebuilders (10) and general contractors (12). In the case of the former, the housing is typically sold on completion to a purchaser who has taken out a long-term loan from a buiding society so the builder is able to repay the bank, normally retaining a proportion of the sale price for profit or use in further building. Clearly the contractor's aim is to minimize the amount, and the length of time, of the loan. Thus any method which will speed up the circulation of the capital, that is to say will shorten the time period between borrowing and completion/sale, will be eagerly considered. One way of doing this is to adopt time-saving (and perhaps sometimes insufficiently tested and supervised) methods of construction such as timber-frame and system building (see Chapter 6). Loans from the banking system to housebuilders may be tied to specific developments in the case of smaller builders, or may be in the form of medium-term, general-purpose finance to the larger well-established companies.

The task of providing short- to medium-term loans (say up to five years) to constructors of housing for sale is undertaken by banks because it does not involve them in the hazardous business of lending long-term money on the basis of short-term deposits. A very large proportion of bank deposits are repayable to customers on demand or within, say, one year. Thus the banking system would be entering into risky territory if it lent out any significant proportion of this money over the long term, say, upwards of five years. Yet this is exactly what needs to be done if major profits are to be derived from developing and managing investment properties. The revenues from a commercial property scheme may not exceed costs for a decade or more, but once they do the rental and asset growth can be enormous. Up to the late 1960s, therefore, the banking system tended to miss out this important source of long-term profitability. Typically a bank would make a three- to five-year loan to the developer to help finance the construction costs of a scheme. The loan might well be secured by a mortgage on the site and it would be made on the understanding that a longer-term lending institution was committed to repay the bank and take over the financing once the development was completed and let. The bank was largely insulated from risk since it probably would not lend much in excess of the potential site value anyway. Once the scheme was let (or, say, 70 per cent let), there was very little risk left for the long-term lender to take either.

The general strategy of the banking system towards investment property prior to the late 1960s and early 1970s boom was thus eminently safe and conservative; but it was also unadventurous and inhibited the banks from participating in the excellent longer-term prospects for rental growth and capital accumulation. In the period 1971–5 the banking system took some dramatic steps to expand this traditional role and learned some salutory lessons. The incoming Conservative Chancellor in 1970, Anthony Barber, set up a working party to examine ways in which expansion might be achieved in the British economy by increasing total lending and thus, in theory, making investment funds more readily available for industry. The banks were only too happy to increase their lending (following the period of tight credit in the late 1960s) but British industry, noting the uncertainties of world trade, did not judge collectively that this was the right time to carry out major investment programmes even though increased credit was available. Property developers, by contrast, were happy to do so since there was a collective optimism that the sharply rising trends in prime business rents would continue (see Rose, 1985). By August 1972 lending to industry was up by only 3 per cent over the past year while lending to property interests was up by over 50 per cent. As a result of competitive bidding, properties were financed or purchased at values such that their current achievable net annual rents represented only a 3.5 to 4.5 per cent annual return (or yield) on the investment. This activity was carried out with money borrowed at between 10 and 15 per cent and on the face of it made little sense. But the generally shared assumption was that the continuing rise in business rents would soon produce a realistic rate of return on the funds invested.

The main clearing banks were too cautious, or too sensible, or too closely constrained by the Bank of England, to become heavily involved in financing or acquiring properties on this basis. But numerous finance houses, which had built up their business on the consumer spending boom of the 1960s, became increasingly and competitively involved. Their status as banks was unclear because of the difficulty in defining, in the then legislative framework, exactly what qualified as a bank. They quickly became known as 'secondary' or 'fringe' banks and as their property involvement expanded they borrowed heavily from the clearing banks at normal commercial interest rates and then lent the money out at 2 to 3 per cent higher. In addition, some of the secondary banks obtained legal permission (under various sections of the 1967 Companies Act) to accept deposits from members of the general public although they were not subject to the same degree of control by the Bank of England as were more recognizably established banks.

The situation, already inherently unstable, turned into a major problem when the international currency crisis of early 1973 helped force up domestic interest rates to very high levels. This was followed by a further severe shock when the Conservative government imposed a business rents freeze, effective in April 1973, as part of its counter-inflation strategy. The assumption of ever rising rent levels fell apart. Many developers and property investors had become heavily indebted at, say, a 10 per cent rate of interest to finance a project showing a 4 per cent net return. This constituted an obvious 'reverse yield gap'. Unable to meet their repayment schedules, they could only hope that the creditor 'secondary bank' would allow them to add the interest to the loan itself. This was a desparate short-term solution and very soon a considerable number of the less prudent property companies had got into an untenable position. The total indebtedness was quickly mounting and could not be reduced from current or forseeable revenues since the office building boom of the late 1960s and early 1970s had produced, in many areas, a glut of office space. This means that the assets themselves (the buildings) could not be sold at anything like their book value since the latter reflected unfounded optimism about their rent-earning potential.

These problems had a knock-on effect as many of the secondary banks had specialized heavily on this type of business and they were faced with massive bad debts. Some of these banks had accepted deposits from ordinary members of the public. Failure to repay could have brought about an embarrassing rush to withdraw money from the banking system in general. This was quickly seen to be one of the most potentially serious banking crises of modern times. The Bank of England and the clearing banks acted by setting up a 'lifeboat' fund to ensure that all small-scale depositors were repaid. (See Figure 4.4.) At its peak, this fund had advanced nearly £1.2 billion to a total of twenty-six institutions – a figure roughly equivalent to 40 per cent of the total capital and reserves of the clearing banks (Bank of England, 1978). A further large sum was provided by the Bank itself as a rash of international bank failures unsettled the capitalist financial system as a whole (see Coakley and Harris, 1983, chapter 4). Various of the property companies themselves, and the secondary banks, went into receivership and the consequent considerable sale of properties led to a general stabilization, or fall, in property values and thus a recovery of property yields from the 3.0 to 4.5 per cent level to a more 'normal' 6 or 7 per cent on prime-quality commercial properties.

The clearing banks and the Bank of England had been both shocked and severely inconvenienced by the uncharacteristic imposition by a Conservative government of rent control, and thus profit-limitation, in the field of investment property – one of the most sacred areas of the free market capitalist economy. They were quick to point out to government the many destabilizing

---

The Times, 1.12.73

CITY FACES MAJOR CRISIS OVER BANKING GROUP'S DIFFICULTIES

BY IAN MORISON FINANCIAL CORRESPONDENT

The City yesterday found itself immersed in a major crisis of confidence, as it became clear that the banking group, London & County Securities, was in serious financial difficulties. Sentiment was also badly affected by the news that a receiver is being sought for Piccadilly Estates (Hotels) (report, page 21).

Under the leadership of Mr Gerald Caplan, London & County has been one of the fastest growing secondary banking operations of the past decade. It held more than £80m of deposits at the end of its last financial year, many of them from the public.

The company announced yesterday that talks were taking place "with a view to seeking means of continuing the viability of the company and the security of its depositors".

It is too early to gauge the full consequences of London & County's difficulties. Potentially,

however, they could affect large parts of the banking, property and investment communities . . .

The search for liquid resources has recently dominated the company's acquisition policy. It bought Drakes, a company rich in cash and property, from the control of Mr Christopher Selmes, one of the City's more controversial entrepreneurs, a year ago. The financial implications of the deal, however, were probably less attractive for London & County than they at first appeared . . .

The effect of the crisis on the property market could be considerable, especially if the company was forced to foreclose on its loans to this sector. In common with many other banking groups of its kind, it relies to a considerable extent on money market funds to finance its lending operations. The market has recently been showing much greater discrimination in its willingness to lend to small banks and lenders are now certain to become more cautious.

For a brief period London & County was heavily involved in the controversial field of second mortgage lending, as a result of buying a leading company in this field called Overseas Financial Trust. After adverse publicity about the rates of interest being charged, however, it withdrew . . .

Figure 4.4   *Following the 'Barber boom' of 1971–3 a number of City institutions lent too heavily into property. Prompt action was required by the Bank of England to maintain financial stability.*

implications of any attempt to impose such controls without giving the financial system adequate time to discount their impact on property asset values. In this they were joined by the insurance companies and pension funds, including many trade union pension funds. As a result, the rents freeze was quickly removed by the incoming Labour government early in 1975. The episode was clearly a costly learning experience for both political parties, for incautious property interests (many of whom lost personal, as well as corporate, assets) and for the banking system as a whole. While the banks have not wholly reverted to their restricted pre-boom role as providers of short-term construction finance, their attempts to secure a share in the equity of the schemes they finance, or to share in future rental growth agreements, have been noticeably more cautious than was their insufficiently considered step, via the secondary banks, into the frantic property boom and slump of 1971–5.

The state

Planning is an activity carried out by the state in the form of metropolitan, county and district authorities under the general supervision of central government. Relations between these various levels of government were, on the whole, amicable and workable between the end of the war and the mid-1970s. This situation, and the balance of power between Whitehall and town hall, has changed significantly in the last decade or so and some brief account is required of why this is so.

Local government goes back to classical times. Self-governing cities preceded self-governing states. Later many cities in Europe achieved incorporated status in the thirteenth and fourteenth centuries and acquired rights to raise revenue, administer justice and carry out such municipal enterprises as wall-building. In Britain the rapid urban growth of the mid-nineteenth century placed impossible strains on the archaic, county-based government structure then in existence and various Acts were passed, notably the Local Government Act of 1888, to create authorities appropriate to the age, to define their powers and duties and to provide for their funding. But for some decades before this (see Briggs, 1963) the growing industrial cities of the Midlands and north had been competing to demonstrate their wealth and civic consciousness. Town halls with grand ceremonial staircases and council chambers, pumping stations with stained glass windows and, more prosaically, vast networks of sewers, provided the tangible evidence of vision, wealth and dedication to progress.

Birmingham was a striking example. Joseph Chamberlain emerged with a Liberal Association and trade union power base to be mayor in 1873. Within three years the private companies providing gas had been bought out by the city, housing studies had been commissioned and a new city centre road and municipal buildings were under construction. Much of this was done with money raised by charging for gas and other services. The watchwords were enterprise, profit and care for all the people. Chamberlain and those around him regarded it as their highest moral duty to provide better living conditions for Birmingham's residents and to be sensitive to their needs (see Figure 5.1). At a stone-laying ceremony in 1873 he said: 'Our Corporation represents the authority of the people. Through them you obtain the full and direct expression of the popular will.' The government of London, as Britain's largest city, gave rise to a particular set of problems which had been discussed for much of the nineteenth century. In the end, despite the disquiet of Salisbury and other Tories, a London County Council with considerable powers was set up. At the first election in 1889, the Progressives, a loose coalition of Liberals and Fabian socialists, won 73 of the 118 seats. From the start they were an irritation and a threat to the Tories in Westminster (see Young and Garside, 1982). At successive LCC elections insults were traded and the Progressives

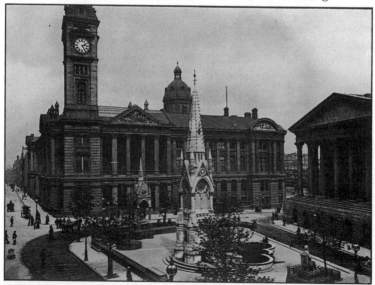

Figure 5.1   *Birmingham Council, led by Joseph Chamberlain, showed what could be achieved by civic enterprise in the period 1870 to 1900. This late nineteenth-century photograph shows the art gallery, the Chamberlain statue and the classically inspired town hall.*

were accused by Salisbury of squandering ratepayers' money on overambitious schemes of civic improvement. One of these was the Boundary Road estate in the East End – one of the most advanced public housing initiatives anywhere in Europe.

Local government, and the LCC in particular, continued to prosper through the period of the First World War. A sizeable public housing drive was one of the 'offers' made in the first postwar election ('Homes fit for heroes') but it foundered by the end of the 1920s, undermined by a combination of Treasury opposition, economic uncertainty and failing political commitment. In other fields, however, the 1930s was a high point of civic consciousness and energy. But the destruction wrought by wartime bombing sounded a death-knell. For many cities the scale of the reconstruction required was such that locally raised revenue could not possibly cover it. The subsequent large-scale central funding (typically 50 per cent or more of local spending over the following two decades) was always likely to be accompanied by moves from the centre to reduce local power and autonomy. In some ways it is perhaps surprising that these moves were not made on any significant scale until they occurred as a response to the crisis conditions of the early 1970s.

The period 1971–4 provided a series of traumatic shocks to the Heath administration. Economic performance was waning. The ill-considered reflation of 1971 had released a mass of lending, much of it into property where it sparked off a damaging boom–slump cycle. The unprecedented house price inflation of 1972 unsettled the owner-occupancy market. The quadrupling of oil prices disturbed sterling and the pattern of trade. Finally, early in 1974 a British government was effectively brought down by the damaging effects of a miners' strike. Later that year a Labour government with a fragile majority was seriously shocked by the well-concealed crises in the banking system.

As one response to this catalogue of near-disasters, the financial establishment began to look more closely at the market-orientated economic philosophies associated with the work of Friedman, an American economist (see, for example, Friedman, 1962). Crudely summarized, Friedman's argument was that the most important component in political freedom was the right of the individual to buy and sell in a market untrammelled by government regulation. People should be allowed to respond to 'price signals' which had not been 'distorted' by government taxation or subsidy. In this way, every individual would be free to express his or her preferences between one good and another. Later works by the Friedmans (e.g. 1980) extended the argument and offered policy prescriptions covering a wide range of social and economic issues. The policy implication of such a doctrine, which in some ways can be traced back to Bentham, is that the state should intervene as little as possible in the market economy. In fact governmental action should be limited to the organization of defence, the maintenance of law and order and the promotion of necessary public works, which are unlikely in the short term to yield a private sector profit. State activity in fields other than these requires a level of taxation that saps individual and corporate initiative and is likely to lead to a waste of resources because centralized planning tends to produce unintended consequences.

The defects of the Friedman position for any administration with social justice anywhere on its agenda can be identified within half an hour by any reasonably competent group of undergraduates. People do not come equal to the market. There has been a pre-history which has conferred enormous differences in wealth, influence and capability to compete. If the state is to play *no* redistributive or protective role, the result is bound to be increasing inequality, costly health and welfare problems and probably a degree of social dissent that will require heavy expenditure on law and order enforcement. These costs are likely soon to outweigh the money saved by not funding social support policies. The notion of pure 'undistorted' prices is suspect anyway if public works carried out with state money have helped to bring some, but not all, goods to the market. The expectation that all participants can acquire perfect knowledge of the market is childishly naïve. In all, the critique is hardly worth pursuing.

The significant point, however, is that a combination of pressure from the City and international capitalist organizations induced or obliged the Labour administration from 1974 to 1979 not so much to adopt the ideas, but to move towards the monetarist economic policies that went with them. By 1975 inflation was running at 30 per cent and there were several commensurately large public sector pay rises. The new financial orthodoxy was that economic salvation lay in reducing the level of public expenditure and thus the amount the government needed to borrow. The result would be to 'free' resources for private sector investment. The reasoning was that the public sector was providing a range of services (health, education, social welfare, etc.) which, in current economic circumstances, we could not afford to finance at their current level. As one Labour minister declared, 'The party's over'. The 1975 sterling crisis which looked heavily stage-managed, in that the Bank of England continued to sell sterling when it would normally have been expected to buy, was constantly linked in government statements to 'excessive' wage demands which were apparently frightening off foreign investors. Demands came from President Ford and Chancellor Schmidt for changes in economic policy. Finally, the currency crisis of the following year was solved by an International Monetary Fund loan which came with very specific directives. The Public Sector Borrowing Requirement (of which more later) was to be kept strictly to lower, pre-set, limits and sizeable cuts (which amounted in all to £8.1 billion) were to be made in the state's spending programme over the ensuing two years (Hall, 1983).

The axe on spending fell disproportionately upon local authorities, and has continued to do so. There are a number of reasons for this. Many local government services were, as we have seen, regarded as partly dispensable. Local government was branded as inefficient because it employed more people than central government per unit of money administered. This is true but cynically oversimplified. Many local government services (such as teaching and social work) are labour intensive because they deal face to face with people. They cannot, unlike some central government activities, be reduced to computer modelling or suddenly made more capital intensive (despite the state-supported boom in computer sales to schools). There were other reasons behind the unease of the City and the IMF at the balance of public to private sector activity. From the end of the Second World War up to the mid-1970s there had been not only a steady growth in public expenditure as a percentage of gross national product, but an increase in the local authority share of this spending. Thus local spending as a proportion of GNP had risen from 10.6 per cent in 1950 to 17.1 per cent in 1975 (Central Statistical Office data). Local politicians got more popular by spending more money – so long as it came from government grants and not local rates. There was, in the eyes of many City and industrial interests, a fatal leakage of 'unproductive' investment via local authorities that was not under sufficient control from the centre.

The advent of the Thatcher government in 1979 simply accelerated all these policy trends. For an anti-labour administration committed to monetarism, local government posed at least three sets of problems – financial, ideological and political. Despite considerable efforts, the outgoing Labour government had succeeded only temporarily in curbing public expenditure. By 1978–9 it was rising again. Local politicians of all parties stand in the 'front line' with the public and they had experienced a lot of criticism at the earlier cuts. For this reason, and often by natural inclination, they were seeking to restore levels of service. Secondly, many local authorities, especially the generally leftish city authorities, were undermining the government's increasingly insistent demands for sacrifice, 'belt tightening', and 'good financial housekeeping'. They were seeking instead, and with some success, to convince their electors that good services are worth having even if they do mean some increase on the rates. The alternatives were very serious, as they could easily show 'pigsty' schools, more children at risk from domestic violence, more old people with hypothermia and more patients turned out of hospital beds and returned to 'the community' far too soon. The Thatcher plea for a return to Victorian values was easily seen as a wish for some people to return to Victorian conditions.

The third set of problems posed by local government is political. Some powerful city councils like the GLC, Sheffield and Glasgow were pioneering alternative social and industrial strategies (Greater London Council, 1985a). Others, notably Liverpool, were seeking crisis-precipitation as a form of resistance. Perhaps more serious is the way that many powerful local authorities can stand in the way of the smooth running of the corporatist state (see Chapter 1). Deals between the government and key lobbies such as the housebuilders are agreed at the centre, in this case over meals at various London hotels. These deals, which in this instance might involve changes in land release policy, cannot be reliably implemented by government if local authorities, often of the left, are seeking to implement their own preferred planning policies. (As Chapter 8 will show, the docklands was not an attractive area to speculative housebuilders until it was 'taken into care' and special inducements such as cheap land were offered.) These political difficulties for the Conservative government added an extra dimension to the previous Labour government's financially based problems with local councils. The new problem was that deals made centrally could not always be delivered locally. The consequence has been, since 1979, a string of measures that would have pleased the ghost of Lord Salisbury. These will be sketched later in the chapter but have been discussed more fully by Duncan and Goodwin (1985b). The measures are about to culminate in the logical final solution – the abolition of the GLC and the six metropolitan counties as a result of what will probably appear in retrospect as a monumental fit of pique.

The central state

Recent theories on the nature and role of the central state (8 in the diagram on pp.68–9) in capitalist systems have been discussed in Chapter 1. The aim now is to give a brief descriptive review of the ways in which various departments of government affect the workings and output of the development system. Most departments of state have some interest in the evolution of the built environment but two in particular affect the rate, mix and locational pattern of new construction. These are the Treasury (in co-operation with the Bank of England) and the Department of the Environment.

The Treasury

The Treasury is often regarded, and certainly regards itself, as the most important department of government. It is responsible for overall financial management of the economy and 'the Treasury view', expressed via the Chancellor of the Exchequer, the Chief Secretary and the various junior ministers, is always a weighty one both inside and outside Cabinet. It is significant that the higher echelons of the Treasury are staffed mainly by economists. Of all social scientists, they are most prone to fall into the trap of 'modelling' the workings of society and believing in the results. The models used by the Treasury can accept only quantifiable data as input. They are also based on fairly naïve theories of human behaviour. It follows that their predictive value is limited since they have taken account of only a tiny proportion of the relevant information. This would not matter if the resultant forecasts were regarded as interesting intellectual exercises. But in fact their output is taken seriously and the 'Treasury model' is used as an important basis for policy formation even though, on many occasions, it turns out to be spectacularly wrong.

The relationship between politicians, particularly the Prime Minister and the Chancellor, and the top Treasury officials is an ever changing one (see, for example, Barnett, 1982; Sampson, 1982; and Pliatzky, 1982). The Treasury view which some authors have

---

Construction News, 28.3.85

WHY THE CHANCELLOR STAYS SILENT ON PUBLIC INVESTMENT

BY JOHN D ALLEN, EDITOR-IN-CHIEF

To create real jobs in the construction industry requires a policy of increasing public investment. That was one subject on which Mr Lawson had nothing to say in his Budget speech.

By contrast the many contributors to the four-day Budget debate that followed had plenty to say about it. At the close the Chancellor still had nothing to say except that he was not prepared to finance additional investment by borrowing.

One reason for this silence is the high level of the government's current spending commitments. Under pressure, Mr Lawson gave one clue to his resistance to more public funding. It was that the £10.5 billion borrowing requirement of 1983-84 was financed at a higher rate of interest than anyone would wish. In short, borrowing is proving expensive . . .

It goes without saying that this is a considerable addition to public current expenditure. The Chancellor is obviously not keen for this growth to accelerate. This is one powerful reason why appeals to fund capital spending by increasing borrowing are falling on deaf ears.

Mr Lawson is being chased on this question of debt payments by the House of Commons select committee, which has been showing signs of impatience with the explanations offered by Treasury ministers. These boil down to the fact that debt interest is not a controllable item in the sense that housing or defence expenditure is controllable. That is, debt interest is not subject to a cash limit.

Figure 5.2   *The Treasury has consistently refused to borrow sufficiently to fund much needed construction activity. The main reason given, as shown above, is that the rate of interest is not controllable under international capitalist monetary arrangements; neither, therefore, is the future public cost of servicing the debt.*

summed up simply as 'saying no' – is relatively stable when compared to the recent extreme swings in economic orthodoxy. (See Figure 5.2.) In some administrations a powerful Prime Minister has dominated a weak Chancellor (notably in the early 1970s). At other times a strong and politically middle of the road Chancellor (e.g. Healey) has been a powerful influence on both the Prime Minister and the Treasury. In the mid-1970s a limited number of top Treasury officials worked actively to precipitate the crisis. Finally, in the Conservative administration since 1979 a Prime Minister temperamentally incapable of living with oppositional views has appointed 'tame' Treasury ministers and economic advisers (some of them with an unpleasantly adolescent sense of humour – see Barnett, 1982, pp. 55–6). There has been an arrogant tendency to listen only to views supportive of the overall 'monetarist' strategy. One result has been considerable disgruntlement in the middle reaches of the Treasury and a high rate of 'leakage' of key information (e.g. the projections of the enormous cost of the growing tax concessions to owner-occupiers), usually to the only sympathetic 'quality' newspaper available.

One of the main tasks of the Treasury, so far as the domestic economy is concerned, is the preparation, every autumn, of the Public Expenditure Review. This culminates in proposals to government about the total level, and distribution, of public expenditure for the financial year commencing the following April. For example, the proposed public expenditure for 1985/6 is £136.7 billion of which £33.1 billion will be spent by local government. The next task is to prepare the annual budget statement which details how the revenue to meet this spending is to be raised. In 1985/6, £127.1 billion was to come from taxes and £2.5 billion from the sale of public assets. This leaves a shortfall of £7.1 billion which needs to be borrowed and is known as the Public Sector Borrowing Requirement (PSBR). This process has been described in detail by Barnett (ibid.). The secretary of state of each of the main spending departments (Health, Education, Defence, Environment, etc.) will have collated the requests from the various areas for which he or she is responsible and will have a target requirement of public funds as a starting-point for negotiation with the Treasury. There follows a series of 'bilateral' discussions in which the Chief Secretary of the Treasury will seek to persuade each spending minister to make do with less. This stage is characterized, as

Rodgers has remarked, by 'horse-trading and ad hocery of alarming proportions' (Rodgers, 1982) and this view is certainly confirmed by Barnett's account. If a minister cannot be persuaded to reduce his or her funding requirement, the issue is referred to a full Cabinet meeting where the chances are that the Prime Minister will support the Treasury view. The pattern of public spending finally agreed, which may in the end be overshot or undershot by enormous amounts, is clearly very significant to all government departments and especially, in the present context, to the Department of the Environment.

Under international capitalist monetary arrangements the British Treasury has clear limits to its autonomy. There are constant external pressures from agencies such as the International Monetary Fund (IMF) and the World Bank. These pressures usually intensify when world and domestic events combine to produce downward pressure on the value of sterling in relation to other currencies, notably the dollar. One standard response is to raise domestic interest rates, so that the financial return on balances deposited in Britain increases. As a result, international funds will tend to gravitate towards London and the buying pressure will support the pound. But the cost of borrowing money at these rates inhibits new investment at home and high interest rates are unwelcome to industrialists (although not to bankers). They are also accompanied by rises in the mortgage lending rate for house-purchase which all politicians recognize as a sensitive matter particularly in the run-up to an election.

When interest rates have been raised to their highest feasible level, and when import controls have been ritually discarded as a solution to balance-of-payment problems, the only answer may be to apply to the IMF for credit with which to pay for necessary imports. This is one way of avoiding payment in sterling and consequent further weakening of the pound. Barnett (1982) gives a graphic account of the British application to the IMF in 1976, the conditions on which the application was granted by the IMF Commissioners and the wearisome and divisive process by which the Chancellor and the Treasury ministers bludgeoned their Labour colleagues into accepting the cuts. The necessary reductions in public spending programmes were achieved but at the cost of deep damage to the relations between the Labour government and the TUC, and with a lasting effect on Denis Healey's chances of winning the leadership (which many would argue had an important bearing on the outcome of the 1983 general election). Ironically, as Pliatzky (1982) makes clear, the IMF loan may not have been necessary anyway since the Treasury estimate of public spending on which the application was based turned out to be £2.25 billion overstated.

The Treasury affects the behaviour of the development system in two main ways; by the fiscal policies adopted, and especially by taxes affecting land and property, and by the funding control exerted over local authorities. To consider fiscal policies first, the construction and finance industries are both sharply sensitive to changes in the level of existing taxes and to the financial implications of new ones. Taxes on property ('rates') have long been a feature of British revenue raising and, despite Mrs Thatcher's personal abhorrence of them, are likely to remain so. The bases on which property is periodically revalued (and the frequency of this revaluation), the ways in which different types of property are treated, whether or not empty properties are taxed, what precise rate of tax (or poundage) is applied and whether or not special concessions apply in certain areas (for example, Enterprize Zones) are all vitally significant to the development system. Other taxes bear directly on land development and property trading. Development Land Tax was the latest in a long line of measures to extract part of the value derived from developing a site; Capital Gains Tax is levied on the realization of an increase in value of assets including property assets (except owner-occupied housing) and Capital Transfer Tax affects property given or willed to another.

In addition to all these, an attempt was made in the 1974 Finance Act to impose a tax on the assessed value of new developments once they had been let for the first time and before they had been disposed of by the developer. This was soon seen to be quite unworkable, partly because it would lead to endless dispute about the taxable value of an asset not yet sold and partly because even if a value was agreed with the Inland Revenue, developers would claim that the building had not yet generated funds to pay the tax. Clearly, in the absence of any actual transaction, the tax would be levied on the *stock* of wealth held rather than on the *flow* of new income gained. It would therefore have introduced a radically new principle into the British tax system – one that would be highly unpopular with all wealth-holding interests.

The effects of fiscal policy on the workings of the development system are highly significant but in view of its complexity the matter cannot be fully discussed here. Even the Pilcher Report (Pilcher, 1975), which was written by a group of property experts, hardly gets into the matter. The history of government legislation in this area is littered with tax measures which missed the target altogether or had quite unintentional effects (see, for example, Rose, 1985) and this reinforces the view that most of the available expertise on the question of taxing land and development profits is on the private, not the public, side of the fence. One well-informed source sums up a discussion of precisely this issue with the brisk comment, 'It must be remembered that the strength of normal market forces may wholly or partially counter the effects of government action' (Cadman and Austin-Crowe, 1978, p. 25).

The role of the Treasury in funding, or more recently not funding, local authorities is an area that is much more open to public comprehension and debate. Central grants to local government are a very visible feature of all capitalist systems although their importance relative to locally raised revenue varies by country. Here they are very important. Britain is a unitary state, rather than a federal structure such as Canada, Germany or Australia, and the tax on property is virtually the only form of locally raised revenue, apart from fees charged for goods and services, available to local authorities. As we saw earlier, there is a well-developed tradition of local public enterprise in Britain although some previously municipal functions such as hospital services, electricity and gas supply and the relief of poverty have reverted to non-elected bodies or the central state. Those that remain within the province of local government, and notably education, housing and social services, have become ever more expensive. In the absence of any powers to raise local or municipal income or sales taxes (cautiously advocated by the Layfield Committee, Cmnd 6453, 1976, but heavily oppposed by the Treasury as a threat to central economic control) it is clear that the delivery of many key services by local authorities is much more dependent on central funding, and thus central influence, than is the case in similar western democracies.

Treasury funding of local government is carried out with a mix of aims in mind, although as we shall see, the mix varies depending upon the complexion of central government. Clearly some local authorities have a much heavier call on their resources, per head of

Figure 5.3   *Run down, but still inhabited, local authority housing in Southwark. The local economy has been in decline for decades and the borough has been starved of funds by central government. Elsewhere in London's docklands similar blocks have been renovated by subsidized private investment to produce 'low cost' private housing, some of which is inhabited by Porsche and Jaguar owners. (© Peter Ambrose 1986)*

population, than others. (See Figure 5.3.) The need for services depends upon such factors as demographic balance, the age of the physical fabric, the state of the local economy, and so on, all of which vary enormously from area to area. Equally some areas have a much greater value of property per head of population than others. This gives them a better base on which to raise rate revenue. As a general rule, the areas with the greatest need in some important respects are those with the least rate-raising capacity. These are typically the older inner city areas. The central grant is, in theory, arranged so as to cancel out, as much as possible, the effects of these inequalities and thus to act as a wealth equalizer between richer and poorer areas.

A second aim in previous times has been to decentralize some of the economic power from the central elected government to the locally elected authority. It is evident that in most situations local representatives are better known to local people and better able to reflect the priorities felt locally than are members of central government. But there would be little point in having this extra layer of government if its capacity to spend, and thus to express political preferences, were to be limited to an income derived entirely from local sources. On this basis the local authority could administer only a tiny range of services and the notion of implementing local preferences would be drastically devalued. A third, related, argument for central funding of local authorities concerns efficiency. It is reasonable to believe that local councillors and officials will have better information about local issues, more time to think about them and thus be in a better position than central government to judge the efficiency, in terms of services delivered per pound spent, of alternative spending choices. The inefficiencies of highly centralized administration are well known and in Britain, which is comparatively free from corruption at the local level, it has been judged to make sense to let local decision-makers decide how best to spend a significant proportion of the money.

In the interests of equity, democracy and efficiency, therefore, a large proportion of local spending has been raised out of general revenue and channelled from the Treasury, via the Department of the Environment, to the local authorities. As we have seen, this spending has increased since the war as authorities sought to meet the public's rising expectations about the quality and range of services required. But in addition to this, a proportion of the expenditure growth has been due to factors which no local authority could control, notably the increased revenue cost of servicing debts resulting from sharp rises in interest rates. The increased borrowing on which this interest was payable had itself reflected a strong tendency by public authorities to replace labour with machinery in the running of many services (for example, water provision, construction and transport have become much more capital intensive). There are, therefore, technical reasons for these long-term tendencies. These have been brushed aside by governments in the past decade in the rising stream of allegations that local authorities have been 'having a party' or are 'profligate spenders'. Public expenditure has been characterized as 'a problem' and something to be ashamed of. Authorities seeking to maintain a good level of services have been characterized as morally reprehensible obstacles to economic growth. Such arguments, which Newton (in Sharpe, 1981) shows to be superficial, have been welcomed by the more conservative elements in the Treasury although there are clear signs that other officials feel the attack may have gone too far.

The overall effect of the recent dramatic changes in policy has been to impoverish local government and to oblige it to withdraw services, in many cases statutorily laid down services, from the public. There has also been a striking change in the balance of *aims* of central government funding. The interests of equity and of local democracy have clearly been downgraded. The new aim of policy control is now paramount. Where government spending has been enthusiastically promoted (as we shall see in the case of London's docklands), the obvious aim has been to increase efficiency – not so much of public administration, but rather of capital accumulation by private investors.

The Bank of England

The Bank of England is formally another branch of the state (having been nationalized in 1946) but it operates with such autonomy, and in such a free market spirit, that it appears more independent of government policy than the central banks of some other western nations. Policy is made by a court of eighteen directors with a heavy private sector, merchant bank, Oxbridge emphasis. There is one token trade union representative but no Treasury director. The Bank carries out a range of functions, most of which are significant in some way to the workings of the property system. In general terms the Bank acts as one of the City's links with government and the Governor has easy access to the Prime Minister. It handles government borrowing and external debts and intervenes if necessary in currency markets to support the pound. It has an important supervisory role in relation to the rest of the banking system, helping to work out legislation to establish precisely what a bank is, supervising the operation of banks by scrutiny of annual accounts and discussion with senior management, seeking to control the total level (and to some extent the pattern) of bank lending, giving a view on the desirability of bank mergers, monitoring the flow of capital overseas and commenting on this flow, and setting interest rates to help regulate the economy. The overall weight of the Bank's intervention in affairs, and the relative strength of the different policies used, varies quite sharply depending upon the general strategies of the government and changing economic conditions.

Some actions by the Bank are crucially significant to the property system. The ease with which capital can be invested overseas, the changing availability and cost of credit and the freedom, or otherwise, of banks to invest in property rather than other sectors are all powerfully conditioned by the Bank and they are all important matters to property interests. In view of the inherent instabilities in the property market the Bank has on occasion been concerned at the amount of bank credit being made available to this sector. Several times in the 1960s the Bank took its normal rather gentlemanly steps to try and restrict the level of such lending. Again in August 1972 it was concerned that if too much money were lent into property, there would not be sufficient available to fuel an upturn in industrial activity. But the main effect of this initiative was not to divert bank funds from property to industry, since industrialists were not yet keen to borrow, but rather to encourage the rapid development of injudicious lending to property by the secondary banks. One implication to be drawn, although it would be disputed in the City, is that the central bank does not have an acceptable degree of control over the pattern of lending by the banking system as a whole. Nor was it, on this occasion, sufficiently competent to foresee the disastrous effects of the massive specula-tion in property which culminated in the need for the lifeboat operation (see Chapter 4).

The Department of the Environment

The Department of the Environment (DoE) is the department most directly concerned with the workings of the property system. The ebb and flow of its intervention in the workings of 'market forces', and thus its changing capacity to affect development outcomes, is one of the key themes of this book. The DoE has grown from the various wartime boards and committees responsible for reconstruc-tion, through the postwar Ministry of Town and Country Planning until now it is responsible for policy in very diverse fields such as housing, planning, roads and transport, public utilities, regional policy, industrial development, pollution control and conservation. Most of these activities are organized and carried out by local or specialist authorities and much of the department's work therefore concerns the co-ordination of activity between various tiers of administration.

The property development system is significantly affected by the spending priorities of the department and by the statutory and informal regulation it exerts. The evolving strategies concerning National Parks, mineral exploitation, motorways, energy production, inner cities, building standards, local authority initiatives and regional incentives to investment, among many others, help to set the context within which property interests develop their own strategies. They constitute 'rules of the game' which have to be more or less observed in the complex processes of accumulating capital via land and property. But equally it would be naïve to conceive of the DoE as the executive branch of a democratically elected and all-powerful state *controlling* such processes of capital accumulation (see the discussion of theories of the state in Chapter 1). To give one example of the ambiguous nature of the relationship between the department and the property industry, the succession of technical guidance papers from the department that led many local authorities to accept insufficiently tested construction methods (for example, some forms of system building for high-rise flats or timber-frame construction) did not emerge from disinterested experts. Individuals with a strong commercial interest in the building systems in question themselves contributed to the discussions on which the advisory documents were based. Many similar examples could be given of the industry helping government to frame the 'rules' and the subsidy structures within which the industry itself operates. (See Figure 5.4.)

There are two main ways in which the DoE interacts with local authorities to provide the administrative framework for the development system: funding and overseeing the land use planning system. Funding will be considered first. The recent sharp move towards constricting local authority spending has already been noted. The aim here is to review briefly the *types* of central grant and the administrative *form* they take. Grants can be general (not tied to any specific purpose), or they can be for identifiable projects. They may, or may not, be conditional upon matching expenditure by the local authority. They can be geared to compensate for locally varying costs or they can ignore such considerations. They can be open-ended in the sense that central government cannot in the end determine their limit (always anathema to the Treasury) or they can be given a fixed limit. Specific grant programmes are designed with a number of judgemental criteria in mind. Such criteria include the extent to which the programme accords with prevailing political philosophies, the feasibility of obtaining sound data on which to make a fair allocation of funds, the ease of grant administration and the predictability of the future public commitment under the programme. The main grant from central government to the local authorities is the Rate Support Grant (the RSG) set up under the 1966 Local Government Act as an amalgamation of several previous grants. The principles upon which the grant is calculated every year are complicated (see Bennett, 1982, chapter 4; or Hepworth, 1980), but in essence the grant seeks to cancel out the effects of the sharply varying tax bases, and spending needs, of local authorities. It also contains an element called the 'domestic element' (about 10 per cent of the total) to reduce the local tax burden on residential, as opposed to all other, ratepayers. This is an anomalous element not found in the grant systems of comparable countries and its main rationale is probably electoral.

As an equalizer of standards of service provision in different local authority areas, the RSG has obviously been of limited effectiveness so far (since enormous inequalities in service provision still persist between authorities). This is no doubt partly because of the immense complexity of measuring a concept such as 'need' and the difficulty of identifying acceptable and unambigiously measurable indicators of the degree of need. But there are also obvious political hindrances to the totally effective operation of what is in essence a redistributional device. Richer areas, no matter what the public stance of their politicians, do not readily agree to receiving less money so that poorer areas may receive more. This essentially conservative (in several senses) attitude has been heavily reinforced by recent political ideologies concerning the supposed 'wastefulness' of authorities who try to maintain a good level of services in difficult situations.

The RSG is a very significant part of total public spending. In fact at £11 billion in 1982/3 it is the biggest single item of government spending after defence and it provides for about 40 per cent of local government expenditure. As such it has been one of the main targets for government cutbacks and it has also been employed as a means of penalizing the eighteen local authorities who have currently (1985) been engineered, by judicial choice of criteria, on to

Building Research Establishment Client Report

Limited circulation

April 1985

Quality in timber-frame housing: interim report

Building Research Station

This report was prepared for the Housing Directorate of the Department of the Environment and should not be referred to in published work

bre BUILDING RESEARCH ESTABLISHMENT

Department of the Environment

Major faults have been found in both the design and execution of timber-frame housing affecting its fire performance, durability, strength and stability. Almost two-thirds of the faults were found to be either universal or common. In all, 75% of the key potential errors listed by the BRE in its 1983 technical appraisal of timber-frame have now been found.

The BRE sums up bluntly by stating that its survey confirms the need for a "radical reconsideration of the way in which timber-frame is currently designed and built".

Building, 9.8.85

FURY OVER BRE LINK WITH TIMBER-FRAME LOBBY

The Building Research Establishment has agreed to collaborate with the timber frame lobby on its controversial study of timber-frame housing . . .

This follows the bitter row between the industry and the BRE over its findings made public in June.

But the membership of the confidential working party, with representatives from TRADA, the House Builders Federation and the NHBC, is already causing controversy over its intentions.

The Association of Metropolitan Authorities has not been invited to attend next month's first meeting, despite local authority housing being a major part of the BRE's study.

This has incensed the association, well known for its critical view of timber-frame. It believes it has now been frozen out of the consultation process following the storm of publicity over the BRE's interim report last June (Building 7 June, pages 7 & 28-29).

Trying to explain why the AMA should have been snubbed, principal policy officer Mike Irvine believes that "the timber frame lobby would have taken particular exception to us being there".

Figure 5.4 (opposite and above)   *A critical report by a Department of State on the implementation of a relatively untested building technology led to a 'bitter row' and demands that the BRE should 'collaborate' with the industry in a 'confidential working party' on which public sector authorities are not invited. Who is seeking to regulate whom?*

the government's 'hit list' for 'overspending'. The grant level is determined annually following discussion between the Secretary of State for the Environment and the local authority associations (which between them represent all tiers of local government). The proposals are then scrutinized, ever more closely since the mid-1970s, by the Public Expenditure Survey Committee. This forms one of the co-ordinating links between DoE policy and central Treasury spending plans. In a following stage the totals of other grants to local authorities, covering special programmes such as transport, are defined and totalled up with the RSG to give the Aggregate Exchequer Grant figure. Since 1976/7 this total has been subject to a strict cash limit, a ceiling which has been set out in advance no matter what the later effects of inflation may be on the amount local authorities have to spend to meet their commitments.

Central funding to local authorities is in a considerable state of flux. There is a constant debate about what local expenditure is acceptable to government as 'relevant expenditure'. Simply defined, this means expenditure on services carried out by local authorities in accordance with their statutory and other duties as agents of central government. But in practice, there is room for endless dispute around a number of issues and particularly about the *standard* of such services, the extent to which users should pay and how much they should cost a local authority to provide. This dispute is unprecedented not only in that it often transcends local party politics, but also in the aggressive and devious tactics used on both sides. Central government has carried its concern about restricting local spending to the point of obsession and has used a range of ethically dubious techniques to hammer local authorities. These include 'creative accounting' by which local authority spending estimates are reduced by government before they are even considered. There are also constant threats to remove councillors, distrain on their personal assets (as in the case of Clay Cross in the early 1970s) and send in central, non-elected commissioners to run local affairs. Some local authorities (notably the GLC, some London boroughs and Liverpool) have attempted to fight back by preparing 'illegal' budgets or reducing the cost of certain services (for example, public transport) to users. The government response has been to abolish the GLC and the metropolitan counties thus removing all 'metro' government completely. Further bizarre suggestions are coming forward from such bodies as the Greenwich (London) Chamber of Commerce who, in summer 1984, offered their services to the Secretary of State as commissioners to run the affairs of the borough. If accepted, this would raise interesting constitutional questions about the nature of British democracy and, in particular, whether the next step might be to abolish elections altogether!

One counter-strategy by local authorities (mostly Labour con-trolled) who wish to maintain a good level of services is to increase local revenue by means of an increase in the rates levy. The government response has been to pass the 1982 Local Government Finance Act which ended the rights of a local authority to raise supplementary rates designed to make up for the penal reductions in its RSG. It also limited the power of higher-tier authorities (the GLC and the metropolitan counties) to 'precept' extra amounts from lower-tier authorities (i.e. the districts, who are the collecting authorities) in order to maintain their levels of service to the public. The same Act, apart from these 'rate-capping' provisions, imposed much more onerous central auditing of local authority spending. Given all these recent developments, the central–local power struggle has become highly charged emotionally, and in this it reflects British politics generally in the mid-1980s. It will be some time before any new consensus is reached about what constitutes an acceptable balance of power between central and local government and about the extent to which local authorities are to remain financially capable of providing the level of service they judge to be appropriate to their particular populations.

The second main task of the DoE is to keep the land use planning and development control legislation under review, to oversee the implementation of planning law and to arbitrate in cases of dispute between applicants and local authorities. The emergence of the planning legislation has been discussed in Chapter 2. Within the broad framework provided by the law, there is much scope for varied interpretation of, for example, what constitutes permitted development under any given plan. There have also been big differences between successive Secretaries of State about what is necessary for them to be 'satisfied' (as required by law) that 'public participation' has occurred in the planning process. Guidance on these, and a great number of related matters, is constantly flowing from the department to local planning departments in the form of circular letters. The department is also responsible for ensuring that local planning authorities (i.e. those authorities defined in law as having a planning function) draw up their plans as required by law. In general terms, the county authorities and the GLC are responsible for drawing up Structure Plans concerning broad future strategies. The district or borough authorities then draw up Local Plans to implement these strategies. The situation is more complex than this, in practice, because the two tiers of local government may have quite different political complexions and development preferences. Either, or even both, of these may conflict with central government's intentions for the area. At the stage of plan-making, however, the Secretary of State is required to approve the Structure Plans submitted by the higher-tier authorities and has the power to intervene if a structure planning authority believes that Local Plans drawn up by lower authorities do not conform to strategic intentions.

The DoE also acts as arbitrator in the case of disputes between developers, the local authority, and interested third parties (for example, members of the public) who have a view on a proposed development. The Secretary of State may intervene either if he or she is convinced that an appeal should be heard against a refusal by a local authority to allow a development, or when it seems clear that there is sufficient public concern to warrant an inquiry at which, in theory, anyone can put a view. The decision whether there is, or is not, sufficient public concern for an inquiry rests with the minister. Public inquiries, which have often become very lively affairs, have many shortcomings as a method of eliciting and weighing the feelings of the population at large. This is to some extent inevitable in view of the increasing complexity of planning law, the very long timescale of any large project, and the difficulty of assessing, at the time of the inquiry, the eventual distribution of costs and benefits. But even allowing for these difficulties, there is much room for criticism about the increasingly technical and legalistic way in which inquiries are conducted. In particular, there is sometimes a failure to compensate adequately for the enormous differences in the capacity to put a convincing case which may arise when the applicant is a large and powerful corporation and the objectors are lay people and citizens' groups. Planning inquiries are also frequently inhibited by the narrowness of their terms of reference. The matters upon which the inspector is required to take evidence and report are often only matters that fall within the strict bounds of planning law. Other issues (such as what will be the effects of the proposal on house prices, or the availability of part-time work for women) may not be regarded as relevant because they are not 'planning matters' and/or no 'hard' evidence can be brought to the inquiry about them.

The local state

The last few years have seen a remarkable growth of interest in 'the local state' (9 in the diagram on pp.68–9), a term brought into prominence by Cockburn (1977) and further discussed by Boddy and Fudge (1981). There are several reasons for this, notably the dramatic issue of Clay Cross. This was a local authority in Derbyshire which had for long been seeking to provide free school milk and keep housing rents as low as possible in the face of central

Figure 5.5   *Local democracy at work. Lambeth Labour councillors express their feelings at a rate-capping debate in 1985. The constant policy of monetarist governments since the late 1970s, strongly resisted by this council among others, has been to weaken the power of local authorities to raise revenue to carry out their duties.*

government policies which moved sharply against such measures in the early 1970s. The confrontation in 1972 (see Skinner and Langdon, 1974) reached crisis proportions with the appointment of a civil service commissioner to impose centrally determined policies. The democratically elected councillors were threatened with the loss of both office and personal assets. No doubt they might in the end have lost their liberty as well but for the reorganization in the 1974 Local Government Act which meant that the authority ceased to exist.

The aim at this point is not to enlarge on the central/local state issue, but to review, in the barest outline, the formal structure of local government in England and Wales (Scotland and Northern Ireland are rather different) and to detail the various tiers of government and their main functions. This is shown in Table 5.1. Local councils are typically made up of seventy or eighty elected members and the statutory powers are vested in the council as a whole. However, such a body is too large to make decisions across

Table 5.1   The functions of local government by type of authority

								Planning				
Type of authority	Number	Rate collection	Arts recreation and tourism	Consumer protection	Education	Environment and health	Housing	Structure Plans	Local plans and development control	Conservation	Social services	Transport
London												
Greater London Council	1		x		x	x	x	x		x		x
London boroughs	33	x	x	x	x	x	x		x	x	x	
Rest of England and Wales												
Metropolitan counties	6		x	x				x		x		x
Metropolitan districts	36	x	x		x	x	x		x	x	x	
Non-metropolitan counties	47		x	x	x			x		x	x	x
Non-metropolitan districts	334	x	x	x		x	x		x	x		
Total	457											

Source: *Local Government in England and Wales*, London, HMSO, 1974.

Note
This table is necessarily a simplification. There are important exceptions. For example, the Inner London Education Authority is responsible for education in thirteen inner London boroughs and certain transport functions are carried out by other levels of government. Over 10,000 parish councils, with limited functions, also exist in rural areas.

the whole range of issues so it is invariably divided up into committees of fifteen to twenty members. Most councillors sit on more than one committee depending upon their background knowledge, interests and stated preferences on election. Each committee will normally reflect the balance of party strength in the council as a whole and be chaired by a member of the majority party. Committee meetings take place in a regular cycle and a report of the discussions and recommendations will be made to the full council for formal decision-making. The matters most relevant to the development system – housing, planning, transport, and so on – are managed by specialist departments in the local authority, each headed by an appointed officer known as a Chief Officer or Director. The senior administrative official of the authority, formerly known by some such title as Town Clerk, is the Chief Executive.

The question of the balance of power between elected councillors on the one hand, and appointed officers on the other, has been debated for several decades now (see, for example, Miliband, 1973, chapter 5). Councillors have a democratic mandate to govern for, normally, four years (although on the basis of perhaps only a 40 per cent voting turnout) but they usually have no training for the task, little technical knowledge and often have to fit in their council duties around the necessity to earn a living. In some authorities a significant minority of them may have entered local politics to further their own interests rather than for any better motives although only a tiny number of councillors have ever been found guilty of corrupt practices. The administrators, on the other hand, are highly trained and (in normal times) permanent officers who are rarely motivated by self-interest, except in the sense of career advancement. The fiction is, as with the civil service, that officers are non-political and exist purely to present information to help councillors make policies and then to implement those policies.

The naïvety of this belief has been exposed and the discussion about the councillor–officer relationship now centres on the way the power balance between them may be shifting and the factors that may be producing a shift. One important factor is the growing complexity of the task of government, and the difficulty of decision-making in the face of the data overkill resulting from the continuing revolution in the techniques of gathering, storing and presenting information. This revolution has already had a number of effects. It tends to focus the attention of the unwary on purely quantitative, rather than qualitative, information; it gives a spurious air of certainty ('if the computer produced it, it must be correct') to data which may have been gathered, and processed, in highly suspect or selective ways; and it can place a greater premium on the policy recommendations of the officers (who are presumed to understand the figures) compared to the view of the elected members (who may not be aware that figures can be used to prove almost anything). This is by no means the only factor affecting the power balance – the sheer time and expertise needed to assimilate the ever increasing volume of legislation and circulars may be another. Nor is it prudent to generalize about the way the balance is moving since it depends so much on the established practices of the authority and the strength of the personalities involved. But the issue should always be kept in mind when considering how any particular local authority makes decisions and, in particular, the part the officers play in policy formulation and implementation.

Cockburn also pointed out in her Lambeth study (Cockburn, 1977) that the 1974 reorganization of local government changed more than boundaries and statutory responsibilities; it brought in a new style of administration. The old municipal titles gave way to a more 'corporate' private sector vocabulary with 'directors', 'chief executives' and 'management teams' of chief officers (who now form a formidable 'power bloc' in many authorities). The new language, and the increasing use of consultants, reflected private sector tendencies as did the new 'info-tech'-based management practices. These tendencies are more than just cosmetic. They seem to reflect a trend towards the blurring, in practice, of the difference that exists in principle between activities carried out with private risk capital – whose sole aim is profit – and activities financed by public money – whose sole aim, presumably, is public service.

If this distinction becomes weakened or lost so too, to that extent, does the reality of democracy based on universal suffrage. This is so since where activities that are publicly funded are carried out with a convincing 'private sector' style, there may be a tendency to narrow the decision-making base – almost as if the funds *were* privately owned. The London Docklands Development Corporation is a perfect example of this trend. It could, therefore, be that what looks like a simple drive to increase the efficiency of local authorities is, in fact, a means of anaesthetizing public awareness of the growing penetration of private sector aims and practices into the field of public administration. The allocational effects of these tendencies might well be considerable and increasing. The decision whether or not to commit public resources to some redistributive programme (pensioners' concessionary fares, means-tested school uniform allowances, etc.) could well be increasingly based on a private sector, not a public sector, ethos. In other words, the key question that may be asked is not 'who most needs help?', but 'is this the most effective way to get a return on new investment?' This argument that there is a connection between the new managerial style and a basic change in the aims and content of local authority programmes is fundamentally important since the underlying meaning of changes in surface style can be easily missed. Arguments that present 'administrative efficiency' as a politically neutral virtue need to be examined very closely.

Returning to the diagram on pp. 68–9, local authorities interact with other elements in the development system in a number of ways. A council, as the freehold owner of a site, may enter into a development partnership with private sector financial and development interests. Because public authorities (unless specially empowered) cannot form their own development company, the usual arrangement is for the council to prepare a 'developers brief' which sets out roughly what form and mix of development it wishes to see on the site. This is then circulated and developers are invited to submit schemes and a financial offer for the lease of the site (typically, for perhaps a term of 99, 120 or 200 years). The lease may be granted in return for a straightforward ground rent, with review periods built in, or the authority may seek to enter into a much more complex arrangement by which it also requires a share of the increases in rents charged to the tenants as the scheme matures. The development scheme and financial bid may later be re-negotiated. The ground rent offer and rent-sharing proposals can be almost infinitely variable and the relative size of the different elements in the case of a mixed development (for example, a shopping centre, plus some flats, plus a new library) can be subject to subsequent bargaining. It can happen that where a developer agrees to include some 'community' content in the scheme, such as a leisure complex, conference centre or even new offices for the

Figure 5.6   *A 'partnership' scheme in Ealing. The local authority acquired the land, much of it by compulsory purchase, and then released the site to the developers. Considerable housing loss was involved.*

authority, the commercial–community mix originally agreed may 'evolve' somewhat over time even though it may have been the subject of an agreement under the relevant legislation (section 52 of the 1971 Town and Country Planning Act). In such cases the delighted headlines in the local paper about 'Town to get new swimming-pool from developer' may become falsified by events. The community element, which was regarded as the 'planning gain' and is part of the understanding on which the consent to develop was granted (see Jowell, 1977), can later be claimed to be not economically viable by the developer or may be relegated to a very late stage in the phasing of the project.

Local authority–developer partnerships are usually formed to carry out commercial or mixed developments where there is the probability of a continuing stream of future revenue. There may also be the chance for the lessee to carry out several redevelopments before the lease expires and the site reverts to the local authority as freeholder (hence the keen interest of developers in leases of 150 or 200 rather than 99 years). By contrast, local authority schemes for housing, roads, schools, and so on, do not command any flow of revenue that is competitive in terms of the investment involved. The profit potential for the building industry lies only in the actual construction, and contracts are awarded for such schemes following a period of competitive bidding. The construction industry is naturally keenly interested in the rate of flow of such contracts. This, in turn, depends increasingly on the amount of local authority spending allowed by central government policy.

As we have seen, local authority spending under most headings has been reduced in real terms in recent years and made much more dependent upon central government scrutiny and approval. Thus transport plans have to be submitted under a Transport Policies and Programmes (TPPS) document every year and housing intentions under a Housing Investment Programme (HIP). Central government normally responds by scaling down the grants to finance such capital programmes and/or by reducing the capacity to raise funds on the capital market by cutting down on loan sanctions, or permissions to borrow (see, for example, Hepworth, 1980, chapter 6). These spending limitations are especially serious to those constructors who have, over the years, tended to specialize in local authority work. They have became very alert to changes in the emphasis of spending under a particular heading. For example, there has been a move in the last decade to fund housing association schemes rather than other forms of local authority housing initiative. Similarly, government policies may increasingly favour the renovation of existing housing rather than the replacement of older housing with new. This will alter the balance and type of building contracts available from local authorities and provide a changing pattern of business for the construction industry.

Whereas the involvement of local authorities in partnership schemes, land acquisitions and disposals and the placing of building contracts is the task of such committees as Corporate Estates or Finance and General Purposes (committee titles vary widely), the granting of consents to develop land falls within the province of the Planning Committee advised by the development control section of the authority's planning department. In general terms, all land development or redevelopment requires planning permission. (There are numerous detailed exceptions such as small additions to residential properties, agricultural buildings, highway improvements, and so on.) An application to develop can be made by anyone, whether the owner of the site or not, although the owner must always be informed of applications made by others. The authority is responsible for informing the public about the application by various means including the posting of a notice on the site and it is obliged to consult the higher planning authority (the county, metropolitan council or the GLC) if the proposal might conflict with structure planning intentions. In this case it becomes a 'county matter'. There may also be a need to consult neighbouring planning authorities, the relevant highway department, interested parish councils or other public bodies as may seem relevant.

Planning authorities also have a general duty, not closely specified in law, to consult 'the public' about applications to develop. The extent of public awareness about proposed developments depends partly upon the enthusiasm with which this task is embarked upon (the applicant in most cases is not enthusiastic at all; for developers consultation equals delay equals increased costs). Planning committees need to be generally satisfied that local objectors have been reasonably dealt with but in the end they are not at any legal risk since if an objector can demonstrate that he or she has lost materially by the granting of a consent to another (for example, in terms of reduced access to property or increased nuisance), then remedy must be sought against the developer, not the local authority.

In very controversial cases which clearly give rise to much public concern or protest, the Secretary of State may be convinced that the application should be 'called in' and dealt with by the department rather than by the local planning authority. In these cases a Public Inquiry may be held or a Planning Inquiry Commission set up (if, as for example in the case of a nuclear power station, the technical issues require expert evaluation). Following a statutory notice period to those considered to have an interest, the inquiry is conducted by an inspector appointed from a panel of qualified lawyers by the Secretary of State. Certain objectors, and other parties with an interest, have a right to appear and others may be invited to give evidence by the inspector. Much of the evidence will be presented by lawyers, qualified planners, economists, and so on, and a good proportion of the debate may be quite incomprehensible to those members of the general public who can manage to attend during working hours. After what may amount to many weeks of evidence, cross-examination, site visits and final statements, the inspector reports, with recommendations, to the Secretary of State. He or she then takes this report into consideration in giving a final decision (which can in some circumstances lead to requests to have the inquiry re-opened).

6
Construction

The construction industry is really a collection of subindustries which produce a varied set of products. At first glance the construction of a house, a shopping centre, or a hospital may all be regarded as broadly similar operations. But to understand the rate of production of these various buildings, their quality and their cost to the user we need to focus on the production cycle of the industry. In terms of the model $M \longrightarrow C \longrightarrow C^1 \longrightarrow M^1$ (see p. 1) it is relevant to consider why any given pattern of investment occurs in construction (whether from public or private sources), who determines the level of the initial amount invested (M) and what sort of capital this is. In the commodity assembly stage $M \longrightarrow C$ we need to know something about the supply of building machinery and materials and the ways that land is assembled. The production process itself $C \longrightarrow C^1$ brings all these inputs together in ways that evolve with new developments in technology. Finally, the realization of the monetary value of the building $C^1 \longrightarrow M^1$ can take one of a number of forms depending upon the nature of the development. As well as considering these various conversions in the production chain, some attention will be given to the adaptations made by the industry as it seeks to protect profitability (the $M^1 - M$ increment) in changing, and latterly very difficult, trading conditions.

The diagram on pp. 68–9 shows the construction industry divided into six separate activities: speculative housebuilding (10), property developing (11), general contracting (12), public authority direct works (13), plant hire (14) and materials supply (15). These represent different lines of work, or *functions*, rather than separate groupings of firms or sectors of the industry. Some large construction firms are involved in all these functions (except direct works) while many smaller companies concentrate on only one or two, perhaps changing their pattern of work over time. This chapter will deal, first, with some characteristics of the construction industry as a whole, then with certain aspects of the production chain and, finally, discuss briefly the four main output functions (10–13) shown in the diagram.

The construction process

Although every building has to be finally constructed on site, the extent to which the semi-finished products can be assembled into components *before* shipment to the site varies considerably. For buildings such as high-rise flats a large proportion of the production can occur off-site. The reverse applies to, say, the conversion of an old Thames-side warehouse into luxury flats. Thus the ratio of on-site labour input to industrialized prefabrication can vary considerably. It also has to be remembered that every site is, by definition, different from all others. The subsoil, aspect, relief and access, all matters of importance to a constructor, are unique to each site and these variations must be allowed for when planning the project. Construction also involves a long timespan between the decision to build, and thus the commitment of some input resources, and the final realization of the product's value on the market. The circulation of the capital, in other words, is relatively slow. This means that the financial calculations necessary in order to decide whether or not the project is worth embarking upon have to be carried out well in advance. This increases the risk, especially since certain of the costs and returns involved in the production of buildings are very sensitive to circumstances beyond the control of the entrepreneur. As an example, the interest rate on borrowed funds can vary sharply between the commitment of M and the realization of M^1.

Buildings are common property in the sense that in nearly all cases they are visible to the general public. The traffic and/or pollution they generate also affects the environment in which the non-owners and non-users live their lives. In other words, they produce a set of costs and benefits for the public at large and this is one of the main rationales for government intervention in the production of the built environment. The producers of buildings, therefore, are necessarily subject to a mass of regulations about density (and thus the potential revenue obtainable from the site), construction materials, building standards, appearance, user activity, and so on, to a greater extent than are the producers of less public goods such as videos or cars.

The structure of the industry

The construction industry is one of the largest in the economy. It employed 1.08 million people in 1983 (the figure was 1.43 million in 1974 so employment had fallen by about 24 per cent in nine years). Several factors have conspired to inhibit the industry's efficiency, although this seems to be more true of its capacity to produce than its ability to make profits. To start with, the industry is highly fragmented in that it is made up of a large number of separate firms carrying out different trades. The official statistics (the *Housing and Construction Statistics* published annually by the HMSO – from which most of the data in this chapter are taken) recognizes three 'main trades' and eighteen 'specialist trades'. Table 6.1 shows some characteristics of the industry's structure and, in particular, the great dominance of very small firms of up to seven employees. Where civil engineering is an important element, that is in two of the three main trades, about two-thirds of firms are of this size. Within the specialist trades (six of which have been selected to indicate the range of variation) up to 95 per cent or more of firms are what would be regarded as very small by the standards of most other large industries. Taking the industry as a whole, this fragmentation has increased between 1974 (76.2 per cent of firms employing fewer than eight people) and 1983 (89.3 per cent of firms now this size). Although total employment has fallen so dramatically, the number of firms has increased from around 93,000 to over 160,000 during this period. The number employing over 300 people has, however, fallen from 437 to 265.

It might be anticipated that although small firms have mushroomed, the big firms have managed to capture a larger share of the work. This is not so. Defining 'small' again as seven employees or fewer, and 'large' as 300+ employees, the share of all work done in the third quarters of 1974 and 1983 respectively was as follows:

Table 6.1 Construction industry: size of firms in different trades, 1983 number of firms

Size of firm	Main trades			Specialist Trades (selected)						All trades
	General builders	Building plus civil engineering	Civil engineering	Plumbers	Carpenters	Glaziers	Heating engineers	Reinforced concrete	Scaffolding	
1–7 employees	57,772 90.0%	2,445 68.7%	1,651 65.8%	14,029 95.6%	9,853 95.1%	3,320 88.3%	7,217 86.6%	379 78.6%	596 76.5%	143,444 89.3%
8–299 employees	6,433 9.9%	1,038 29.1%	827 32.9%	642 4.4%	506 4.9%	432 11.7%	1,098 13.2%	94 19.5%	175 22.5%	16,887 10.5%
300+ employees	71 0.1%	78 2.2%	32 1.3%	— —	— —	6 —	20 0.2%	9 1.9%	8 1.0%	265 0.2%
Totals	64,276	3,561	2,510	14,671	10,359	3,758	8,335	482	779	160,596

Source: *Housing and Construction Statistics*, London HMSO, 1984.

	1974	1983
small firms	11.6%	24.0%
medium firms	48.9%	49.0%
large firms	39.5%	27.0%
	100.0%	100.0%

This is a curious feature. In almost all other large industries, for example the manufacture of cars or consumer durables, the long-term trend has been for an ever larger market share to be captured by a small number of very large corporations. Discussion of certain other features of the British construction industry may help to explain why this was not occurring in the industry in the 1970s.

The nature of demand

Uncertainty about the long-term flow of work is one of the ever present hazards. Over the last century or so very large periodic variations have occurred in the rate of construction of the built environment. Explanations have been offered in terms of economic theory, since both short- and long-term cycles in the rate of investment and activity seem endemic to capitalist systems, and also in terms of waves of technological innovation. For example, certain key changes in technology, such as the national electricity grid and the rapid development of car production, helped to engender a sudden surge of suburban industrial and housing development in the interwar period. Similarly, the spread of electronic data handling and exchange could theoretically mean more home-based work and a reduced need for specialized office space in future years.

In the shorter term, fluctuations occur in the effective demand for new owner-occupied housing. These depend heavily upon the flow of purchase funds available from the lending agencies. This, in turn, depends on the success of these agencies in attracting deposits in competition with the many other agencies (including the government) seeking to attract savings. The competition becomes more frenetic in periods of rapidly changing interest rates. The industry itself cannot control any of these factors; it can only react to their effects. One effect is that when the flow of purchase funds is high, houses can be sold at a price well in excess of total production costs. In the reverse conditions heavy losses may be sustained and housebuilding firms will if possible adapt their methods and/or contract their programmes (if they foresee the problem) or risk going out of business (if they do not).

Firms specializing in public sector contracts have similar difficulties, although they result from a different set of factors. As was made clear in Chapter 5, public expenditure programmes in housing, health, transport and other social fields which require construction to be done have been heavily cut back since the mid-1970s. To some extent these cutbacks in government programmes may have been predictable, but to a greater extent they are the result of changing policy preferences by government. Such preferences are notoriously difficult to predict because of the wide variety of factors to which governments have to respond. Official figures show that there has been a sharp reduction (in real terms) in new construction orders obtained from public sector sources between 1974 and 1983. Within this overall contraction, however, marked differences have occurred. Public sector orders for new offices, health facilities and airport construction have kept up well, but the value of new public sector housing construction fell, in real terms, by about 40 per cent between 1974 and 1983. There is no certainty that these priorities may not be completely reversed in the next five years – with important implications for construction firms specializing in one or other of these construction types.

The construction cycle

Sources of initial capital (M)

For a building cycle to commence there must be a supply of initial capital. This may be from either a public or a private sector source. Public expenditure on construction can flow through a number of channels (see diagram on pp. 68–9) to public authority direct works departments (13), through contracts placed with private sector builders (12) or via 'partnership schemes' where a local authority carries out infrastucture work before leasing out a site to a private developer (11). The factors conditioning the level and pattern of public expenditure on construction have been discussed in Chapter 5. In the private sector capital to initiate construction work comes mainly from one of three sources: retained profits from previous construction (or other) activity, loans (from 4, 5 or 7) and funds

Construction News, 28.2.85

BARRATT FACING UPHILL STRUGGLE

BARRATT Developments, the country's largest housebuilder, will show very poor returns in March for the first half of the current financial year, according to a report from market analysts Savory Milln.

The stockbrokers also predict that Barratt will be unable to pay a dividend for the year, despite an improvement in the second half. The report says: "Full year earnings look due to fall below the £13.5 million mark required to cover a maintained dividend."

Defensive

Savoury Milln also forsees that the recent change in Barratt's marketing image will take a long time to succeed. The stockbroking firm says the company's promotion is now essentially defensive — in the wake of the adverse publicity of two World in Action programmes — and this has not only detracted from Barratt as the most approachable housebuilder but has also enabled the competitors to catch up with their own incentive schemes.

Barratt is also beset with debt problems. The massive investment in land and production in the UK to meet the ambitious target of 18,000 homes a year has sent borrowings up to more than £150 million, around two-thirds of shareholders funds.

The drop in the new housing market has consequently put pressure on the company to clear stocks. While the four-year mortgage subsidy has been discontinued, Savory Milln anticipates that prices discounting will persist in one form or the other until the end of the financial year and that profits on sales will not rise much above the current level of £1,000 per unit.

Profits from the US operations are unlikely to alleviate the difficulty, although they doubled in 1983/84 to £4 million and could rise further this year. The interest on the £60 million US debt will limit the net contribution.

Despite the pessimistic outlook and the current low share price, Savory Milln does not consider Barratt a likely target for a stock market predator.

Figure 6.1   *Barratt, one of Britain's largest 'volume housebuilders', is heavily dependent on borrowed money.*

invested by shareholders (via 6). Retained profits are re-invested to some extent in most capitalist enterprises. The unusual feature of the construction industry lies in the balance of the other two types of capital. Most construction firms, and certainly most of the larger ones, tend to be *highly geared* – i.e. in the capital they are using there is a high ratio of loans to money subscribed by shareholders. (See Figure 6.1.)

This gearing strategy confers several advantages. It gives greater flexibility for increasing or decreasing the amount of finance being used in the light of variations in demand. This is so because it is usually much easier to raise new loans (or repay old ones) than to issue new stock. Adequate security for borrowings is usually available. A high proportion of most larger builders' assets is in the form of a landbank rather than production assets such as plant and machinery. This landbank will have been acquired over the years partly to ensure a flow of, say, five to ten years' worth of future building land but partly also with a view to its use as mortgageable security for further borrowing. In addition to these advantages, high gearing often means that strategic decisions concerning the running of the company can more easily be kept within the control of the owners and managers rather than shareholders – especially if the shareholding is not too widely spread.

But one important consequence of a high reliance on borrowed money, rather than money subscribed by shareholders, is the greater sensitivity to changes in the cost of existing borrowings that results from changes in loan interest rates. Whereas the rate of dividend paid to shareholders can be determined by the firm itself, the cost of borrowed money cannot. This was not an important consideration in periods of stable interest rates. But the last two decades have seen almost unprecedented fluctuations in rates as the international financial agencies have struggled to stabilize wild swings in the relative value of key world currencies. Some states (notably the USA and the UK) have also used interest rates as important regulators of their internal economies. The result has been an additional hazard to those construction companies, probably the majority, who depend to a high degree on loan rather than share capital. These enterprises, if they are to be profitable, need to achieve a rate of return on capital employed that is higher than the cost of borrowing it. If this latter cost is, say, 15 per cent as it has frequently been, the task of achieving a return higher than this has often been difficult if not impossible.

Land assembly and materials supply (M $\longrightarrow$ C)

The initial capital is used partly to assemble the necessary land and to buy building materials. It is self-evident that each building uses a piece of land – equally relevantly it usually prevents alternative uses occurring on that land for the period of the building's existence. Getting hold of suitable amounts of land in suitable locations is an ever-present problem for constructors. Equally important, the constructor must make an accurate assessment of how much to bid. Generally speaking, the market value of any site – whether as a capital sum or a stream of revenue – is conditioned by the net income derivable (i.e. after allowing for construction costs) from the most profitable building that can be placed upon it. The highest possible use, in other words, determines the value. In some cases this value is fixed in the transaction by which the constructor acquires the land just prior to the commencement of the construction. In these cases the bid for the land has been made with fairly precise knowledge of the future revenues or market price obtainable from the building to be constructed. In other cases land now being developed may have been acquired at some point in the past (perhaps as long ago as the Norman Conquest or the Crusades) with no precise idea about its future value. This does not invalidate the principle that at any particular point in time the market value of a developable site, whether it changes hands at that time or not, depends almost totally upon the expected revenues (less the necessary construction costs) that can be derived from whatever building can be built upon it.

This value level tends to ripple outwards by a 'spatial contagion' effect (often formally reinforced by the zoning carried out by land use planning). Once a particular site has had its value fixed as a result of a consent to develop, the potential value of other similarly zoned sites in that locality may *tend* to be viewed as roughly of the same order, even in advance of any formal consent to develop being granted. Thus the addition of a building, or complex of buildings, which introduces a new set of high-revenue uses into an area often leads to a drastic reorganization of local land values. Thus new 'commercial centres' are born.

The assembly of the necessary building materials is usually a more straightforward task than the acquisition of a suitable site for building. The materials supply industry (15 in the diagram on pp. 68–9) has a number of characteristics which make it rather different from most other branches in the construction sector. Building requires an enormous range of commodity inputs. Aggregates, stone, bricks, cement, tiles, timber, hardboard, glass, gypsum, structural steel, ceramics, plastics and at least two dozen other commodities are used even in quite simple buildings. The supply of many of these commodities is dominated by a limited number of producers, or even by one market leader. For example, as at 1985 Redlands dominate the European market in roof tiles and three firms (Blue Circle, Rugby Portland and Rio Tinto Zinc) virtually control the supply and pricing of cement. English China Clays lead the field in concrete-block production and, with Tarmac, are the largest producers of quarried materials. In brick production the London Brick Company are almost the sole supplier of general purpose Fletton bricks and a limited number of other suppliers (Streetley, Armitage and Blockleys, etc.) dominate the production of other bricks. Apart from the much higher degree of oligopoly evident in the materials industry compared to the building industry, the former is much more capital intensive than the latter. It is also much more internationalized – inevitably so since world supplies of some of the main building materials, such as timber and aluminium, are heavily dependent upon a few source countries.

Changes both in construction techniques and in architectural fashion produce quite large swings in the demand for various materials. In recent years the growth of timber-frame construction in speculative housebuilding produced a surge in demand for timber. By 1982 around 25 per cent of all speculative housing starts were using timber as the inner skin of the walls. Following media exposure of the damp penetration and rotting risks associated with this form of construction, the use of the technique declined until by May 1984 only 16 per cent of housing starts were using this method. There has also been a design swing towards the use of facing brick finishes instead of 'harder' materials such as concrete and glass in shop and office developments. Similarly, structural steel frames have recently been gaining at the expense of poured concrete in the construction of buildings over six storeys high. This trend can be seen to some extent as part of the overall drive to increase the use of prefabricated components rather than methods which depend on a heavier use of labour on site.

The organization of production (C $\longrightarrow$ C¹)

The actual construction process is organized in Britain largely on the basis of contracting and subcontracting to carry out a particular project. Under this system specialist firms come together for a specified time period in order to produce a building or set of buildings. On the completion of the project, the association ends until another scheme, probably using a different combination of firms, is commenced. An obvious alternative arrangement would be for sets of large builders and specialist firms to combine on a permanent basis into large integrated corporations which would be capable of carrying out all the varied operations in a construction scheme. This does, of course, happen and a proportion of total construction work is done in this way. But it remains a surprisingly small proportion and the pattern of large building firms sub-contracting with small specialist firms remains the dominant one (see, for example, Smyth, 1985, chapter 3).

Part of the explanation for these arrangements can be found in the varying pattern of demand to which the industry is responding. Historical data show that the building industry has, for at least a hundred years, been a prey to large cyclical variations in demand or, perhaps more accurately, large variations in the rate of flow of new investment into it. One consequence of an uneven, and to a large extent unpredictable, flow of business is that the industry must collectively keep to some overall strategy which enables it to guard against overcapacity and to survive through the downturns in demand/investment. One way for the large builders to do this is to make the pattern of association with specialist trades as free of permanent commitment as possible; hence the pattern of association by periodic contracts to carry out specific projects rather than by merger or takeover of ownership. The results of mergers could be (and sometimes are) corporations that have an overcapacity in periods of demand downturn.

The British construction industry displays a particularly low ratio of fixed capital employed to output achieved (see Figure 6.2). In 1977, construction accounted for over 7 per cent of the gross domestic product, but it used only 1.2 per cent of the nation's stock of productive capital (plant and machinery) to do so. Clearly the industry appears undercapitalized and labour intensive. In fact it is one of the largest employers of all with 1,084,000 employees in 1983. Of these, 814,000 were employed in the private sector and 270,000 in the public. Both sectors had contracted drastically since 1974, the private sector rather faster than the public. Of the total employees, 782,000 were classed as 'operatives' and 302,000 as 'other staff'. The number of operatives had contracted much faster

Figure 6.2   *The British construction industry is heavily under-capitalized and relies on labour intensive methods. Although there is claimed to be a strong demand for new private housing in London's docklands, and although there are several hundred thousand construction workers unemployed, there were very few people working on this site in Wapping.*
(© *Peter Ambrose 1986)*

than the other staff, especially in the private sector. The number of managerial and technical staff had actually increased by 8 per cent between 1974 and 1982.

One of the peculiarities of the British construction industry lies in the casual basis on which much of the labour is employed and the coexistence of a very high rate of unemployment with a chronic shortage of skilled workers. The causes are complex but centre around the 'labour only subcontracting' system, known as 'the lump', by which much of the labour input is provided – especially in the field of speculative housebuilding. Under this system the main contractor (say, a housebuilding firm) does not employ workers on a direct and permanent basis, but supplies the plant and materials and offers a subcontract for the workers' labour only. The sub-contract is likely to be for a specified project or projects, and payment may be either a fixed sum or a sum per amount of work done. The subcontract may be with individual workers or with a

---

Construction News, 6.12.84

OUT-OF-WORK COSTING £600m

CONSTRUCTION'S unemployment is costing the government £600 million. This was the blunt message delivered to Lord Young — the government's new unemployment supremo — by Michael Millwood, president of the Building Employers Confederation.

He said that 400,000 workers, 20 per cent of the industry's total workforce, were now on the dole and the government saw no real return on the unemployment benefit it paid out.

"Yet at the same time we see mounting evidence of urban decay and of a worsening problem of disrepair in homes, schools, hospitals and factories," he said.

"Around one-quarter of all private housing is in serious disrepair and we face major problems in the public sector where we need to spend an estimated £10 billion to rectify defective housing.

"Reports from the government's own inspectors show that many of our school buildings are in an appalling condition — one in four schools is overcrowded or has outdoor toilets and nearly a million children study in temporary accommodation.

"Half of our hospitals were built before the First World War, three-quarters of them before 1939, and capital spending within the NHS has almost halved as a proportion of total NHS spending since 1974."

He passionately believed there was a grave mismatch of resources.

"It cannot be good husbandry to pay 400,000 construction workers to do nothing, while the nation's building stock slides further into decay. We are running up ever larger bills for the future for the lack of preventive maintenance now," he told Lord Young.

Figure 6.3 *Unemployment in the building industry has risen sharply since the late 1970s and the industry is constantly pointing out that more capital spending by government is vitally necessary.*

firm which itself organizes groups of workers offering only their labour and hand-tools. A variety of arrangements is possible, most of which are, in reality, sub-subcontracts. A number of consequences flow from these arrangements. Many workers feel that the system offers them better earnings than could be achieved in permanent employment. Equally, many contractors clearly see benefits in the flexibility which results from being able to offer more, or fewer, labour subcontracts so as to match the volume of demand, rather than to carry a permanent workforce on the payroll. But critics of the system, notably the construction unions, see serious long-term disadvantages. The system makes it extremely difficult to ensure a high level of unionization in the industry since there is little continuity of the workforce and much of the labour input is by casual or itinerant workers.

An associated point made by Ball (1983) and others is that the use of the lump system, rather than a system of permanent employment, enables employers to maintain a much greater degree of control over strategic investment decisions and the conditions of employment. This, in the opinion of many, is at the root of the poor provision of training programmes and the patchy employer support for the training courses that are on offer. This, in turn, has led to a chronic shortage of skilled workers in the industry. There is a plausible argument that if all building workers were permanent employees of building companies, then the latter, as employers, would have more interest in ensuring the necessary level of skill in their employees. At present the counter-argument, that the lump system minimizes short-term labour costs, clearly looms much larger in the calculations of many employers. What suits most individual employers does not, however, seem to add up to advances in the performance of the industry as a whole. It is widely believed that the lump system produces, overall, less efficiency, less skill, less commitment to the project in hand and more delay in the completion of projects.

There is a related point concerning safety and conditions of work – areas in which improvements might have been expected had the workforce been well organized into unions able to negotiate improvements in these fields. Certainly average hours of work, including overtime, have fallen drastically from 55.7 per week in 1974 to 48.0 per week in 1983 (*Housing and Construction Statistics*, 1984). But this reduction reflects a fall in demand for labour over this period rather than true gains in terms of a shorter working-week. The accident record of the industry remains 'dismal' (Leopold, 1983) and a 1980 survey by the Construction Industry's Manpower Board showed that 25 per cent of skilled men over 50, and 44 per cent of unskilled in this age-group, reported some disability that prevented them from working at the rate they would wish. Many in the industry retire early, often without the benefits of an occupational pension scheme because of the casual basis on which they had been employed. Many others turn to occupations with better working conditions. Certainly Leopold's work shows that whereas two industries with broadly similar risk content (the railways and mining) had managed to reduce their rate of fatal accidents considerably since the war, the death rate in the building industry has remained more or less stable.

The forms of realization ($C^1 \longrightarrow M^1$)

In any form of development initiated within the private sector, the whole point of the exercise is to realize an $M^1 - M$ increment – to end up with more money than one started with. But this increment can take at least four forms. It can be a once for all speculative gain or a stream of future revenue or an increase in book value assets or the profit element in a fixed payment for work carried out under a contract. For purposes of comparison the stream of revenue can be 'capitalized' or imagined as the capital sum that would yield this stream of money at the ruling rate of interest. Alternatively, the once for all gain, or rise in assets, can be turned into a stream of revenue by investing it at the same ruling rate of interest. Either way the ultimate aim is the same; to maximize the $M^1 - M$ increment per unit of capital employed per time period of its investment. The latter point is important. A return of 20 per cent on capital employed over a two-year period is not as successful an outcome as an 11 per cent return on the same amount of capital over a one-year period (assuming one can repeat the performance in the second year). We consider the various forms of realization in the next section.

What of construction that is funded and carried out entirely within the public sector? Can such activity be said to yield a 'return' – even if not in the form of $M^1 - M$? In the larger sense of the amount of social benefit achieved (better health, education or movement of vehicles) it seems reasonable to make assessments of the relative rate of 'social return' derivable from specific public projects. In fact if this could not be done, there would be no rational basis for deciding to go ahead with one public project rather than another. But the argument gets more complex. To what extent does public money spent on building a Channel tunnel benefit the profits of haulage firms as distinct from saving the time and money of individual holidaymakers? To what extent is public investment in low-rental housing reducing living costs for the poor as distinct from damping down the wage demands they make of employers? Until we have vastly more sophisticated analytical procedures, these questions cannot be answered (except polemically) and the crucial issue of who reaps the major share of benefit from public sector construction expenditure will remain unresolved.

Specific functions within the industry

We can now give some consideration to each of the four main output-producing functions shown in the diagram on pp. 68-9: speculative housebuilding, property developing, general contracting and public authority direct works.

Speculative housebuilding

The speculative housebuilder (10 in the diagram) puts together finance, land, labour, 'off the peg' designs, material inputs and a planning consent so as to produce houses which, he hopes, will sell as soon after completion as possible for some figure in excess of the combined cost of the inputs. He goes through a four-stage process of project evaluation, site preparation, house construction and final sale (usually through an agent). Much of the entrepreneurial skill lies in the first stage which involves negotiation with the planning authority, usually to fix the maximum permitted amount of development on the site, cost projections, analysis of the likely demand for the houses and calculations to ensure that, so far as can be foreseen, the total sale value will exceed total costs.

The larger regional or national builders tend to acquire land, or take an option to purchase, as and when it comes up for sale in favoured urban-fringe locations. The vendors are likely to be farmers, or farming companies, or the land may form part of some large estate which finds it convenient to sell or possibly the owner may be some public authority. Whereas the larger builders may then hold this land in their 'landbank' until conditions are right for construction (or resale) smaller locally based builders tend to get into construction only as and when they can acquire suitable sites. Ideally the site purchased will be zoned for residential development and already have at least outline consent to develop (an application can be made by the prospective purchaser as well as the owner). If the future development capacity of the land is known, its market value can be more accurately fixed. The vendor will – or should – be advised by his estate agent while the purchaser will embark on a set of calculations. These will take into account the probable total revenue from the eventual sale of the houses, from which will be subtracted the total construction costs, the cost of the borrowing to carry out the project and the profit required. The 'residual' figure will be the upper limit of the worth of the land to the purchaser. If the valuation reached by the vendor's estate agent is within negotiable range of the prospective purchaser's, the sale can be made.

Ball (1983) has carried out much recent research on the structure and operation of the speculative housebuilding industry. He distinguishes, on the basis of survey data, various categories of builder ranging from the 'petty capitalist' (employing very few people, building up to twenty houses per year and financing new starts from the sale of completed houses), through small family firms, firms for whom housebuilding is a side-line to some other activity, to 'large capital' housebuilding firms who, between them, dominate the market. He quotes data for 1978 which indicate that 47 per cent of total housebuilding was carried out by builders producing more than 250 houses per year (see also Fielding, 1982). Few, if any, of these latter are housebuilders pure and simple. Some (such as Wimpey Homes) are subsidiaries of large construction groups and others (New Ideal Homes owned by Trafalgar House – see Figure 6.4) are part of massive multipurpose conglomerates. While all these larger firms hold several years' supply of land in their landbanks, most of them still operate only at a regional scale. Only Wimpey, Barratt and Tarmac, the three largest in 1979, worked on a national scale at that date.

Many of the larger housebuilders also operate as developers of industrial and commercial property (see the following section). They may be able to carry out periodic development using finance from the sale of houses, thus obviating the need to borrow. An additional advantage is that the steady stream of revenue derived from a rental development helps to even out the lumpy cashflow from house sales which, as we have seen, can fluctuate unpredictably. It seems likely, for these and other reasons, that an increasing market share of all construction may in future be achieved by groups which combine the capacity to carry out both speculative housebuilding and property development. The activity cycle of

Construction News, 9.2.84

MERGER AT TRAFALGAR WILL AID INNER CITIES

BY MARTIN WALLER

The decision by Trafalgar House late last year to merge its property and housebuilding divisions into one entity came as little surprise to watchers of the shipping-to-construction conglomerate.

What was perhaps surprising was the announcement that the merger would take the group further into the development of derelict inner city areas in the housing and property fields, particularly retail.

New Ideal Homes, Trafalgar's housebuilding subsidiary, had traditionally been associated with large-scale developments well outside the main cities like the giant Goldsworth Park estate near Woking which is due to be completed in 1986.

Not so, says David Calverley, managing director of the new division, Trafalgar House Property, and formerly head of the housebuilding division. He said that New Ideal's south east subsidiary now builds around 50 per cent of its output within the Greater London Council area, against 10 to 15 per cent three years ago.

The group currently has a number of inner city renovation schemes under way — typically one in Camden, North London, where an old lorry park is being converted into 60 flats.

The merger is seen as a response to changing conditions in the residential and commercial property markets. The trend in retailing and refurbishing property and tailoring new schemes towards specific tenants' requirements, rather than the large-scale developments of recent years.

There is also a move towards mixed schemes, incorporating elements of housing and industrial or commercial use. Mr Calverley puts this down to a "revolution" now occurring in traditional work patterns, with people wanting to live closer to, or even in the same development as, their workplace.

"The demarcation lines between commercial, residential and industrial property no longer apply to the same extent. The margins are becoming blurred," says Geoffrey Carter, chairman of the new company and originally managing director of the property side.

Figure 6.4   *The larger multi-purpose conglomerates such as Trafalgar House are in a position to diversify their construction activity and make the most of market trends in different sectors of construction. The merger may well aid Trafalgar House as well as the inner cities.*

these two activities is often out of phase and a capacity to switch effort from one to the other is an important safeguard in periods of uncertain demand.

Property developing

The developer (11 in the diagram on pp. 68–9) brings together a site, finance, an architect, a planning consent, a construction contractor and marketing and management skills to produce a building having a capacity to generate a stream of future rent income – either for himself or some purchaser of the building. The activity can be carried out on a large scale by an organization occupying only a small suite of offices, having a very narrow ownership base and employing only a handful of people. The site may have been acquired freehold at some point in the past (probably with old, lower-revenue, buildings upon it) or it may be acquired just prior to the development or it may be leased over some appropriate period – the longer the better – from the freehold owner. If this owner is a public authority for whom the developer is initiating and/or carrying out a project, the arrangement is known as a 'partnership' scheme. The financial offer made for the site by the developer, whether to lease or to purchase, will need to be carefully worked out in the light of the future annual rent revenue potential of the completed building, the cost of the finance and construction and the rate of return the developer expects to obtain on the capital committed. Assessment of each of these factors is complex and demands considerable expertise. A simplified version of the calculations involved is given in Cadman and Austin-Crowe (1978).

One of the main aims of the developer is to reduce the degree of risk inherent in the situation. This can be done in various ways. If the scheme is a partnership in which the local authority, as freeholder, has a financial interest (such as ground rent payments and some share of the rental income of the buildings), the risk element is much lower. The authority clearly has an incentive to see the scheme succeed and can, for example, commit public money to improving the access to the development or prohibit subsequent developments which might affect the rentals achieved by the scheme. The risk can also be considerably reduced by the careful preparation of the contract with the builder, especially in relation to specifications, costs and completion time.

Perhaps most of all, the success of the scheme is made much more likely if a good proportion of the office and shop space is pre-let to reliable tenants. These might include the authority itself, a government department or perhaps one of the major retailers, say

Boots or Martins, who can act as 'anchors' to the scheme and attract other retailers because of the business they are known to generate. The most prestigious retailers of all, for example Sainsbury, Marks & Spencer, C & A, and Tesco no longer fulfil this function since they often initiate and carry out their own development on their own freehold sites. Despite these safeguards, risk can never be entirely removed and changes in factors such as the cost of borrowed money or rent levels in the locality, which depend on the evolving pattern of demand/supply and accessibility in the area, cannot be controlled by the developer.

The arrangements for financing developments have become much more complex in recent decades. Up to the early 1960s the pattern was relatively straightforward. Few developers could finance schemes from retained profits because few developments were sold on completion. The construction costs were usually financed by a bank loan which, on completion of the scheme, was paid off by taking out a long-term, fixed-interest loan from a financial institution. If the developer needed to sell, there were tax advantages in selling the company which owned the building rather than the building itself since there was no tax on buying and selling shares. The main aim of the lending institutions was to arrange for perhaps 15 or 20 per cent of their total investment portfolio to be in the form of loans to, or shareholdings in, first-class property schemes.

From about the mid-1960s onwards various changes occurred. The inflation rate, and with it the borrowing rate, began both to fluctuate and to climb. Long-term, fixed-interest lending made little sense because interest rates might increase soon after a loan was made. Several large insurance companies, notably Eagle Star, the Prudential and Norwich Union, began to initiate their own property developments on a large scale. Most of the other institutions began to seek more active participation in property schemes. Rather than acting simply as lenders, they became interested in acquiring a larger shareholding in property companies (thus inducing many of them to become public companies) and in drawing up financing agreements which gave them a share of the future rental growth of the buildings. In these ways they have benefited from the increases in the *asset value* of the developments as well as from the revenue growth. Finally, a number of development companies have been taken over by their creditor institutions, often because they have run into difficulties in continuing loan repayments. This recent growth of a wide variety of linking arrangements between finance interests and developers has meant that although financing and development are still quite separate *functions,* as shown in the diagram (pp. 68–9), the ownership and management distinction between the institutions that carry them out is now frequently fogged. Many large developments are carried out by multipurpose issuing house/evaluation/investment/development combines or consortia who are capable of raising money in various financial centres and developing on a multinational scale. In many ways the swashbuckling scene of the one-man development empires of the interwar and postwar years, as depicted by Marriott (1967), has changed to something much more complex and international.

Another of the developer's tasks is to oversee the work of the architect. The architect's job is to design the scheme to a brief which specifies particularly the amount of lettable space required (upon which the calculations about the financial viability of the project depend). At the design stage there is close consultation between the developer, the architect, the consultant engineers and the local planning authority who have, in theory, already specified such matters as the upper limit and type of development allowed. Questions of storey height, appearance, materials, access, local traffic generation and many others are all dealt with in continuing discussions between the developer, the construction professionals, the chosen building contractor and the planning authority. If the project gives rise to considerable public concern, because it is likely to produce a considerable increase in traffic density or is held to be visually undesirable, local opposition may persuade the Secretary of State to call a Public Inquiry. This will produce delay and could lead to some change in the content of the scheme, thus affecting potential profitability even before construction is commenced.

When the project is completed, the developer may realize the M^1 – M increment (assuming it is positive) in a number of ways. If the site has been leased, the developer benefits from what is likely to be a growing difference between the net rental income received from the building and the ground rent payable to the freeholder. The latter may have negotiated a rent-sharing agreement, in which case the revenue growth is shared between the two parties in accordance with the agreement. Or the developer, if freehold owner of the site, may be the sole beneficiary of the rising rental income (and thus the

increasing asset value) of the building. Commercial developments
may be expected to have a revenue 'life' of twenty, fifty or even a
hundred years and their initial cost is fixed at the time of
construction. This means that the greater the rate of inflation, the
more the current, constantly renegotiated, revenue from the
building will exceed the current real cost of servicing the borrowing
which initially financed the scheme. This is likely to be true even if
the loan was on a variable, rather than a fixed-interest, basis. As a
final variant on the M^1 – M realization the developer may sell the
freehold of the project to the financier (or someone else) and then
lease back the building and manage the lettings. In this case, as in
the first case, the level of the developer's profit depends upon the
difference between the revenue obtainable and the cost of leasing
the building from the new freeholder.

The pattern of client demand to which the developer is responding
has changed considerably in recent years. The typical suburban, or
county town, high street is increasingly dominated by branches of
building societies, estate agents, travel agents and shops selling
electronic or high-technology consumer goods. The form of
development reflects more and more the requirements of the 'one
stop' car-borne shopper. Covered malls with adjacent multilevel car
parking are to be found immediately adjacent to many old-
established shopping streets or, alternatively, in some easily
accessible location on the urban periphery. Airports have become
more important than railway stations as locators of high-technology
research and development, manufacturing and associated office
space. In fact at present higher office rentals are obtainable in parts
of Slough (close to Heathrow) than in Holborn. Three of the largest
developers, Land Securities, Hammerson and MEPC, together with
companies in the Trafalgar House group, continue to dominate the
office and shop development market while Slough Estates are the
leaders in the growing field of high-technology factories.

General contracting

A building contractor (12 in the diagram on pp. 68–9) operates quite
differently from a speculative housebuilder or a developer (See
Figure 6.5). Typically he tenders for a construction contract which
has been placed on offer either by a public authority or by a
commercial developer. His task, simply stated, is twofold: he has to

tender in such a way that he wins the contract, and he then has to ensure that the amount he receives under the contract exceeds the total cost of carrying it out to the satisfaction of the client. Successful tendering is, therefore, the first essential. It has often been pointed out that the system of matching clients to contractors by a process of competitive tendering has many disadvantages. If, say, five or ten firms tender for the same job (as is frequently the case), not only do the tenders often vary to a quite baffling degree but all the unsuccessful tenderers will have invested a large amount of time and effort for no purpose. At least one official report (the Wood Report of 1975 on public sector building contracting) identified current tendering procedures, rather than fluctuating demand, as the source of most uncertainity and discontinuity of work for the individual firm. There remains, of course, the strong probability that 'competitive' tenders are often submitted after informal discussion between apparently competing firms – some of whom may be keen to win the work, or to develop in a particular area, and some of whom may not.

Part of the contractor's management skill lies in keeping a good 'mix' of contracts in operation to ensure that the contractor's various resources of labour, plant and expertise are not left idle, but are employed as much as possible on one or other of the contracts in hand. Equally important, the flow of income from the various contracts should be as continuous as possible. Wide fluctuations in payment can lead to periods of very low income followed by periods with excessive income ('excessive' because it may lead to a greater tax liability in that particular year than would otherwise be the case). Generally speaking, realization of the $M^1 - M$ increment is by instalment. Payment is made to the contractor monthly on the basis of work completed to the client's satisfaction, but subject to some retention of funds until overall completion in case of inadequate or late work. Clearly the contractor will be anxious to minimize the use of his own (or borrowed) funds and will seek both to delay his payment for materials for as long as possible and to obtain the bulk of payment from the client as soon as possible. He is likely, therefore, to overstate the cost of the work in the early stages (foundations, etc.) and understate the later stage work (finishing, etc.) This strategy, known as 'loading', results in a more advantageous cash flow for the contractor.

Contracts can be carried out on a wide variety of bases, all coming

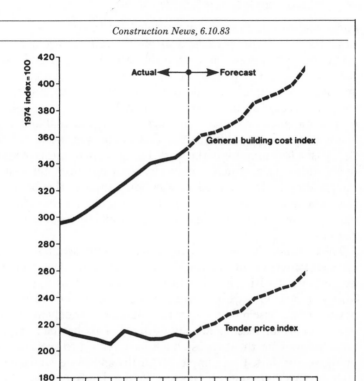

Construction News, 6.10.83

BUILDERS' MARGINS TAKE A TUMBLE

Building contractors' profit margins have fallen dramatically over the past three years, says a report from the Building Cost Information Service. Although tender prices indicate a maximum drop over the period of seven per cent, contractors' costs have risen by no less than 23 per cent.

The situation is unlikely to improve for at least two years — and possibly three — says BCIS, an arm of the Royal Institution of Chartered Surveyors.

Only a minimum recovery in market conditions is expected in the next couple of years, the survey predicts. As a result tender prices are likely to stay fairly closely linked to building costs with no resulting improvement in contractors' profit margins.

Figure 6.5 *Contractors have suffered a squeeze on profits in the early 1980s. It has been necessary to adopt specific strategies to remain profitable.*

under one of two main headings: Joint Contracts Tribunal and 'design and build' (or 'package deal'). In the JCT arrangement the promoter, or developer, is responsible for the design and close specification of the project; he obtains the necessary planning approvals and his professional team, led by the architect, supervises the progress of the work. In the 'design and build' contract, which normally applies for simpler buildings such as industrial units, the contractor is responsible for the design, the approvals and for the satisfactory progress of the work. His task, therefore, is to work to an outline brief which will specify what the promoter wishes the building to do, and produce a building to meet this brief. He carries a larger share of responsibility should the building be unsatisfactory or late in completion than would be the case under a JCT contract.

The contractor's client may be a private sector developer or one of a wide variety of public authorities, such as a central government department, a nationalized industry, a local authority, a public utility or the Housing Corporation. The total flow, and the pattern, of work from these public sources has fluctuated widely in the last decade or so for reasons already outlined. This has had varying repercussions for those firms which have tended to specialize in public sector work. For example, McCarthy and Stone, who are the largest providers of sheltered housing for the elderly, have benefited from increased government interest in this field and have recently doubled their profits as a result.

In 1964, a key report (Banwell, 1964) drew attention to some of the inefficiencies inherent in the dominance of the competitive tendering/contract system. The committee took the line (perhaps prompted by some of the larger contracting interests who helped to bring about its setting up) that there was too much competition for contracts. The trend since then has been for the repeated use of contractors who had given previous satisfaction and the increasing use of 'approved lists' of contractors by public sector clients. One consequence of these changes in procurement strategies seems to have been that various of the larger contractors, benefiting from the more reliable flow of public sector work, have succeeded in securing a larger share of the market in public sector construction. This seems to provide some support for the view that a change from competitive tendering to some more reliable means of obtaining contract work might well lead both to more stable workflows and to some reduction in the extreme fragmentation of production effort in the industry generally.

Direct labour work

Direct labour organizations, or DLOs (13 in the diagram on pp. 68–9) are local authority departments which carry out building work, including maintenance and repairs, for the authority. Most of their work is related to the statutory functions of the local authority (housing, highways, etc.). They had their origins in the 1890s following the various Acts which set up the British local government structure. Many of the newly constituted authorities (led by the London County Council) found that the service given by private building contractors was unsatisfactory and too costly. As one history of direct labour puts it: 'The contractors need for profit was at variance with the objectives of local government' (Direct Labour Collective, 1978). Arguably this observation is still largely true today, and the tension inherent between the service provision aims of public authorities and the profit-maximizing aims of private contractors is still clearly evident.

Direct labour organizations are, in most respects, the complete antithesis of the private construction industry. They employ building workers (around 200,000 in the late 1970s) on a permanent basis as distinct from subcontracting for their labour. This means that, in general, workers are more highly unionized, have access to more training opportunities and enjoy better career benefits such as long service bonuses, holidays, welfare facilities and pension rights. Partly for these reasons, and partly because public authority employers make correct income tax deductions and national insurance contributions for their workforce (which are widely evaded under the 'lump' system), extra labour costs are involved in direct labour construction. But the profit appropriated by private contractors, and the delays, poor work standards and increased accident costs often associated with construction carried out by the private sector, can be avoided. There is, in fact, overwhelming evidence that direct labour organizations save building costs in the long term, and often in the short term, and are usually able to carry out projects (or complete those left unfinished by a bankrupt contractor) at well below the average price tendered by the private sector.

In the face of this situation the private sector of the construction industry has mounted a continuous campaign against DLOs. The virulence of this campaign is a clear indication of the threat to profitability inherent in the direct labour method of organizing construction. The attack centres on the alleged inefficiencies and high costs of DLO construction and stresses the value of competitive tendering by private sector firms. This attack loses some of its force given the considerable body of evidence that private sector firms often collude informally about tenders for particular contracts. It is also clear that over the last decade the total flow of construction business has fallen considerably. With less work to go round, there is bound to be deep private sector unease about work done for local authorities by their own 'in house' building departments.

In the mid-1970s, the Chartered Institute of Public Finance and Accountancy, which incorporates the views of some public sector accountants and treasurers, called for some changes in DLO procedures. The general idea, borrowing from a private sector ethos, was to make DLOs operate more closely to a 'profit and loss' model and to become, in a sense, local authority trading departments or enterprises whose main aim was to make 'a profit'. Given that DLOs, from the beginning, existed to 'de-casualize' employment, to ensure better pay and conditions for employees, and to provide better-quality work than the private sector (thus saving on subsequent maintenance costs), it seems clear to critics of this view that to apply the narrow logic of the market is to erode these principles. A paper 'profit' or 'surplus' can be attained, as it often is by private sector firms, by skimping on quality and/or worsening the conditions of employment of the workforce. To insist that public services departments must compete for work by tendering in the market, and then make a certain percentage return on capital used, is as contradictory and detrimental to users' interests in this field as it is, for example, in running the railway system. In both cases a satisfactory public service cannot be maintained, nor the interests of employees protected, by a strict project-by-project (or train-by-train) profit and loss approach.

Adaptation strategies to the post-1973 slump

The construction industry has reacted in a particular set of ways in the face of the recurring uncertainties and fluctuations in demand for its product since the recession began in the early 1970s. Unlike the consumer electronics industry, its main response has not been to enlarge its market or reduce its costs by technical innovation. Certainly it is not averse to such strategies and there have been periods when new technologies have been applied on a large scale, but this has often been with insufficient field testing and disastrous and costly results. For example, many local authorities are only now counting the enormous cost, variously estimated at between £10 billion and £20 billion, of repairing and renewing the high-rise blocks of flats built with the concrete slab/wall-frame system

---

Network, April 1984

STUMBLING BLOCKS!
NATIONAL TOWER BLOCKS CAMPAIGN

"THERE ARE PROBLEMS FOR VIRTUALLY EVERYONE WHO LIVES IN A SKY BLOCK . . . PEOPLE OFTEN FEEL IMPRISONED, CUT OFF AND ALONE . . ."

It is no longer denied by any responsible body that much of the system built housing built in the 50s and 60s has proved to be a disastrous experiment in social and environmental terms; the problems are particularly acute in the high rise housing schemes — especially those within the poorer communities. Ronan Point and the deliberate demolition of two Birkenhead tower blocks (less than 20 years old) bear witness to

the social tragedies of the problem.

The National Tower Blocks Network — formed from a conference held in October 1983 which attracted 170 different groups — has contacted the National Planning Aid Unit and an initial meeting between the groups has already been held. Both groups have made a firm commitment to aid each other and see their work — particularly in the building of volunteer networks — as mutually beneficial.

If one of Planning Aid's main objectives is to promote the TCPA's grassroots — or 'Bottom Up' — approach, then our link with the National Tower Blocks Network could prove invaluable.

The Network has now produced a newsletter The View which seeks to coordinate information throughout the country.

Figure 6.6 *Many of the 1950s and 1960s tower blocks were produced using techniques that were insufficiently researched and with inadequate on-site supervision. The social and economic cost is now being counted.*

The Guardian, 2.1.86

COUNCIL AWAITS GO-AHEAD TO GIVE ESTATE AWAY

BY GEOFF ANDREWS, LOCAL GOVERNMENT CORRESPONDENT.

A Conservative-controlled city council is likely this month to sanction the giving away of a block of 520 council flats and maisonettes, said to be worth £5 million, to a developer.

Barratts is waiting to hear whether Mr Kenneth Baker, the Environment Secretary, has approved its offer to take over the Portsdown Park Estate, in Portsmouth, and to spend £8 to £9 million on refurbishing it to provide homes for sale or letting through a housing association.

Homes on the estate, a grim fortress of brick and concrete on an exposed site above the city, have leaked badly since soon after the estate was completed 20 years ago. It also suffers from vandalism and other social problems.

Portsmouth City council maintains that it cannot afford to remedy Portsdown Park's faults and that the Barratt scheme is a realistic way to make the most of a badly flawed development.

Last October, Mr Ian Gibson, the leader of the council, told Mr Baker that Barratts would sell a proportion of the existing units outright after refurbishment, and make the rest available through a housing association or a mix of shared ownership and fair rent lettings.

The Labour minority on the council opposes the transfer and says that the city would have to pay out around £300,000 in compensation to residents moved into other council accommodation while Barratts refurbish their homes for sale.

The council would have to pay off £475,000 a year in debt charges, but would lose more than that in rent income. The full refurbishment scheme is due to begin in nine months.

One Portsdown tenant, Mrs Mary Woodward, a leader of the residents' action group, said yesterday that the Barratts' plan was "financial lunacy."

Sheila McKechnie, director of Shelter, which is campaigning against council estate disposals, described the Portsmouth plan as "an extreme example of the way some councils are proposing to dispose of estates to developers at the expense of tenants and ratepayers."

Figure 6.7   *... but construction companies can pick up some reasonable bargains from friendly councils*

introduced in the early 1960s (see Figures 6.6 and 6.7). The 1965 subsidy arrangements gave local authority housing departments every incentive to build high. The government subsidy per housing unit varied from £20 per annum for four-storey blocks up to £45 per annum for ten-storey blocks. In the same year the authorities were urged by government circular not to do any evaluations of the new industrial building system themselves, but to rely on the technical advice produced by the National Building Agency – the latter, of course, relying to some extent on the expertise of people with a commercial interest in promoting the new systems.

Mistakes on a similar scale could possibly be occurring now in the speculative housebuilding field. As we have seen, certain leading housebuilders (notably Barratt's) have invested heavily in the use of timber framing for the inner skin of the cavity wall (Cullen, 1982). Again, advice from official sources has given a certain technical respectability to the method. In fact it is true that the use of timber rather than building-blocks for the inner wall can give greater strength to the building. But it is important to use properly seasoned timber, to keep it dry on site and to attach the waterproof lining correctly in the construction stage. Several television documentaries have shown quite clearly that these precautions have not, in every case, been observed. Damp penetration and rot may lead to heavy repair costs for thousands of home owners in five to ten years time. It may well be, therefore, that two of the main innovatory technologies introduced into residential construction over the past two decades have backfired badly. If this is so, and given the huge investment required to introduce a major new building technology, it is hardly surprising that the rate of innovation in the industry is so unimpressive. Nor, as we have seen, has the industry reacted (like the car industry) with a massive move to world-scale concentration of ownership and the seeking out of cheap labour areas for component production. Clearly the nature of the product is different. It is difficult, although not impossible, to envisage a large market share of world construction being captured by a handful of large corporations, or a system by which a British housebuilder uses windows made in Brazil and tiles made in Formosa.

Instead of these theoretically possible strategies, the industry has responded to the unpredictabilities of the market by sharpening its capacity to switch effort in at least four ways: between different forms of construction, between building and land dealing, between construction and quite different activities, and between home and overseas markets. It has also redoubled its attempts to stay 'light-footed' in terms of finance and labour arrangements (as already discussed) and has increasingly adopted, as a fifth strategy, various devices to reduce its overall borrowing requirement in view of the high and unpredictable cost of finance.

The first strategy, therefore, has been for firms to improve their capacity to undertake differing forms of construction work in response to changes in demand. Information on these changes over the past decade can be gained from *Housing and Construction Statistics*, and some reference has already been made to changes between 1974 and 1983 in the pattern of public sector contracts on offer. Trends in the private sector were similar. New orders increased by 183 per cent (at 1983 prices), but within this gross figure housing orders increased by 345 per cent and orders for industrial premises by only 50 per cent. Information on the way that different firms adjusted their activity to this sharply varying pattern of demand can be gained by examining the annual reports and accounts of a selection of the large construction companies, especially those with a mixed construction and civil engineering output. Clearly firms such as Laing or Costain, which established themselves in the field of interwar speculative housebuilding, have diversified and can now compete for a wide range of different constructional and engineering contracts. Similarly, in the late 1970s firms that had been specializing in motorway and trunk-road projects (such as Monk and Marchwiel) reacted to the cutbacks in the roads programme by moving into the speculative housebuilding field.

One very lucrative strategy has been for firms to move into the field of repairs, renewals and maintenance. The continuing success of the conservation lobby in many historic towns has produced more business for firms capable of producing renewed, and possibly increased, rentable floorspace while retaining the outer shell of a Victorian or Georgian building. Similarly, the amount of public money channelled into home improvement grants – which has ebbed and flowed but on the whole increased – has produced a great deal of renovation work in the private housing sector. But the main opportunities for firms capable of a wide range of construction work probably lie in the needs of public sector clients. A study carried out late in 1983 by the National Federation of Building Trades Employers (*Construction News*, 26 January 1984) concluded that local authorities required to have about £5 billion-worth of construction work done per year. Of this about £1.9 billion was for new buildings, of which direct labour organizations currently do about £0.3 billion, and £3.1 billion was repairs and maintenance work, of which DLOs do perhaps £2.0 billion. (Clearly, whether intentionally or not, the construction industry ensured a good flow of future renewal work when it used inadequate technologies and methods to build the high-rise blocks of the 1960s and early 1970s.) New rules framed by the government as part of their drive to dismantle public sector building departments mean that private sector constructors will, in future, be in a better position to compete for the £2 billion or more of work currently carried out by DLOs. Firms capable of undertaking both new build and repair/maintenance work are likely to benefit considerably from this drive to privatize construction activity.

The second adjustment strategy has been to switch effort and investment away from construction and towards land dealing. Unfortunately, although there is considerable inferential evidence that this is happening, it is impossible to be precise about the extent. This would require the level of investment and profit in these two fields to be separately identified in the published accounts of construction firms, which they are not. Even if they were, the book value profit on the sale of a piece of land acquired, say, ten years ago would vary a great deal depending on the accountancy conventions adopted and the rate of tax applicable to this particular form of profit. The general observation can be made, however, that highly inflated development land values (and therefore an enhanced possibility of profiting by dealing in such land) are certainly to some extent a consequence of the 'rationing' of building land inherent in land use control. Since it appears to have become much easier in recent years to overcome or bypass zoning (Rydin, 1983), some of the heat may have been taken out of the market in development land. As a result, land dealing, as opposed to construction, may have become less attractive. On the other hand, the industry is currently claiming that in some areas the shortfall in land zoned for housing has led to a scramble for sites which has pushed prices up to £500,000 or more per acre. It makes no sense for land acquired with borrowed money at this price to lie idle in a landbank. It is, therefore, probable that much of the land held is 'old' land acquired at much lower prices which give some scope for future trading at a profit. The issue requires further research.

There is considerable evidence concerning the third strategy: the growth in multipurpose conglomerate groups of companies capable

of switching into, and out of, construction activity. In the mid-
1970s there was a spate of mergers and takeovers involving firms
which had previously specialized in construction (Ball and Cullen,
1980). Some examples will show the range of diversification
strategies adopted. Two housebuilding firms (Galliford Estates and
Bovis) were taken over by large and diversified groups (Sears
Holdings and P and O Steam Navigation) which grew up originally
in other fields of activity but which wished to develop a housebuilding capacity. By a reverse process, in 1972 a firm which was
originally a specialist housebuilder (Crests) merged with a yacht-
building firm (Camper Nicholson) to form a group which has since
that time expanded by takeovers into engineering and optical
equipment. Blue Circle, the cement suppliers, had a different
strategy in mind when they took over Armitage Shanks, who
produce ceramic sanitaryware, in 1980. It was found that 75 per cent
of sanitaryware was being sold to the home improvement, rather
than the new-build, market and this was a way of evening out group
activity during downturns in the demand for new construction.
Taylor Woodrow examined another possibility early in 1984; they
considered taking over and running some small power stations
being sold off by the Central Electricity Generating Board as part of
the privatization drive. At much the same time Bellway, another
housebuilder, was acquiring a 26 per cent stake in the Falmouth
Container Terminal scheduled to open in 1987.

Trafalgar House, Britain's largest conglomerate, have been active
in acquiring construction firms. They have interests in shipping,
aviation, hotels, oil and gas and a turnover of around £1.0 billion
annually in construction. The group as a whole is not heavily
dependent on loan capital, as opposed to equity capital, and this
relative immunity to the effects of steep rises in interest rates gives
it considerable advantages over other constructors. It has recently
acquired Comben, the specialist housebuilder, and apart from thus
doubling the group's landbank it aims to increase house production
from 2000 per year to 4000. It is also significant that in 1984 the
group merged its property development and speculative housebuilding companies into a single organization largely because it
judged that the opportunities opened up by inner city renewal will
call for an integrated mix of the two forms of activity. Since the head
of the group, Nigel Broakes, was for some years also head of the

London Docklands Development Corporation, the judgement is probably well founded.

A final form of organizational response to the difficult trading conditions of the past decade has been to go out of business altogether. Official data on insolvencies in the industry indicate that an average of 900 to 1000 construction companies went into compulsory or voluntary liquidation each year during the latter 1970s and the figure rose sharply in the early 1980s. A roughly similar number of self-employed builders also went out of business. Many of the latter no doubt retired early or were skilled tradesmen who moved out of an entrepreneurial role and into employment with a larger firm. This switching into and out of self-employment is a marked feature of the industry and skilled carpenters, brick-layers and even electricians can, in certain states of the market, acquire sites and carry out a development of ten houses or so on their own account and with very little capitalization involved.

The fourth adaptation strategy available mainly to the larger firms in the industry has been to seek business overseas (see Figure 6.8). Table 6.2 shows the source areas of contracts obtained by British constructors in three selected years over the past decade. It is significant that in 1979 the incoming Conservative administration virtually abolished exchange controls and greatly facilitated the international flow of capital. This may well be one of the main factors behind the acceleration that has occurred since that date in the amount of overseas business undertaken. It is noticeable that very little of the total overseas work has been gained in Europe. One knowledgeable housebuilder considers that this reflects, as much as anything, the linguistic limitations of British management. But there is, on the whole, surprisingly little cross-border contracting in the EEC, possibly due partly to the conservative attitudes of private and public promoters in Europe. The largest growth area for overseas work before 1979–80 was the Middle East but this growth slackened in the early 1980s. The most striking recent expansion in overseas contracts has been in Africa and Asia, followed by America and Oceania. Certain British constructors have been especially active in seeking overseas work. Barratt's, Lovell's and Wimpey have all entered into the American housebuilding market, either directly or by the acquisition of an American subsidiary, while Costain has acquired an interest, via a subsidiary, in the Alabama coalmining industry.

British business

Weekly export and industrial news from the DTI 25-31 October 1985 £1.25

Britain's £2.4bn business: construction overseas

Above: commercial centre in Manama, Bahrain by Jalal-Costain, (left); housing in Oman by Wimpey.

Above: Aga Khan hospital, Karachi (left), and Jumoro bridge, Ghana (above right), both by Cementation International.
Below: tuned track athletics facility at Yale University by En-tout-cas; airfield work on Ascension Island by Costain International and Tarmac Overseas.

Figure 6.8   *The British construction industry has been very successful at building up its overseas business, expecially since 1979*
Source: British Business, 25–31 October 1985

Table 6.2   Value of contracts obtained overseas by British construction companies, 1973–4, 1979–80 and 1982–3 (£m. at current prices)

Source area of contract	1973–4	1979–80	1982–3
EEC	11	27	19
Rest of Europe	51	82	36
Middle East	214	652	776
Rest of Asia	14	89	362
Rest of Africa	138	203	826
America	54	274	455
Oceania	75	58	258
Total	557	1,385	2,732

Source: *Housing and Construction Statistics*, London, HMSO, 1984.

The fifth and final adaptation strategy has been to seek out and develop new ways of reducing the borrowing requirement or, which is nearly the same thing, to shorten the time period over which M is turned into M^1. Given the great increase in the cost of borrowing since the early 1970s, it is obvious that users of loan funds will try to minimize their dependence on borrowed money and to make each £1 borrowed work harder and faster. To some extent the moves towards industrialized building and timber-frame construction can be seen as attempts (once the initial investment in the new methods has been made) to speed up the circulation of capital. Similarly, the front-end 'loading' of contract costing is an attempt to keep borrowing to a minimum by improving cash flow.

There has also been a noticeable move over the past decade or so to hire construction plant and machinery rather than to use more capital by buying it. Ive (1980) has shown the growing significance of plant-hire firms in the overall process of production. As he points out, such a policy helps to guard against any production over-capacity. In effect, what happens is that the plant-hire firms, many of which are actually owned by the major construction groups, take on the capital outlay involved in purchasing and hiring out plant and machinery and hope to make an economically viable return by achieving a more intensive rate of use than would a general contractor. The risks inherent in this activity, given the considerable recent fluctuation in the volume of construction work, are obvious. The following figures show the value of work done by

plant-hirers for selected years over recent decades (at 1980 prices)
(see *Construction News*, 18 October 1984):

1967	£601.9m.
1970	£866.4m.
1973	£1030.2m.
1976	£760.3m.
1979	£923.1m.
1982	£812.4m.

The effects of the post 1973 construction slump are clear, although
the recovery in recent years has been somewhat stronger than for
the industry as a whole. The danger of having considerable capital
tied up in plant and machinery is somewhat less acute in this
industry than in many others because of the relatively slow rate of
obsolescence and technical innovation (although in recent years
there has been a rapid development of powered access platforms). It
is also true, however, that slightly outdated plant can be acquired
fairly cheaply, often from overcapitalized or bankrupt building
firms, and hired out at a rate that undercuts that for the most
up-to-date equipment.

The ownership of the plant-hire industry is much more highly
concentrated than that of the building industry as a whole. Ive
(ibid.) quotes a NEDO report which estimates that the seventeen
largest firms account for three-quarters of the business done, and
nine of these, which account for half the output, are part of
multinational corporations. These firms are therefore in a good
position to shift their current effort, and future investment, from
one country to another depending upon the state of the local
construction cycle. At the other end of the scale, and usually
outside the membership of the Construction Plant Hire Association
(CPA), there has been a considerable recent expansion of small
plant-hire shops, most of them geared to the needs of small builders
and do-it-yourself exponents. The industry, in common with most
of the construction sector, is in some difficulty. Although in recent
years the specialist hire firms' share of all the total net investment
in plant and machinery carried out by the construction industry
has risen sharply to about one third, firms which cannot easily
switch their effort on a regional or national scale are exposed to all
the dangers of overcapacity and cut-throat competition. As a result
the CPA, as mouthpiece for the industry, has for some time been a

voice in the general chorus calling upon government to increase public capital expenditure (if necessary, at the expense of public revenue expenditure). Under present policies the industry appears to be in for some hard years yet.

In the drive to reduce borrowing there have been some advances in marketing the completed buildings, especially in the speculative housing field. Certain of the larger housebuilders (notably Barratt's) have offered 'extras' in the way of carpets and kitchen equipment as part of a 'package deal' for the purchaser. This has backfired to some extent because some first purchasers have found that the value of the house, on an early re-sale, has been several thousand pounds below what they paid. The extras clearly did not impress the second purchaser. Barratt's have been driven to make a public offer to re-purchase some of their houses at the original sale price. Some housebuilders have agreed to accept a purchaser's present house in part-exchange for a new one. This has led at least one firm (Homequity Relocation) to take these traded-in houses off the builders' hands for 88 per cent of the current valuation. They then seek to dispose of them by sale to relocating executives, presumably at full market value. The same firm is offering to buy, then lease back, the show houses that most builders keep open on their new estates. All these devices are clearly intended to speed up the M^1 realization and thus to reduce borrowing.

PART III
The system in operation

This part of the book deals with land development in the 1980s in two key 'arenas'. Over the past two centuries the most profitable arenas for development have varied depending on patterns of demand and changes in production and transportation technology. During the rapid urbanization of the later decades of the nineteenth century rented housing was a fruitful field for investors. Sometimes these were the actual builders but often they were business or professional people who acquired or promoted a handful of houses for the rental income. Between the wars, the speculative development of suburban houses for sale, plus investment in rentable shopping developments to serve them, became a key activity. The late 1960s and early 1970s was a period of frenetic activity, especially in London, for city centre commercial developments both for rental return and capital growth. Millionaires were produced by the dozen until the instabilities inherent in the activity began to take their toll late in 1973.

The two arenas selected for study in Chapters 7 and 8 include some elements of these earlier episodes, but there are also new aspects which make them distinctive. Chapter 7 deals with the 'green belt' areas around many of the larger cities. Here a battle is being waged between the housebuilding industry, led by the 'volume' builders, and more or less everybody else (except the government) over the amount and location of land to be released by the planning system for housebuilding. Chapter 8 deals with what is often called Europe's largest redevelopment opportunity – London's docklands. To set the scene each chapter includes a brief sketch of the historical background, and lists and describes the chief participant interests with some reference to case studies.

The aim of the analysis is to show how some of the interests identified in Part II combine, or come into conflict, in specific situations and especially to assess the extent to which planning is still able to achieve its aim of ensuring orderly and democratically accountable land development. To recognize that there are a number of interest groups engaged in conflict is not to subscribe to the pluralist interpretation of the state referred to in Chapter 1. Pluralists might expect the outcome of the interplay of interests to be tolerably 'fair' and consensual (because the groups between them represent more or less all interests and have reasonably equal access to power). The two chapters seek to show that neither the underlying conditions nor the outcomes accord with a pluralist perspective.

7

The war for Jenkin's ear:
development on the urban fringe

The problem of how best to manage the outward extension of urban areas, to reconcile the aims of those seeking suburban homes and those seeking to farm and preserve the countryside, is as old as urban growth itself. Similarly, the idea of 'green belts' around cities to prevent them coalescing goes back to biblical times. But for a number of reasons the issues have become more urgent, and more politically visible, in the last two centuries of urban/industrial growth.

Mineral and fossil-fuel-based production technologies tended to bring about disproportionately large agglomerations of people in the areas where these resources occur – hence the crowding of 30 to 40 per cent of the population of Britain on the coalfield regions, which are something like 10 per cent of the area. The total population has increased enormously since the 1780s, and until quite recently most of the growth was in this 10 per cent plus London. Non-residential uses – roads, railways and high revenue commercial developments – have tended to occupy city centres, thus forcing much of the housing growth to the peripheries. Simultaneously advances in public and private transportation have stretched the tolerable limits of the journey to work to something like 40–50 miles along the main road and rail arteries, and the very linearity of these arteries has produced 'ribbon' developments which have had disproportionately adverse affects both on agriculture and on the amenity value of the countryside. Finally, in the eighty years or so since Ebenezer Howard's seminal work, there has been a strong body of opinion in favour of the controlled exodus of population from the urban centres to 'satellite' towns located in, or just outside, the green belt cordons.

Given some of these trends, and despite the excellence of the intentions, there was always the potential danger that these satellite towns (of which eight have been built around London alone) would coalesce with neighbouring towns, or with each other, or that the outgrowth at the fringe of the major city would threaten to reach them. This potential danger has become more real in recent decades, especially so since the advent of a government in 1979 explicitly and ideologically opposed to intervention in market processes. In taking steps to move towards a 'free for all' development situation in this sensitive arena, the Thatcher government has succeeded in offending more or less everybody except the speculative housebuilders. Those offended include large numbers of natural Tory supporters in the shire counties and prosperous commuter villages. As a result, a number of unusual alliances have been formed to modify the rate at which the regulation of development is being dismantled. At the time of writing the political career of one ex-Environment Secretary lies in ruins and there are clear signs of yet another U-turn in policy.

Five separate interest groups can be seen interacting in the 'greenfield' arena. ('Greenfield' is a better term than 'green belt' because not all the area involved is formally designated as green belt under the planning legislation.) These interests are land investors, farmers, speculative housebuilders, conservationists and planners. The first three are driven wholly or primarily by the need to accumulate a maximum rate of return on capital invested while the motivations of the last two, although varied, are not primarily capital accumulation. All five interests frequently claim to act in the interests of a sixth – the general public. The nature, strategic intentions and manifestation of each of these competing interests will be discussed separately, as will their relationship (given the claims to be acting in the general interest) with the state.

The land investment interest

This interest is by no means confined to agriculturalists, although farming is one of the ways in which it is realized. Land investment means committing money into the ownership or leasing of land with the object of achieving an annual rate of return, or capital growth, as good as or better than that achievable in alternative fields (such as industrial investment). The return may be in the form of agricultural revenues from owner-occupier farming, rental from a lessee or proceeds of the sale of minerals or other resources. Or, given proximity to some growing urban area, it may be in any of these forms plus a steep growth in capital value as the land 'ripens' towards development. In several of these forms, especially the last, the time horizon of the investor may need to be long-term and that is why, in recent times, the large financial institutions have been increasingly active as investors.

For much of the urban/industrial era since the 1780s, certainly up until the last decade of the nineteenth century, the land investment interest was loosely synonymous with the 'landed aristocracy'. Much of the land was in the freehold ownership of the major or minor landed gentry, who had acquired it at various points in the past sometimes going back to the Norman Conquest or the Crusades. The landed interests achieved a satisfactory return from own account farming (and/or the sale of mineral rights where possible) or from the rents of tenant farmers. These, in turn, achieved a living by the sale of crops produced by a large, low-paid agricultural labourforce who lived on a modest and insecure income from their labour. As the nineteenth century advanced a proportion of these latter bought or rented smallholdings – often using money earned outside agriculture, perhaps from labouring on railway construction – and became small proprietors themselves.

For a century or more the advances in the techniques of production, and especially the need to use new forms of crop rotation and commit capital to mechanization, had been prompting a move towards the enlargement of holdings – a move which found its legal expression in the succession of Enclosure Acts. By 1873, when a tolerably accurate land ownership survey was held, a highly concentrated ownership pattern had emerged and the land investment interest was embodied largely in a few thousand substantially large owners. Agriculture, or mineral extraction, seemed the natural way for these interests to preserve and increase their inherited wealth. In political terms their concentrated ownership of land as the key input factor enabled them both to dictate the form of the production process and to dominate the social relations of production in both these industries. Farmworkers, by their spatial dispersal and dependence on land owners for both work and accommodation, found it difficult to organize so as to gain a larger proportion of the considerable wealth created by their labour.

In the forty years or so after 1873 the picture changed dramatically. A string of years with bad weather for the cereals harvest in the 1870s plus the growing price competitiveness of foreign wheat and meat led to the sharp reversal in fortunes known as the Great Agricultural Depression. For the first two decades of the depression, the landed interests appeared to bear the brunt of the effects. The Second Royal Commission on Agriculture found, in 1894, that many landlords had drastically reduced the rents charged to tenant farmers. Despite also reducing expenditure on the estates (and thus reducing their long-term value as investments) falls in net farm income were common and varied up to 60 per cent and more. One inevitable reaction was to seek to disinvest in land and a steady movement of farm sales began, usually to the tenant farmers.

This move had other motivations behind it. The Liberal Party policy around the turn of the century included sinister proposals to tax wealth, particularly in the form of land (see Rose, 1985), and this was a prospect that many large land owners, already buffeted by years of depressed revenues, could not face. They sought to realize the wealth in land and transfer it into stockholdings in commercial enterprises, often overseas. Although the Great Depression was temporarily halted by the abnormal demand produced by the First World War, it set in again in the 1920s, with the consequence of further falls in land prices. In a sense it is still with us, and it is arguable whether it would pay farmers to produce food at all in this country were it not for the very high level of subsidy received.

The outcome of these processes is significant for the line-up of interests in the conflict over greenfield areas (see also Goodchild and Munton, 1985). The long depression largely removed one force, the landed aristocracy, from the scene. Something like 65 per cent of farmland is now worked by owner-occupiers. Most of the rest is owned and managed by investors such as farm management companies (often foreign owned), well-off individuals with funds available for tax-effective investment and certain of the large financial institutions discussed in Chapter 4 (notably pension funds). To all these, and especially the last group who as trustees of money for others can afford to take no other attitude, investment in farming activity is purely instrumental. The level of investment simply reflects the best judgement they can make about the likely rate of return from, and capital value growth of, the land. These judgements tend to be unclouded by any notion of the value of farming 'as a way of life'. In fact capital growth is most likely to occur if the land is converted from farming to some more lucrative use such as housing.

There has been, therefore, since the turn of the century, a significant shift in the nature of the groups pursuing land investment profits. Their characteristics and motivations are quite different from those of the late-nineteenth-century landed aristocracy (Barlow, 1985). They are likely to assess more professionally the relative profitability of farming vs non-farming uses. If the land remains in farming, they are likely to pursue strategies that optimize the rate of return given the 'environment' of subsidies and tax legislation created by government at various levels. Very often these strategies will lead to greater capital intensification or the application of new management methods. Or there may be moves to buy more land to enlarge and rationalize farms. This is one reason behind the increase in real prices in agricultural land from an index value of 100 in 1973 to 248 in 1983 (Ministry of Agriculture Index). It is often difficult to justify paying the current high prices for additional areas of land unless the cost can be spread by increasing the efficiency of the enlarged unit as a whole and this usually requires yet more capital- and energy-intensive farming methods. As a result of these developments, farming has now become one of the most capital-intensive industries in Britain – more so, ironically, than the housebuilding industry that is competing with it for land in many greenfield areas.

The implications of these changes for the conflict arena we are concerned with are clear. The historic participants in land investment, the landed aristocracy, could be expected to keep their money in farming, despite the quite sharp swings that have occurred in prices and rates of return, because land ownership was the ultimate source of their social status and political dominance, both locally and nationally. They were part of a three-tier rural social system of landlord, tenant farmer and labourer that went back to the Middle Ages. But a variety of circumstances has caused them to be replaced by own account farmers and management or trustee institutions who are capable of playing a variety of investment markets (Northfield Committee, 1979). Simultaneously, over recent decades rates of interest available on perfectly safe investments elsewhere have both risen to unprecedented levels and fluctuated sharply. The range of alternative investment opportunities is bound to be more varied when 10–13 per cent can be achieved safely somewhere in the international finance market than when – as was true for most of this century – the investor was looking for perhaps a safe 5 per cent. The opportunity cost of sub-optimal investment has grown, and the sharp fluctuations in the rate of inflation have made it all the more important to pursue an investment strategy that protects capital from negative real rates of return. These circumstances, and the advances in information technology that facilitates market monitoring, mean that the long-term attraction of British agriculture to investors cannot be assumed. It is now dependent on a number of factors far removed from the social and political aspirations of the former landed gentry.

Farming interests

This broadening out of land investment interests has made it easier to identify farming *per se* as a separate interest. This has been manifested in a more specifically agriculture-based defence against the powerful development pressures at the urban fringe. In view of recent national debates about the role of British agriculture the argument is not as persuasive as it was. The industry has always lobbied effectively and enjoyed the ear of government. It has argued, correctly, that labour productivity has increased faster in farming than in most other industries. Compared to 1952, productivity had increased by a factor of 4.33 by 1979 while employment had fallen to 40 per cent of the earlier level (Fothergill and Gudgin, 1982). The effects of the U-boat blockade during the war, and systematic postwar policy, have meant that we now produce 65 per cent of our temperate foodstuff requirements compared to 35 per cent in 1939. But the industry is still only a tiny part of the total economy, employing perhaps 2 per cent of the workforce and producing a similar percentage of gross domestic product. Also, as we have seen, the landed aristocracy (its historic advocates) have partially disinvested and probably also lost some influence with government. The industry stands open to attack as never before, especially since entry into the EEC has given a greater political visibility to the crucial issue of farm subsidies.

The attack has been mounted by Body (1982, 1984), among others. Aggressively rebutting the arguments about growth in productivity, the protection of the balance of payments and the strategic need for a high degree of self-sufficiency, the critique has argued that the apparent 'success' of British farming derives largely from a massive level of protection and price support, the cost of which comes directly from public funds and the consumer's pocket. Virtually everything about the situation is wrong. In 1980/1, £1928 million had to be spent in subsidy to give farmers a net income of £1162 million. This vast amount of money could have been invested in British industry and employment creation. It could have been used to stimulate lower-cost agriculture in Third World countries. Much of the subsidy must, anyway, be going through the farmers' pockets and ending up in the profits of ICI, Shell, BP and Fisons, the main suppliers of fertilizers, and some of it must be inflating land prices. (There is an interesting parallel here between this point and the point made in the housing literature (e.g. Ambrose, 1976) that the roughly comparable owner-occupier housing subsidy must be inflating development land prices.)

These criticisms are impressively backed up by the figures. Only about 17.5 per cent of farmland in England and Wales is classified as grade I or II (roughly speaking, as 'high quality' for farming). Yet perhaps double this proportion is used for crops. To get an apparently 'efficient' return from the grade III areas, a very high level of energy and capital input is required. The finance to pay for this has come not only from the escalating public subsidies, but also from a twelvefold increase, in real terms, in City lending to agriculture since 1947. Further hidden subsidy has resulted from the tax advantages granted to agriculture – the partial avoidance of Capital Transfer Tax and the low average tax payments in the industry. This artificial support of total farming revenue, which would apparently be heavily negative without it, has also distorted the underlying asset values of land since these are arrived at by capitalizing the value of current revenues. It has even been suggested that the increase in the aggregate value of farmland since 1945 is £40 to £60 billion *more* than it would have been had commodity prices not been supported.

There is no sign of any abatement in the rate at which money is being poured into British agriculture. Between 1979 and 1981 (as revealed in a parliamentary answer) public expenditure for farming support increased in real terms by 13.9 per cent – about the same as the *decrease* over the same period in housing investment. Body (a farmer and a Tory MP) concludes:

The British farmer, that symbol of rugged independence, is now – I hate to say – far more of a charge on the state than a worker in any of the ailing, government-subsidised shipyards or car factories or docks which we hear so much about. (Body, 1982, Introduction)

The similarity to the favoured position of the house-purchaser, another 'symbol of rugged indepedence', is again striking.

In this situation of developing public awareness, the farming lobby has to choose and mount its arguments about land loss with some care. On the basis of the figures above, which are not of course unchallenged, it would arguably be cheaper for the nation if a proportion of farmers working grade III or worse land were to stop their current high energy farming practices altogether – thus saving public subsidy and part of the foreign exchange cost of the imported fertilizers they are necessarily using to achieve current yields. This land could then be farmed at a level more appropriate to its intrinsic quality or made available for other uses. The industry must either rebut these arguments, using figures that are more convincing than those used by the critics, or shift the ground of the argument towards the strategic desirability of high levels of self-sufficiency. Less tangibly, it might argue the importance of farming as 'a way of life' or as some aid to the long-term good ecological management of the countryside as an amenity. This latter point is difficult to make convincingly given the effects that current intensive farming practices often have on, for example, the local ecological balance and hedgerow protection.

The National Farmers' Union (NFU) is the main advocate of farming interests. It has historically good relations with government and a high level of protection for agriculture is built into the postwar planning system. Much development for agricultural purposes is exempt from the planning legislation and non-agricultural development proposals involving the loss of 10 acres or more of farmland are subject to what amounts to a Ministry of Agriculture right of veto. This close relationship becomes clearly visible at Public Inquiries when the NFU often act in a 'consortium' with county or district planning authorities to prepare and present evidence. But even before this stage is reached, the NFU often makes a pre-emptive input into Structure Plan preparation by identifying parcels of land for development that could be lost to farming with little or no adverse effect.

The NFU, as protectors of the farming industry and custodians of the 'national farm', have strong opinions about the rate of release of farmland for urban development. This does not mean that they will battle over every acre, but that they will have in mind the implications of development proposals for the farm(s) concerned and also for the viability of farming in the area generally. They judge the latter point to be very significant and underweighted by the planning system, certainly at the district and and national level. From their accumulated experience of farming, they are aware that the invasion of farmland by housing can have adverse effects equivalent to perhaps double the acreage actually lost. Houses mean people, and people mean more walkers and trespassers, more gates left open and crops trampled, more dogs and litter, and more expectations that the adjacent land will provide amenity of some kind.

Apart from these local effects, there are a number of likely spillover effects at a subregional scale – a scale ill-served by the planning system which is based on county areas with boundaries which mostly go back to the Middle Ages. These consequential effects of housing development include more loss of land for schools, hospitals, electrical substations, and so on. Land may also be needed for more roads and here again the effects may be disproportionately large. A bypass may be built some distance outside the new urban periphery. This often fragments farms and places the farmland between the periphery and the bypass under increasing pressure until eventually it, too, is taken for development.

All these factors taken together mean that the annual loss of farmland to development, while conceded by the NFU to be low in a historic context, is having serious and disproportionate effects on the efficiency of farming in and around the greenfield areas. In the view of the NFU, compartmentalized thinking in the planning system sometimes fails to assess these effects correctly. The union's position is also frequently undermined at the local level by urban-fringe farmers who are sometimes, understandably, falling over each other to sell parcels of land development at prices which can give them hundreds of thousands of pounds in the bank for the sale of a few acres. These proceeds, invested at 10 per cent or more, can give them security for life.

Housebuilding interests

to expand owner-occupancy we need to bring prices down...land prices must come down to reduce house prices. (*Housebuilder*, May 1984)

The aim of the housebuilding industry is simply to achieve a maximum return on capital committed to the construction and sale of housing. In the greenfield areas (as in most others in Britain) this housing is normally built speculatively, that is in advance of sale, and it is normally sold freehold. Although the aim is straightforward, it would be wrong to see the industry as a monolithic entity. As Chapter 6 made clear, housebuilding is carried out not only by a handful of 'volume' builders (who do, however, have a very large market share), but also by hundreds, or probably thousands, of smaller concerns. At present (1985) the House Builders' Federation estimate that between 120 and 200 affiliated firms are active in any given year and they recognize that there are many other active smaller builders who are not affiliated to their organization.

The source of funding and parts of the market 'targeted' by different builders varies enormously, so does the variety of options available to the individual organization. At one extreme is the small one-man or two-man firm building, perhaps, six houses every other year and filling in with maintenance and extension work. At the other extreme is the large firm with an annual programme of 10,000 units, structurally part of a group including companies with a much broader range of interests on an international scale. One important point for the analysis of greenfield development is that while housebuilders at these two extremes, and all those between, are likely to be interested in different types of land, they may also be in conflict over particular sites. The resultant competitive bidding may well establish a new benchmark for land prices.

A house, once built, is by definition immobile; so is the local physical and social infrastructure of roads, schools, parks, and so on, without which people will not want to live in it. But the employment that helps to locate people – and their capacity to raise a mortgage – in an area has become highly mobile, especially since the advent of the recession in the early 1970s. Thousands of jobs can materialize relatively quickly in a growth area; equal or greater numbers can be lost with spectacular speed elsewhere. The

Construction News, 18.5.85

THE WORSENING WORK DIVIDE

Contractors working in the north of England will be hit hard by a worsening north-south divide in the late 1980s says a report published this week by research organisation Industrial Futures. Work, says the report, will become increasingly concentrated in the South-east of England.

Summarising its conclusion, Industrial Futures argues that regional activity broadly depends upon a region's existing wealth and fortunes, its population growth and on government policy.

These factors determine the share of the national cake for a particular region and in turn the demand for new construction Income growth. Because the existing poor economic state of the northern areas of the UK is unlikely to change from internal moves Industrial Futures says that any major change in fortunes can only come from increased spending by central government, which is unlikely under present policies.

But, the South-east does have an internal growth which is likely to help it continue its momentum, although there may be some slowing down in some future years.

The comments are all made in the report entitled "Regional Construction Outlook". Subscribers to it, at a cost of £450.00 will be given a wad of figures for the different regions of the UK plus an analysis of construction activity. The value of the report, however, must surely lie with its statistics, although based on an Industrial Futures computer model they can only be proved correct after the event.

The broad conclusions can be drawn, it could be argued, from data already available.

Industrial Futures finds that with Private sector activity concentrated in the south one would expect land prices to be sharply driven up. Public sector construction would ordinarily be required to cater for this continuing population by building hospitals for example but the tight control of public expenditure means that existing facilities will simply have to be stretched further instead.

So we have confirmation of two factors already well known within the industry:

1. Government spending on capital projects is unlikely to increase
2. The construction industry in the south is likely to be more active than in other regions.

Figure 7.1 *Increasing economic disparities between the various regions have important implications for the housebuilding industry.*

housebuilder has little or no interest in the latter areas. He is not directly concerned with repayment defaults due to falling employment since the existence of the hire-purchase system, the building societies, has isolated him from such losses. He has, by contrast, the greatest possible interest in the growth regions. (See Figure 7.1.) He is not even particularly concerned with the *stability* of the growth for the same reason that the long-term risk of a reversal of fortunes and default on payments is borne by the purchaser-borrower and the mortgage lender, not by the builder-vendor. The difficult trading conditions of the past decade, and the rapid fluctuations in the fortunes of particular regions, have meant that some more sophisticated understanding of locational trends in employment is now necessary to protect profitability. In particular, if the industry wishes to attract more first-time purchasers, without which the whole sector would begin to shrink, it is necessary to produce medium- to low-cost housing within commuting distance of employment growth points. This more precise understanding of the significance of work/housing co-location has led the industry, in recent years, to seek a closer relationship with government because local and national agencies of the state are the source of statistical projections, development policy and infrastructural investment – all matters of increasing concern to the industry.

Government has been ready to listen. The Tory Party is strongly committed to the ideology and political leanings associated with home ownership (despite the enormous subsidy costs involved). It has for half a century or more clearly perceived owner-occupancy as a weighty political inhibition to the development of any collective radical politics. It is even being used at the time of writing (October 1985) in a Tory conference speech as a counterbalance to the damaging effects of the Keays revelations (Keays, 1985). There is political point in this. There is no way that the individual mortgage-payer can negotiate about the general level of prices for the product; and endlessly repeated interviews on picket lines with returning strikers who have a family and mortgage to support demonstrate the inhibitions that loan-encumbered ownership has produced on industrial activism. Since the mid-1960s, on more pragmatic grounds, the Labour Party too has accepted owner-occupancy as the 'normal' tenure. Thus both main parties regard the housebuilding industry as the favoured deliverer of the 'property-owning democracy'. Lobbyists for greater equality in society (for example, Child Poverty Action Group) have also frequently seen home ownership as a way of spreading wealth more fairly. This is a difficult claim to evaluate. Quite possibly the distribution within the top 60 per cent of the wealth-holders (i.e. the home owners or purchasers) has been equalized but the gap between them and the other 40 per cent has almost certainly been widened by regressive tenure-based subsidy arrangements, especially since 1979.

Whatever the detailed position may be, the industry badly needs the ear of government and in the early and mid-1980s it is easy to see why. The recession has brought high interest rates which can be crippling to firms operating on a high ratio of loan to share capital; there has been Treasury-backed rumbling about the enormous and escalating cost of the purchasers' tax concession, moves by the federal authorities to cancel this concession in the United States, and falls in real wages or unemployment for millions of current and potential purchasers. Furthermore, as shown in Chapter 6, the industry has not had the will or capability to update its production methods which remain, on the whole, strikingly low-tech. Its biggest advantage at the moment may lie in a government that is explicitly anti planning and pro free market and which seems willing to be pushed into a line highly advantageous to the industry over the crucial matter of land release in the greenfield (and dockland) areas. (See Figure 7.2.)

Clearly all construction requires land. But to a housebuilder land is more than something to build houses on. An adequate stockpile of developable land enlarges the range of future options available; land as an asset can be offered as security for loans, land as a commodity can be traded, land can appreciate dramatically if acquired at one use value and upgraded, with a planning consent, to another. The urge to acquire the landbank of a smaller builder is often the main reason for a takeover bid. The time, trouble and money involved in acquiring land when suitable sites are scarce is one of the four main items in the housebuilder's cost structure. The other three – finance costs, materials costs and labour costs – are set to a greater or lesser extent by forces outside the industry itself and in more or less competitive markets. But land costs, whether in greenfield or redevelopment situations, are the product in Britain of a much more regulated market. The supply of suitable development land in the areas that the industry regards as 'right', that is where it sees a market of potential purchasers, is not fully elastic; it is regulated to a degree by the planning system (Barrett and Whitting, 1983).

Thus the significance of the land release squabble, to be

192 *Whatever Happened to Planning?*

Construction News, 17.10.85

MORE LAND AVAILABLE FOR PRIVATE SECTOR

The Government is to step up pressure on councils to sell housing land to the private sector.

That was the promise from Environment Minister William Waldegrave in response to housing debate at Blackpool last week.

Pressure to sell the land was "the other side of the green belt story" — and would help protect green belts from housing development pressures, he said.

The Government had details of some 120,000 acres of public land — "most of it's in towns and 60 per cent is owned by councils. So far we had got them to sell 20,000 acres, and put another 8000 acres back to use.

"It's not enough. If necessary we will use the law — the 1982 derelict land act — to make them sell. All their land must be bought back into use," he warned.

He attacked housing record of the last 20 years. But he said "we have got to show that if you put private money and good design and planning on a human scale together, you can turn the tide in the cities."

London's docklands was a good example of how a "no-hope area" could be turned into "the biggest urban renewal project in Europe."

In a reference to nuclear power, he said: "nuclear waste is now kept perfectly securely and no hazard to anyone. And we are completing our studies into disposing of it finally and safely."

Figure 7.2 *The government is ready to compel the sale of publicly owned land in order to 'bring it back into use'. It is reassuring, incidentally, to learn that nuclear waste is 'no hazard to anyone'.*

examined later in this chapter, is rooted in a chain of logic. The industry needs to sell more of its product; but given the chronic recession, real wages among the prime client groups are not rising fast enough (if at all); therefore, to protect profitability and increase sales the product needs to be made available at a lower price; but the industry can do nothing to cheapen finance or home-loan costs and little to cheapen materials and labour costs. It has, in its own view at any rate, cut production costs to the bone. But land costs could probably be cheapened dramatically (or so it is widely believed) if the planning system zoned, or released, something like 5000 acres more building land in the 'right' areas each year. If this were to happen, the scramble for land from competing builders, and

New homes make the housing ladder work.

Figure 7.3   *The combination of a speculative market in building land and a low wage economy results in difficult access to reasonable housing. The homely symbol of the ladder acts as a legitimating device.*
Source: Homes, Jobs, Land, *The House Builders' Association, 1985*

farmers, would be lessened, norm-setting 'idiot bids' would not be made, the heat would be taken out of the market and Sir Lawrie Barratt's public-spirited complaint, made on behalf of eager but frustrated purchasers, that the land cost element is now pricing people out of a home, would be answered. (See Figure 7.3.)

The message from the industry, as loudly proclaimed in successive issues of the industry's mouthpiece, the *Housebuilder*, is clear. The planning system, while worthy in many ways, is outdated and blinkered. It thinks too much of environmental protection and too little of the actual configuration of effective demand for new housing. It is adding to the country's housing problems by not releasing the 'correct' amounts of land in the 'correct' areas as assessed by the industry. It is keeping jobs 'locked up in filing cabinets'. It is holding back the recovery of the economy by making housing impossibly expensive in growth areas such as Berkshire. It is not sensitive enough to the market. In a word, it is inflexible. It therefore requires the expertise of housebuilding interests at certain crucial points, notably when an assessment of local building land availability and market demand is made during Structure Plan preparation (see Cuddy and Hollingsworth, 1985). Everybody could then enjoy the comforts and benefits of home ownership, although 'Only by using cheap land could we build houses in which the living rooms were bigger than the garages' (T. Baron, chairman, Christian Salvesen: *The Post*, 28 July 1984). The housebuilding industry, like the farming industry, looks very much now as if it claims to embody 'the national interest'. Since the two industries are locked in diametrically opposed conflict in the greenfield areas, one or both of these claims must be open to question.

Conservation interests

The idea of protecting the countryside against the all-devouring tide of urban development is not new. But the matter has been given much greater urgency since cities lost their self-defining walls (only around a hundred years ago in the case of many European cities such as Paris or Vienna) and since explosive urban growth and developments in public and private transport facilitated a flight to the suburbs. This flight was repeatedly self-defeating. No sooner had one prosperous ex-urban group achieved their semi within easy reach of green fields than another lot arrived and the green fields were built over. Nor was the development pattern rationally concentric. It spread out along the arterial roads and neutralized the agricultural and amenity value of a disproportionate amount of rural land. The arguments for policies to prevent these effects were, by the end of the Second World War, virtually unanimous. To argue against the idea of rural preservation would have been like arguing against goodness or motherhood.

The Council for the Protection of Rural England (CPRE), which recently and significantly substituted 'Protection' for 'Preservation' in its title, has for fifty years or so been one of the most powerful voices of the rural conservationist argument. It has been supported on a number of issues by bodies such as the National Trust and the Country Landowners' Association. For most of the postwar period the council has shared much common ground with the official planning bodies such as the Town and Country Planning Association although clear tensions exist between them over some strategic issues. For example, in the wake of the 1942 Scott Report, differences arose over the extent to which 'new towns' or expanded towns should be built on agricultural land to house the overspill population from the cities.

The CPRE is far from being a purely negative conservationist body manned by bumbling blimps. It is true that the regional organizations which do most of the 'legwork' on contentious greenfield issues owe a great deal to retired service personnel. But many of them are well capable of seeing the issues in broad perspective and most of them seem very opposed, perhaps by both temperament and training, to governmental action that short-cuts established planning procedures, appears to manipulate statistics and negates or ignores clearly expressed local opinion. On all three counts there has been plenty to object to in the 1980s. The collection of interests commonly to be found fighting against development under the CPRE umbrella is often quite varied. There are still plenty of dyed-in-the-wool defenders of the rural way of life and the hierarchical social relations that go with it. There are agricultural landlords and farmers to whom an influx of 'townies' means more damaged crops and worried sheep. There are also, it is often alleged, prosperous ex-urbanites who, having achieved a state of leafy seclusion in some pretty village, bidding up the price of property beyond the pockets of the locals in the process, are now concerned to stop any more development. But in the council's central office the concern is with broader issues. Arguments are being developed against the current official misuse of data and the illogicality of spending public money on new infrastructure to service greenfield housing when existing facilities lie underused in the inner cities. In recent media discussion of the issue (for example, the BBC Radio 4 debate about the green belt on 15 September 1985) the director of the CPRE found much common ground with the director of the London Housing Aid Centre, a voluntary body campaigning for more low-rent inner city housing. Both argue that the release of more green belt land is irrelevant to the solution of Britain's most pressing housing problems and that development allowed in peripheral areas will have the effect of sapping future investment for the rehabilitation of inner cities. Such an alliance, and such a breadth of interest by the CPRE, would have been difficult to envisage even ten years ago (see Council for the Protection of Rural England, 1981).

Planning interests

Most professional planners and many members of planning committees, if pressed to define 'the planning interest' in the dispute about rates of greenfield land release, might well maintain that they are taking the balanced, long-term, rational, disinterested 'public benefit' view of the problem. Clearly material self-interest is not (or of course should not be) the main motivation when plan-making or dealing with a development application. In this respect planners differ from the land investment, farming and housebuilding interests to whom one outcome rather than another has clear implications for wealth accumulation. The practising planner can claim that he or she has no such special interest and, moreover, that the information base on which he or she is making decisions is a more rounded one than that available to commercial interests.

In specific terms the structure-planner is seeking to draw up and articulate a development pattern that incorporates the principles of orderly, balanced growth (or, in many cases, decline). Thus change in local employment should ideally be matched by changes in the availability of housing, schools, medical facilities and shops in the area. In this process it is necessary to reconcile as much as possible the various competing interests. There are a number of factors which have always weakened, and now threaten almost to neutralize, the planner's capacity to carry out these tasks, particularly in the arena we are concerned with. Many of the investment decisions that have implications for the pattern of settlement have been made pre-emptively by powerful bodies such as water, power supply or transport authorities who have little or no democratic accountability. In the absence of any unitary or regional planning structure, some key decisions affecting the development pattern of, say, a county are made by an elected county committee, some are made by a national Department of Transport, some (for example public housing investment decisions) are made by district councils and some are made by statutory, non-elected suppliers of infrastucture. The planning system is supposed, somehow, to harmonize the workings of all these agencies and produce a consensual outcome.

The housebuilding lobby has recently become a more coherent and insistent voice in the general confusion. It would be wrong to present it as a single voice because the lobby includes various bodies such as the House Builders' Federation, the Federation of Master Builders and the National Federation of Building Trades Employers. Each tends to represent a different sector of the industry. But the lobby's voice, if not in unison, is at least in tolerably close harmony. It requires of the planning system the delivery of a sufficient supply (perhaps five years' worth at current building rates) of good housing development land in areas where the industry judges that amount of housing can be sold. If possible, it requires this amount of land release without the aggravation of appeals or lengthy arguments at Examinations in Public. This rather narrow requirement is in sharp contrast with what the planning system might regard as desirable since if land is to be released for a given amount of housing it needs to be matched with new land for industry, schools, retail facilities, open space, and so on. The conflict is between the industry's short-term requirement to maximize capital accumulation by constructing and selling the maximum number of houses and the planners' requirement for orderly balanced development.

In the frenetic lurch towards a more free market approach under the radical right administrations since 1979 most of the long-term underlying weaknesses of the planning system have become cripplingly apparent. Land use *control* powers are much weaker than the powers based on land ownership. Few planning departments actually own land, and if they do, they are no doubt under pressure to sell it. Their actions have always been indicative and reactive, rather than prescriptive and initiatory and now they have become more so. As relatively small spenders planning departments have been soft targets in the onslaught by national government on virtually all local authority activities. As deliverers of relatively shadowy 'quality of life' benefits – orderly and balanced patterns of development and environment protection – they hardly weigh in the 'profit and loss' scales adopted by government when compared to departments that produce a measurable output like education or roads. (By the same thinking, 'humanities', including planning, courses in higher education matter less than accountancy and engineering.)

The arguments are not all one way. The structure planning system has some inbuilt inflexibilities. As a county-based democratic institution it has always, very reasonably, had regard first and foremost to *local* needs as expressed by indices such as local housing waiting lists, and so on. But over the years the county scale has become inappropriately small. Labour market areas, perhaps the most appropriate units for implementing planning policy, have got larger while counties have stayed much the same. Employment levels, especially recently, have risen and fallen on a scale which is bound to have transcounty implications. The housebuilding industry itself has become steadily more national, and even international, in its own perception of where new housing can most profitably be built. There is a lack of any adequate regional or subregional structure to match the industry's developing capacity to think, and make demands, at this scale. This technical weakness has, in today's conditions, rapidly turned into political vulnerability. In at least one county (Devon) there are serious proposals to abolish the planning department altogether. The 'planning interest' in many authorities has now been reduced to a fight for professional survival. The former role and authority of the planning system as an umpire, with the Department of the Environment on hand as a tournament referee, has been undermined. Not only are line calls increasingly questioned, there is now a clear threat to hijack the umpire's chair.

Estates Gazette, 18.5.85

GREEN BELT OR IVORY TOWER?

OPINION

The harsh criticisms being aimed at the enterprising proposals put forward by Consortium Developments to build a series of private new towns in the South East, such as the Tillingham Hall project just unveiled near Thurrock in Essex, are only to be expected. In an era dominated by conservation, the new is automatically suspect. Yet it is ironic that, despite a certain amount of self-satisfaction for other accomplishments, British town planning is primarily respected abroad for one outstanding achievement — the New Town story, closely linked with its directly-related forerunner, the Garden City movement.

Both, in their time, had their detractors. Ebenezer Howard's new-fledged concept struck conservative critics in 1898 as being absurdly Utopian, while confronting the idealists of the political left with a threat to their revolutionary panaceas. New Towns, in their turn, have on the one hand been labelled elitist, while on the other they have been accused of producing a drab uniformity of design and lifestyle.

Echoes of such censure resound in the present reaction to private new town development proposals. There is also an outcry at what is seen as a deliberate desecration of green belt strategy. Little has changed since Lewis Keeble described green belts as "a faint substitute for regional planning", for while no one would deny the need for protection of the countryside, too rigid and unselective an approach devalues the whole currency of rural conservation. Indeed, it can be suggested that a positive and far more discriminating attitude towards rural preservation would generally be accepted. This could readily complement the promotion of a planned concentration of new developments, suitably equipped with a proper level of public services and demonstrating a true regard for urban design and landscape. Surely this must be better than the lasting rash of shoddy infill schemes and peripheral estate developments which have disfigured too much of the Home Counties. Equally, the argument that privately-sponsored new communities will act as leeches, sucking the lifeblood from inner city areas, overstates the role they might play and misunderstands the nature and scale of urban decline.

Figure 7.4   *A respected property journal making a case for private sector new towns. The comparison of what is proposed with the concept of the socially balanced New Town, as developed in the post-war years, is not entirely convincing. Who is to provide the investment for the 'proper level of public services'?*

Greenfield land release in the mid-1980s

The five interests listed above, and others less clearly articulated
such as construction labour and local political groups, confront
each other in the greenfield arena. One of the main 'rules of the
game', to which at least lip-service is paid by all, is the need to
protect rural amenity by some form of 'green belt' around built-up
areas. The concept of ensuring continued contact between urban
dwellers and the countryside goes back at least to Robert Owen and
other 'enlightened' entrepreneurs. Ebenezer Howard advocated
'green lungs' (see Figure 7.4). In this century, in 1933, Unwin
proposed a 'green girdle' around London and this was enacted in the
1938 London County Council Green Belt Act. Finally, in 1947 the
Town and Country Planning Act gave local planning authorities
statutory powers to designate and protect green belt areas. The
main aim of the legislation was not to ensure 'recreation areas' for
city-dwellers, but to prevent urban areas from coalescing. It was to
be a 'girdle' rather than a 'lung'. It has already been noted that the
recreational use of urban-fringe land presents potential problems to
farming interests. 'Recreation' often means litter, gates left open
and trampled crops while the need for maximum access implies
that 'green fingers' should penetrate into urban areas whereas the
farming interest lies normally in minimizing the length of the
urban fringe. Given the power of the farming lobby, it is perhaps not
surprising that recreational objectives never figured as an aim in
green belt policy.

   Green belt preservation has been, on the whole, a successful
feature of the 1947 system (see Hall *et al.*, 1973; Munton, 1983).
Growth pressures in the buoyant regions have been immense but
they have tended to leapfrog over the green belts and find
expression in development just outside (see Spence *et al.*, 1982).
Thus green belts have been under pressure on both their inner and
outer peripheries. Despite this, and the fears in the case of London
that the Greater London Council set up in 1963 would pose the
same kind of overspill threat as the London County Council many
decades earlier, the green belt policy held. In fact many planning
commentators have made the point that whereas in the 1930s the
concept was for major city green belts with a width of about five
miles, designated areas in current Structure Plans are sometimes
more than twice that distance across. No doubt, one powerful

element in this defence has been the Tory support in the shire counties and outer suburbs for a heavily restrictive approach to land release policies. But given the new freebooting era after 1979, it was inevitable that this situation would be opened up. A Department of the Environment draft circular prepared in December 1982 (but not released, significantly, until after the June 1983 election) signalled a new willingness to relax green belt policies. Its release followed very shortly on the publication of plans by a powerful group of volume housebuilders – Consortium Developments – to build up to fifteen 'new towns' of 15,000–20,000 population on sites not initially identified but all to be within thirty miles of London. Each town would need a greenfield site of 700–1000 acres. If carried out in full, this programme would be similar in scale to the postwar London new town programme, as originally conceived. Consortium Developments were at pains to make clear that their scheme was not simply to build yet more suburban estates. They proposed 'balanced communities' with matching employment and social

---

Estates Gazette, 11.5.85

FIRST SHOT IN CONSORTIUM CAMPAIGN

BY TERRY CUNNEW

Consortium Developments, formed in August 1983 to promote the development of new country towns to meet the perceived demand for new homes in the South East, has fired the first live round in its campaign.

This week it put in its application for outline planning consent for a new community of 14,000 population in Thurrock, south Essex. Thurrock District Council has already expressed its opposition to the plan, which is for the development of 760 acres at Tillingham Hall, in the green belt between Basildon and the edge of Greater London.

Because of this opposition, the proposal is almost certain to go to a public inquiry and — even if the go-ahead is finally given — it is unlikely that the first homes would be available until the late 1980s.

Consortium Developments is an alliance — holy or otherwise, according to the point of view of the observer — formed by nine of the country's leading housebuilders. The aim is to try to meet the continuing demand for new homes in the South East, which it sees as being far greater than national or regional estimates have suggested.

Figure 7.5   *In an almost unprecedented move, nine highly competitive housebuilding firms have joined forces to try and steamroller a more rapid rate of land release.*

infrastructure and they have made varying offers to contribute to the costs of providing primary schools and other necessary services. (See Figure 7.5.)

Although by no means the first shot in the war for the ear of the unfortunate Jenkin (see Rydin, 1983), the Consortium Development proposals had a catalytic effect. More or less everyone, except presumably Mrs Thatcher, was uneasy about the proposals – although the opposition was on sharply differing grounds. To the planners in the areas concerned, the proposals were a blatant challenge to the carefully worked out land development policies, each subject to painstaking public participation, contained in the relevant Structure Plans. To the farming interest the risks of land loss and farm dislocation were obvious – although to some individual farmers the prospect was somewhat less negative and one commentator remarked on 'farmers queuing up to sell to Consortium Developments'. The Council for the Protection of Rural England from the beginning mounted a spirited and reasoned attack on both the circular and the development proposals, which were clearly seen as linked, while the GLC, the Association of Metropolitan Authorities and other local authority associations challenged the thinking in the circular. Finally, and embarrassingly, the unrest of a significant number of Tory MPs surfaced at the 1983 Party Conference. The result of these pressures was a clear 'own goal'. The draft circular was withdrawn in November 1983.

In the next few months there was furious activity on all fronts. It was announced early in 1984 that the House of Commons Environment Committee was to study the issue of green belt release. The House Builders' Federation redoubled their lobbying, reiterating their case that increased land release was in the national interest because if the industry could not secure land, it could not build sufficient houses to enable the boom areas to grow at their 'natural' rate. *Building* (9 March 1984) referred to a 'land famine' and a chain of events where fewer housing starts meant higher prices, fewer sales and, significantly, a drop in the share price of house-building firms. In the same issue Sir Lawrie Barratt claimed that 'Land prices have escalated out of all recognition' (i.e. up by 50 to 100 per cent in the previous twelve months). By April 1984 the *Housebuilder* was broadening its attack on the 'poor condition of the planning system'. The system, it argued, tends to impose long lists of 'wordy, irrelevant conditions' with consents. (But the

Estates Gazette, 21.9.85

SPEYHAWK PROPOSE 740-ACRE BERKS "VILLAGE"

BY ALEX CATALANO

The current controversy over where new development in Berkshire should be sited is likely to heat up a degree or two with Speyhawk's application for permission to build an ambitious "village settlement" and associated industrial and commercial scheme at Great Lea, south of junction 11 of the M4.

The proposal covers some 740 acres of mainly agricultural land bounded by the M4 on the north, the Reading/Basingstoke railway line to the west, Fullers Lane in the south and the A33 Swallowfield Bypass to the east. The housing element of the scheme, about 3,500 units, will cover 350 acres, and 280 acres are set aside for open space to assure "a high quality of environment".

There will also be a local centre for shopping and recreational facilities.

Speyhawk are also applying for permission to develop the 100 acres to the east of the housing for commercial and industrial uses. This part of the scheme is near junction 11 of the M4 and includes a 1.075m-sq ft business/industrial park, 250,000 sq ft of shopping and leisure facilities and a 100,000-sq ft hotel/conference centre . . .

Speyhawk's scheme is in conflict with the current draft version of Berkshire's structure plan, which is now out for public consultation. Although the county had originally earmarked the Great Lea area for housing, objections from Wokingham District Council and others caused Berkshire to drop the site.

Berkshire is also opposed to industrial development south of the M4. As we reported on August 17, there is already another business park being proposed on 200 acres north of the motorway near junction 11.

Figure 7.6 *Another attempt to breach structure plan policy on land release. The site is highly attractive to the developers since it lies adjacent to the M4 and a mainline railway. In this case the revenue derived fron the proposed commercial/retail/leisure developments will help provide funds for the housing component.*

example described as 'infamous', that access should be available by wheelbarrow to the rear of a house without going through the living room, did not perhaps warrant such censure.) In the subsequent issue there was an article advising housebuilders how best to keep an eye on the process of Local Plan preparation in their area. Such plans, it was pointed out, are not subject to approval by the Secretary of State in the way that Structure Plans are. They are therefore much more a product of local decision-makers who, by implication, can be more easily influenced, although 'Unfortunately the Plan process has now some fairly clear rules for public participation'.

In subsequent months the industry began to articulate its critique of the system in terms that were both broader and more strident. District councils, in their local plan preparation, were accused of 'parochialism', in that they worked out their rates of land release with too little regard to events across their borders and in the subregion generally. The aggregate effect had been a long-standing underprovision of housing land in the whole area south-east of a line from the Avon to the Wash. It is a significant reflection of the recent striking polarization in the fortunes of regions that the industry currently has little interest in areas north-west of this line except for 'niche' markets in prosperous rural areas around, for example, Manchester. Thus, argues the industry, the system as a whole has been slow to perceive and adjust to the overall pattern of employment growth and decline. The rather perverse point has also been made that district councils have been too ready to keep to an inflexible line, respond negatively to proposals and to let matters go to the Department of Environment on appeal. In doing this they have been 'passing the buck'. Issues that should be weighed and arbitrated locally (in the direction of freer release naturally) have been decided centrally, with less regard to the local balance of development needs which, by implication, the housebuilders are best able to judge. The industry has also made the related point that uncertainty about the future status of specific parcels of land currently designated as green belt has led to increased levels of financial speculation in green belt areas generally. It would be better to reduce the extent of such designated land in a 'once for all' release operation and then to give absolute protection to the new, reduced green belt areas. This argument has a 'last territorial demand' air about it.

In June 1984 the House of Commons Environment Committee report was published. This took a fairly protectionist line and reflected the CPRE/planning view rather than the housebuilders'. The *Housebuilder* was disappointed. It argued (July–August 1984) that the report 'ran away from key questions' and placed 'too much emphasis on Green Belt inviolability'. But the following two circulars, 14/84 on 'Green Belts' and 15/84 on 'Land for Housing' offered more hope. The latter of these required the planning system to cater more directly for *demand*, made reference to the possibility of private sector new towns and directed that housing land should be released, so that a five-year supply at Structure Plan building rates should be available. These circulars could be, in the industry's view, 'a big breakthrough' if the builders acted together to convince the planners at the local level. But if the local planners could not be convinced, then the case could be made when the Plans were subjected to their Examinations in Public. The minister has the power, on receipt of the panel's report from such an Examination, to increase the housing land allocations before giving the required ministerial approval to the Plan. The rallying-cry rang out in the *Housebuilder* for September 1984. The House Builders' Federation would be represented at all Examinations to ensure that 'all relevant planning and environmental matters are properly considered'; in the end, 'the names of North East Hants, Leicester-shire [etc.]... will read like battle honours in possibly the bloodiest war that has been fought since the 1947 Planning Acts came into force'.

The industry's strategy for the war consisted of at least three tactics: an excursion into housing demand analysis, moves to ensure that members of the industry participated in local land availability studies and the setting up of a 'fighting fund' to assist in the expert presentation of the industry's case at planning inquiries and Examinations in Public. The industry entered on the first tactic in mid-1984 with some trepidation since it recognized that the term demand means different things in different contexts and that the range of factors affecting the level of demand in a strict commercial sense is an enormous one. Assumptions need to be made about future levels of population, household numbers, borrowing capacities, the availability of housing in other sectors and the rate of formation and dissolution of household units. Moreover, to be valid evidence in support of its case there would need to be a regional dimension to the demand projections.

The industry soon found itself in the statistical and political minefield that is familiar territory to social analysts and forecasters. Official figures are constantly produced, constantly challenged and constantly reviewed. For example, in December 1984 the Department of the Environment projected that there would be an extra 543,000 households in the south-east region over the period 1981–91. In May 1985 the Department amended this projected increase to

720,000. Following some close questioning concerning the reasons for the change of plus 33 per cent, the department explained that it was largely a technical matter to do with changes in the age bands adopted in the calculation. Meanwhile, in the figures produced to support the case for a new town at Tillingham Hall, in Essex, Consortium Developments estimated that the change would be plus 884,000 households. One problem is that the eventual number is not an independent entity, but will itself be partly a product of the estimates made about it – and the policies adopted by private and public agencies on the basis of those estimates. One prominent spokesman for the building society movement goes so far as to take the view that the amount of new housing demanded is, in fact, the amount actually sold. The market, in other words, is a perfect mechanism and simply clears itself at the appropriate price level. Clearly this should not be all that housebuilders want to know as they do their forward planning since they presumably need to make reasonable estimates of *how much* new housing needs to be sold at that price level to give an acceptable aggregate return on capital invested. It is not, however, clear that this *is* their present concern since the industry seems to have taken the collective view, no doubt based on its own demand assessments, that in certain high-growth greenfield areas of the south-east it can sell as many houses as can be produced. Whatever sense this might make in financial terms, it makes little sense in planning terms.

The second issue over which the industry has sought to develop and argue an independent view is that of building land availability. Indeed the industry has gone further and claimed that:

> objectivity in the assessment of the forward supply of land can only be derived from Joint Studies undertaken with housebuilders' representative organizations, thus emphasising the Housebuilder Federation's important role. (*Housebuilder*, November 1984)

Thus the planning system can apparently no longer be regarded as any kind of objective or balanced arbiter unless helped by the industry. The issue of land flow is simple in principle (five years' forward supply of land has been accepted as desirable) but endlessly complex in terms of actual measurement. Even by 1981 there had built up what the Federation of Master Builders termed 'a serious conflict of opinion' between the department and the industry about the availability of land for speculative housebuilding. There had been a number of joint studies on this issue from the mid-1970s onward but the department's Circular 9 of 1980 gave the issue greater political visibility and encouraged more research. For example, in April 1981 the Federation of Master Builders polled some of its members and obtained 455 usable responses. Most of these were small builders operating without the cushion of a landbank. Of those replying, 85 per cent reported an acute shortage of land and 65 per cent tended to place the blame on planning restrictions. Only 20 per cent realized that they could participate jointly with planning authorites in analysing land availability (although such studies had been going on for a number of years with the very active participation of some of the volume housebuilders). Results similar to the first two of these have been repeated in subsequent studies by the industry.

The conclusions of Serplan (the London and South-east Regional Planning Conference), set out in a series of annual reports, have been different. The July 1984 report, *Housing Land Supply in the South East*, argues that in the 'outer metropolitan area' and the 'outer south-east' the aggregate housing land provision in the relevant Structure Plans is in excess of the recommended five-year supply by 35,000–40,000 sites. Moreover, the report found that there was rather more land available for private housebuilding, and less for local authorities, in the total figure. The situation in Greater London was less clear because only about one-third of boroughs had carried out a joint land availability study. The general view of the GLC, however, was that the rate of housebuilding in London was being inhibited more by a lack of finance and investment than by a lack of land. This whole line of argument has recently been dimissed by a major housebuilder with the brisk comment, made privately, that 'Serplan is rubbish'.

There are a number of reasons for this sharp discrepancy in view between the industry and the planners and most of them were identified in a consultants' report produced by Coopers Lybrand early in 1985 following the analysis of eighteen Structure Plans. 'Demand' to a housebuilder is an area-specific, even a site-specific, concept. To a structure planner it is something to be assessed, largely from population and migration projections, at a county scale. In addition, it is difficult for all parties to assess what effects increased supply itself will have on future demand. In terms of economic theory, some equilibrium should be reached. In reality, growth often begets growth. As a result, in the consultants' view, in some areas such as small villages and high-growth 'corridors' land provision fell far short of demand; in others such as isolated towns and on large estates the planned provision was overgenerous. There is also a difference in perception about what constitutes an 'available' site; an area might be technically available if zoned for housing but builders may doubt the marketability of houses built there. The report also agreed with the industry's view that regional strategies, never strong under the British planning structure, had become increasingly vague. There were conflicting messages from the department's, and other, ministers about some of the implications of the M25 motorway and about the desirability of large-scale development east, rather than west, of London. (See Figure 7.7.)

The industry's recent moves to carry out more thorough analysis of both demand and land availability have probably changed its collective thinking in a number of ways. It may well have

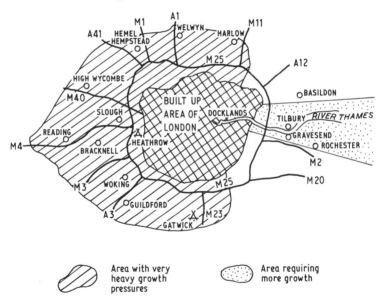

Figure 7.7   *One of the effects of the recent large-scale roadbuilding has been to produce a growth imbalance between the areas east and west of London. In the absence of any strong regional planning agencies this problem can be 'solved' only by massive infrastructural developments such as, possibly, the Channel Tunnel – although this may not help north Kent and south Essex.*

concluded that there are so many imponderables and uncertainties in the situation that precise measurement, let alone accurate prediction, is not a realistic aim – both depend on the assumptions you choose to make and how you decide to weigh the various factors. This being so, influence stems more from assembling a plausible case and then exerting pressure at the right time and place than from spending a lot of time and money trying to get closer to some objective 'truth'. Thus having established demand as a relevant concept for plan-making, having secured its role on joint industry/local planning land availability committees, and having tooled up its research capacity, the industry's next logical move was to ensure that its case could be put at the right place and time and in the right terms. The place, for the moment, has been identified as the Examination in Public of Structure Plans. The industry, or at least the House Builders' Federation, has therefore set up a 'fighting fund' by raising a levy of £5 on each house built by its members in order to cover the cost of more expert professional representation at EIPs. Thus the ammunition collected in the form of better demand and land availability assessments can now be fired by some bigger hired guns.

Case studies

We conclude this chapter by looking very briefly at a few cases from around the Home Counties and elsewhere. This will fill in some fine detail to complement the more general level of analysis. For example, the issues were sharply apparent at the July 1984 Examination in Public of the Stage 1 Alterations of the North-east Hampshire Structure Plan, which covers the Fleet, Hook and Yateley districts. The Alterations were to update the Plan for the period 1982–91. Consortium Developments, to whom reference has already been made, had a keen interest in the area as a possible site for one of their 'new towns'. The volume housebuilders in the consortium, between them responsible for about 30 per cent of the industry's total output, had employed consultants Conran Roche to look for suitable sites in growth areas, with good transport links and a 'pre-history' of large-scale development proposals. Hook had been identified by the London County Council as a new town site in 1961. The town was never built in the form proposed, but some kind of 'pre-history' was established. Letters expressing the consortium's interest in the purchase of land were sent to large land owners in the area. It became apparent that the consortium had in mind a 'new town' of 5000 houses adjacent to Hook and were, in addition, seeking to build 1000 new houses in Fleet and 500 in Yateley.

At the July 1984 Examination in Public the County Planning Officer for Hampshire stressed that the north-eastern area of the country could not possibly cope, in the 1980s and 1990s, with the sort of growth it had experienced in the 1960s and 1970s. He detailed the very limited possibilities for new development in view of the amount of land in the hands of the Forestry Commission and the Ministry of Defence. In addition, considerable areas of land were designated as Areas of Outstanding Natural Beauty and there was a clear responsibility to protect them. The Chief Planner stressed also the uncertainties of regional strategy for the south-east; the need, as he saw it, to redress the growth imbalances between the areas west and east of London, and the rationality of making better use of sites in existing urban areas before taking more large areas of greenfield agricultural land. He drew attention to the Department of the Environment's own view (in their evidence to the House of Commons Environment Committee, for example) that there was adequate land already zoned in the south-east region to meet housebuilding demands for the foreseeable future. These arguments were backed up by other bodies, both statutory and voluntary. The Mid-Southern Water Company put the view that 'if there is major development a new reservoir would almost certainly be needed'. The West Surrey and North East Hampshire Health Authority (part of the South-west Thames Regional Authority) also confirmed that 'The region is unable to meet the needs of additional growth' and in their view a large growth of population would be 'disastrous' in terms of the level of health care that could be provided at current resource levels.

At an administrative level there had been much dismay in at least one of the three constituent district authorities at the apparent unwillingness of the Department of the Environment to deal rationally over the questions of Local Plan making and development proposal appeals. In 1980, following the submission of the Structure Plan, the Secretary of State had sought arbitrarily to add a further 4000 houses to those proposed. This was subsequently brought down to 2500 following strong representations by local planners. No guidance was offered about where in the three districts this extra development could be located. The house-building industry interpreted this change, quite rightly, as a signal that appeals against refusals to develop would be sympathetically considered by the Secretary of State. The consequent appeals were dealt with in such a way that, in the view of some local planners, any attempt to carry out a logical and responsible planning process in compliance with statutory guidelines was totally undermined. Many members of the districts' planning committees also felt that the local planning process was degenerating into a mass of un-coordinated *ad hoc* decisions. There was a strong feeling that important questions were either going by default or were being settled over their heads.

The Hampshire branch of the Council for the Protection of Rural England (CPRE), with assistance from head office, spelled out some of the weaknesses of the presumption in favour of allowing development at a rate well in excess of planning intentions. It argued that pro-development assumptions about the rate of out-migration from London were becoming more shaky and that Greater London's own potential contribution to its housing problems was being undervalued. Strong restraint on the urban peripheries could, it was argued, be an important factor in steering development back to the cities where it was sorely needed. It had serious doubts about the developers' offers to meet the capital costs of new infrastructure; for example, by providing serviced sites for primary schools, clinics, and so on. Even if substantial contributions were made towards the capital costs of these facilities, the revenue costs remained to be borne by the local authorities. In any case, asked CPRE, how rational was it, no matter who was paying, to invest in expensive new infrastructure in greenfield areas when there was still a mass of sewers, schools and water mains available in areas of London that were losing population? Might it not be better to spend a lesser sum of money putting these in order and enlarging their capacity?

When the Examination was finished, the report of the Panel of Inspectors was sent to the Department of the Environment on 26 October 1984. Some internal ministerial agonizing, and pre-sumably some lobbying, then went on because the report had still not been published by mid-June 1985 at which point a local MP asked a question in the House concerning its whereabouts. In July the Secretary of State's proposed modifications to the Plan were published. Predictably these plumped for a rate of housebuilding between those advocated by the planners and by the House Builders' Federation – but nearer to the latter's. There the matter rests.

A second illustrative example is provided by the case of the proposed development at Tillingham Hall, in Essex. In May 1985 Consortium Developments made an application to Thurrock Borough Council to develop a new town with a projected population of 14,000 on a 760-acre site situated four miles from an M25 intersection. The project would involve the investment of £400–£500 million. The aim was to produce a 'balanced community' rather than a dormitory suburb. There was to be a range of housing types selling from £25,000 to £65,000 and the expectation was that 2000 jobs would be created in the town within a decade. Although most of the development was naturally to be carried out by members of Consortium Developments, 10 per cent of the land was to be made available to local builders. Consortium were to provide the physical infrastructure for the town and to contribute to the cost of one primary school and a health centre. The applicants, who held options to purchase from the two farmers who between them owned the site, were willing to spend up to £500,000 to finance the process of obtaining planning approval.

Although most of the Tillingham Hall site is only grade IIIb or IIIc agricultural land, the NFU has joined forces with Essex County Council to oppose the proposal. The agricultural agreement is that although the site itself is only 760 acres, it is located in the centre of an area of open land about 6 miles across. To insert a town at this point would be to produce a 'ring' of farmland about 2 miles across which, in view of the urban-fringe effects, would be both difficult to farm efficiently and very vulnerable to further development pressure. There is also the question of the fragile viability of other small settlements in the area. Given no expected increase in education resources, which existing village schools would have to be closed in order to staff the three primary schools proposed for the new town?

The questions raised by the proposals in north-east Hampshire and Tillingham Hall are absolutely typical of those raised in countless other greenfield areas. Structure Plan land release policies are carefully devised following lengthy consultation with as many as possible of the agencies who will need to provide water, health care, education, welfare, and so on, to the incoming population, and with a view to the long-term conservation of environment and agricultural activity. Over the space of a very few years, and in obvious deference to market forces, these long-established planning procedures have been directly threatened in a succession of cases. Those with the 'planning interest' at heart will need to redouble their efforts in the 'bloody war' now being waged in this arena if the cavalier charge of the housebuilding industry is to be contained.

The second London blitz: redevelopment in docklands

London's docklands cover sizeable parts of five Thames-side boroughs. The area has strong traditions which die hard. To those who grew up downstream of London Bridge and within easy reach of the river the docks were a fact of life. The sight of the line of working cranes seen over the endless terraced housing of Bermondsey, the smell of leather tanning, soap and biscuits, and the sounds of foghorns on murky nights were an unforgettable part of childhood. It is true that those born south of the river and owing allegiance to Millwall and the New Cross speedway team had little love for the aliens on the north shore who supported West Ham. But there was more to unite the two than to divide them – as became apparent in a thousand ways during the 1940–1 London blitz.

The sense of community, which has brushed off to some extent on the successive immigrant groups who for centuries have settled in the area, is still a force to be reckoned with. The folk memory is a tangible factor. It has its roots in a tradition of shared involvement in dock-based economic activities and a militant and articulate labour movement. It also shares an inheritance of hardship and a sense of having suffered knocks that goes well back into the last century. This is where much of 'outcast London' was to be found, where Dickens and Mayhew observed the poor, where typhus and cholera raged into the 1880s and where Booth and Marx, from their differing perspectives, reflected on the consequences of mass urbanization. Here in the last two decades of the nineteenth century a rotting mass of poverty was discovered at the heart of the world's richest empire.

Despite the best efforts of the charitable housing trusts and the pioneering attempts of the London County Council (LCC) and some of the boroughs, the appalling legacy of the Victorian era could not be put right overnight. In fact matters were, if anything, getting worse between the wars. In 1933 a report entitled *The Housing Horrors of London* revealed that the LCC itself admitted there were a quarter of a million living in slums. There were over 18,000 cases where a family of six or more were living in two rooms. It was common for a spouse and children to share a bed with a tubercular patient. The health risks were enormous. An LCC official conceded that 'practically all Stepney is a slum' and that thousands of people pulled their beds out into the street on warm nights to escape from bugs and vermin. An ex-nursing sister who had worked in eastern Europe and China came to the conclusion that nothing she had seen equalled 'the filth of the vermin-infested slums of London'. In the following year the Mansion House Council on Health and Housing reported that the excess of separate households over separate dwellings in London had *increased* by well over 200,000 between 1911 and 1931. Financial crises and Treasury policy had restricted public investment in housing and London local authorities, compared to those in other major British cities, had consistently made a very low charge on the rates to finance housing. This poor record had not been sufficiently counterbalanced by voluntary sector or co-operative activity, as was common for example in Holland and Germany. The Mansion House Council concluded that a single Greater London housing authority was needed to complement the efforts being made by the existing 113 housing authorities.

The 1933 report had made reference to another problem. Although in Poplar the LCC had succeeded in rehousing over 1200 families in new estates between 1925 and 1930, there was by the early 1930s practically no vacant land left in the borough. As a result, 'Rehousing is possible only by previous clearance'. Or, the report might have added, by seeking land in the outer suburbs where housing could be built for the overspill population. But here the theme of opposition to the 'townies' – still to be heard – came loud and clear. One suitable site was located just adjacent to Osterley Park, west of London. But the aristocratic owner, Lord Jersey, strongly objected. He had recently spent large sums improving the estate and LCC housing development within visible range would seriously affect his 'amenities'. The LCC looked elsewhere and found a suitable 1000-acre site near Ilford, in Essex. In this case Ilford Borough Council attempted to prevent the development by seeking to purchase the site themselves (the freehold was owned by the Crown). After a long struggle and a public inquiry, the LCC won this battle.

Later in the 1930s there was much discussion of the possibility of building a set of 'satellite towns', rather than isolated out-county estates. Those proposing such ideas were branded as hopelessly unrealistic or worse. One such visionary, Abercrombie, argued that the planning problems of the London region should be looked at as a whole and that some kind of commission should take over from the Ministry of Health and be given the task of devising and implementing a coherent regional strategy. For this he was branded by Berry (the Labour LCC town housing chairman) as totalitarian, un-British and in the same fascist category as Mussolini. It is interesting to reflect that within ten short years, and following a war to defeat fascism, an Abercrombie-type commission was hard at work implementing a new town programme not only around London, but also in several of the regions.

Thus by the outbreak of the Second World War London's housing problems, and especially those of the East End, were well documented. The root causes of chronic underinvestment in low-rent housing, overcomplex administrative structures, land shortage in inner areas and resistance to overspill by outer areas had been well established. The war was to have a profound effect on all these and for a brief period in the 1940s it looked as if the collective determination engendered during the conflict to do away with the 'bad old days' might enable solutions to be found. This has not, of course, happened, but Hitler's bombs did at least open up the land question. During the war the scale of destruction was considerable, although nothing like that anticipated when the war began. The City of London itself suffered the greatest proportional destruction to its physical fabric but few people lived there and the impact was primarily on the level of economic activity. Of the London boroughs, Stepney and Shoreditch each lost over 20 per cent of their buildings as a result of bombing and other dockland boroughs such as Poplar, Bethnal Green and Bermondsey suffered almost as heavily. By contrast, boroughs elsewhere such as Westminster and Hammersmith lost only 4 per cent or so of their fabric. In the dockland areas as a whole, something like 1250 acres were still vacant, war-damaged or built over with temporary buildings in 1949.

Clearly the unwelcome attentions of the bombers, using a bombardment technology that peppered the areas around the prime targets, did at least produce the beginnings of an answer to the land shortage problem – although of course much housing was lost in the process. The key issues were posed in the popular magazine *Picture Post* (3 January 1941). What basically were we fighting for? For a return to a system of uneven growth, poor housing and an environment destroyed in the search for profits? On what political, financial and administrative bases should reconstruction proceed? Would it be on a basis which would solve the festering problem of bad housing conditions in London's docklands, to which graphic illustration had been given in previous editions of *Picture Post* (see, for example, 1 April 1939)? During the war, as we have seen in Chapter 2, much attention was focused on these issues. Reith, as Minister of Works, asked for a plan for London's postwar development. It was produced by Forshaw and Abercrombie (1944) on the assumption that 'new legislation and financial assistance would be forthcoming'. London's main problems were identified as depressed housing, traffic congestion, poor open space provision and too much intermingling of industrial and housing land uses. This diagnosis conditioned the proposed solution so far as the East End was concerned. The key idea was to open up the river, 'London's most beautiful and most neglected open space'. Public open space, then only 9 per cent of river frontage, was to take up 30 per cent. There was to be no public or business building in any of the LCC boroughs downstream of London Bridge and the open space and community facilities to be plentifully provided were to be designed for the needs of local residents.

In retrospect, and in view of what has been happening for at least two decades, this was a breathtakingly naïve prospect. But it rested on two forgivable assumptions: that the docks would continue to operate, and that we were fighting a war to achieve the kind of society where powers and benefits would be more evenly distributed – an aim not explicitly shared by Churchill, as Chapter 2 made clear. The authors realized that the implementation of the plan would require interventionary legislation, in both land use and financial fields, going far beyond the 1932 Town and Country Planning Act. Significantly, photographs of Moscow were used as illustrations of what could be done. The plan argued that it was easier to carry out one large publicly guided reconstruction effort, comparable to that which produced Haussmann's Paris in the 1870s, than to have endless piecemeal schemes each producing a set of claims by owners concerning their lost development rights. The cost of a large 'one-stage' public initiative would be considerable but it was argued that much of the proposed redevelopment would have to happen on one basis or another anyway, an argument which misses several key points about the nature of capitalist systems. Rather more tellingly, it was pointed out that to carry out a one-stage public acquisition of land and then to implement the necessary redevelopment would cost only what several weeks of fighting the war was costing. To reflect on this is to reflect on the size of the planning opportunity that was lost in the postwar years.

During the first two postwar decades it became clear that many buildings in docklands, which had been inherited from the Victorian era, had outlasted their usefulness. The role of London as the hub of world trade was already undermined. An overcapacity in both upstream dock space and warehousing slowly became apparent. Some manufacturing activities were attracted out to the new towns and other peripheral sites offering more cost-efficient locations. Much canal and railway related land began to fall derelict. Many of the commercial and industrial buildings destroyed by bombing had become obsolete anyway and for many enterprises the state compensation for loss of buildings and plant could be more usefully invested elsewhere. The overall result, in the postwar decades, was a gradual growth of a development 'vacuum' in the old-established dockland areas. (See Figure 8.1) These trends were accentuated by changes in sea transport technology. The growth of containerization, and the resultant premium placed on easily accessible deepwater facilities downstream, rather than on the obsolete and congested docks upstream, began to have its effect. East India Dock was closed in 1967 and trade in the other upstream docks began to fall (Hardy, 1983). These trends were not confined to the major rivers of Britain, or even Europe. The massive new waterfront commercial developments in, for example, Detroit, Chicago and Toronto all stem partly from the same capital-intensifying trends in transhipment technology.

In the late 1960s the planners of the recently constituted Greater London Council began to look seriously at the growing dereliction

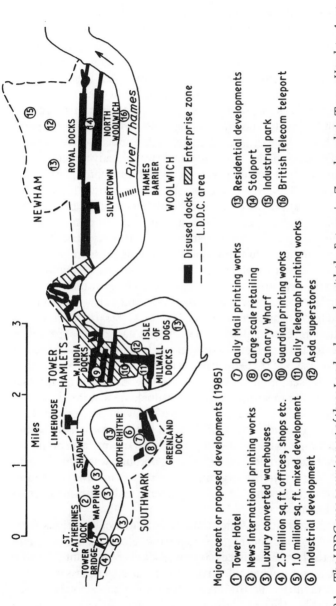

Major recent or proposed developments (1985)

① Tower Hotel
② News International printing works
③ Luxury converted warehouses
④ 2.5 million sq. ft. offices, shops etc.
⑤ 1.0 million sq. ft. mixed development
⑥ Industrial development
⑦ Daily Mail printing works
⑧ Large scale retailing
⑨ Canary Wharf
⑩ Guardian printing works
⑪ Daily Telegraph printing works
⑫ Asda superstores
⑬ Residential developments
⑭ Stolport
⑮ Industrial park
⑯ British Telecom teleport

■ Disused docks ▨ Enterprise zone
--- L.D.D.C. area

Figure 8.1   The LDDC area occupies part of three London boroughs with the Enterprise Zone largely in Tower Hamlets. As at mid 1985, 149 separate development schemes were built, under way, or proposed. The pattern of employment, housing and service facilities is overwhelmingly related to profit maximization rather than locally expressed needs. Although virtually the whole area will be within 15 minutes of the City by public transport, the pattern of development becomes less intense and 'commercial' with increasing distance downstream from Tower Bridge.

east of the City (Eversley, 1975). It was evident that the issue had regional and even national implications. This was one of the few areas (Croyden Airport was another) where large-scale development could occur without taking green belt land. Much of the urban fabric had been destroyed, or was in obsolete uses. The redevelopment of the area might require substantial state funding both in view of the scale of the problem and because of the national benefits which might flow from certain forms of development, for example national trade and exhibition centres. The Forshaw–Abercrombie notion of redevelopment for local people was already undermined – as was the future of jurisdiction by the individual boroughs over an area which the GLC felt should be planned as a larger unit.

The Metropolitan Structure Map, which formed the basis of the 1969 Greater London Development Plan, showed almost all the docklands area as zoned for industrial and commercial use. But this took insufficient account both of the growing pressures for more housing and recreational development and the decreasing interest of industrial investors in the area. Conflicting intentions were emerging faster than the plans which, theoretically, should have been mediating between them. The GLC Strategic Planning Committee recommended (in 1970) that large areas be made available to Tower Hamlets to build public housing as part of a drive to house 67,000 people in up-to-date dwellings and with a heavy public sector emphasis. The Port of London Authority, as a large land owner in various parts of the docklands, wanted half the same area to be developed speculatively for owner-occupation. This would mean that adjacent areas of land in their ownership would acquire a higher value by 'contagion' effect deriving from an influx of higher-status people. Tower Hamlets borough was torn between the clear duty to rehouse large numbers of lower-income people and the desire to attract higher-status property and activities so as to increase its rates base.

While these matters were under discussion, calculations were being made about the cost of acquiring, clearing, draining and servicing the large areas necessary for producing both more housing and more jobs. Considerable investment was also necessary in the transport facilities of the area. The total figure involved was estimated to be at least £1 billion. It was clear that there could be no competitive short-term return on an investment of this scale and the feeling quickly grew that heavy involvement by a supra-borough agency of some kind was inevitable. This meant either the GLC or a specially appointed development corporation with generous state funding, wide powers and, to be realistic, considerable representation of private sector interests at board level. The precedent for such a body went back to the new town corporations of the heady postwar years.

London's docklands had come to be recognized as 'the largest redevelopment opportunity in Europe' by the early 1970s. The range of interests involved, and the pre-existence of a sizeable population with strongly assertive political traditions, produced a situation of bewildering complexity. A stream of reports and plans emerged from a succession of agencies during the 1970s. Travers Morgan, the consultants appointed by the government in 1971, were directed to analyse the issue specifically in the context of the 1970s Burns Regional Plan with its emphasis on development in south Essex linked to Maplin as London's third airport. But the implications of thinking at this scale, which was miles removed from Abercrombie's notion of development for local residents' interests, alerted opposition in the dockland boroughs. The issue was clearly, and correctly, seen as one of politics, not of planning – if the latter was taken to mean, as it frequently was at the time, the making of a neutral, 'rational', choice between competing options. For example, the production of a good low-rent council house and of a penthouse flat selling for £200,000 can both be seen as rational, depending on the criteria of rationality one feels moved to adopt. But the choice between them, or at least the order in which resources are made available to produce them, is essentially political.

The consultants reported in January 1973 with a range of options, none of which could be regarded as a comprehensive plan. Nor did they please most local people. A stream of publications emerged from groups such as the North Southwark Community Development Group and from the Southwark and Canning Town Community Development Projects, both appointed by the Home Office. As a further response, the Docklands Joint Committee was set up jointly by the GLC and the five boroughs most concerned. It produced the London Docklands Strategic Plan in 1976. These various documents identified a key dilemma and led to a sharp division of opinion. Loyalties were, and still are, divided between those who welcomed *any* development, including office blocks, because it meant jobs, and those who wished to maintain an employment structure closer to the industrial traditions of the area. In the sphere of housing there was conflict between those who wanted much more speculative private development to produce a more 'normal' tenure balance, and those who wanted more low-rent, local authority housing. Unfortunately, partly as a result of the pattern of subsidies offered by central government, several of the boroughs had opted for the development of high-rise flats on a massive scale. Not only did one of these blocks (Ronan Point) partially collapse in 1968, but many of them now require either vast expenditure to restore them to habitable condition or, failing that, demolition.

The 'homes vs offices' issue transcended any simple dispute about which pattern of land use might be accepted as 'the best'. It was about who controls power and resources and was very clearly seen as such by most local activists and community groups. This raised sharp dispute about who could most validly claim to speak for the local 'community' – democratically elected representatives or community group leaders. It also led to confusion about who should be 'scapegoated' for unwelcome decisions: local planners or more distant and shadowy forces in 'the City'. Hopefully, previous work (see Ambrose and Colenutt, 1975) may have shed some light on these issues. The interlinked problems of how to get more state money without allowing more external control, how to raise more revenue from rates without having the area dominated by activities ill-suited to local needs and how to ensure genuine participation in decision-making by local people formed a Gordian knot by the end of the 1970s.

The advent of a government of the radical right in June 1979 cut that knot. Within months, powers were being proposed to set up Urban Development Corporations, with centrally appointed boards and access to state funding. One such was to deal with London's docklands. In one sense this solution had been canvassed since the Abercrombie days of the late 1930s and it had already been adopted for the new towns programme. In fact it is instructive that this same constitutional device has been interpreted alternately as 'totalitarian' in the late 1930s, a socialist intervention in the 1946 new towns programme and a tool by which capitalist forces can dominate development in London's docklands in the 1980s. Much depends on the politics, and the configuration of forces, of the day. The 1979 philosophy clearly saw private investment as the only saviour for the inner city areas and the purpose of the new corporations was to do everything possible to get private and institutional money into the area. They were to be, paradoxically, public sector agencies to ensure minimal public intervention in land development processes.

The setting up of this type of urban development corporation under the powers of the 1980 Local Government, Planning and Land Act was a significant shift of policy away from the area-based, positive discrimination approach of, for example, the Educational Priority Areas. The 1980 Act was explicitly about relaxing planning controls, forcing the sale of public land, setting up inducements for private capital and controlling public spending. The 1982 Local Government Finance Act called for much closer auditing of local authority finances – in effect, an audit of policy not just of money (Duncan and Goodwin, 1985b). Large sums of public money, no longer to be available to democratically elected local authorities, were to be channelled to a centrally appointed corporation. The massive land infrastructural programmes which had for at least a decade been seen as necessary were to be publicly funded but with the aim of releasing prepared land on attractive terms to private developers and builders. The general view of the government was that local interests must be subordinated to the national good. Ministerial pronouncements became steadily more hysterical. The 'municipal Marxists' who wished to offer subsidized public transport and job-creation initiatives were bent on some kind of takeover of national politics. Some protection must be offered by central government: 'Parliament has always had a historic duty to protect the people from the oppressor' (quoted in *Guardian*, 12 October 1983). The GLC was a prime target, it had been 'creating poverty, killing industry, breaking the law and helping criminals' (*Guardian*, 15 March 1982). London was 'in the hands of Marxists bent on revolution. It must be defeated. So we shall abolish the GLC' (*Guardian*, 18 March 1982). Not all government supporters saw it this way, however: 'I have been years in local government and have not come to Parliament to turn a partnership into a dictatorship' (Tory backbencher, *Guardian*, 9 July 1980).

The arguments were fully aired in a House of Lords inquiry, held in February–May 1981. Despite the patronizing acceptance that local opposition was 'perfectly genuine', and an assurance that 'the committee understand – and indeed sympathise with their attitude', it was concluded, on balance, that the case for a public sector corporation had been made. The London Docklands Development Corporation (LDDC) was, therefore, set up in July 1981 under the chairmanship of Nigel Broakes, an entrepreneur not unknown to the City. The board of directors was made up of carefully selected local politicians plus various private sector representatives (see LDDC *Annual Reports*).

This brief account of the planning history of docklands reveals a more complex situation than that in the greenfield arena. There are more identifiable competing interests at work. They include central government in the shape of the LDDC, land owners, property developers and investors seeking rental returns and capital asset growth, speculative housebuilders, other commercial interests (for example, building contractors, airline entrepreneurs, etc.), the planning system in the shape of the boroughs and the GLC and, because the area has been lived in for a long time, an articulate local population. As in the greenfield arena, most of these interests can be categorized into two groups on the basis of their funding, control and intentions. There are the capital-accumulators (developers, housebuilders, contractors, etc.) and the others (planners, local people, etc.). At the present time there is a third group – nominally public sector corporations who act as if they were private sector entrepreneurs (the LDDC, and the Port of London Authority). The following sections of the chapter will deal briefly in turn with most of these interests (see also Goodchild and Munton, 1985, chapter 8).

The central government interest

> This is the closest to total dictatorship any British government has ever come and I am totally and utterly opposed to it. (Leader of a docklands council, May 1980; he subsequently joined the LDDC board together with two other local council leaders)

The 1980 legislation that led to the setting up of the urban development corporations (UDCs) and Enterprise Zones had two main aims: to shift the power balance from local to central government, and to encourage private entrepreneurial 'flair' and capital as regenerators for 'problem' areas. The latter aim can best be achieved, in the eyes of the 'new right', by short-circuiting established planning, fiscal and participatory barriers and thus allowing business interests to work in a land and property market 'undistorted' by regulatory measures. The other aim, to centralize power in Whitehall where it is beyond the reach of high-spending local leftist politicians (or 'municipal Marxists'), has been a consistent element not just since 1979, but since the financial crisis of the mid-1970s, the massive IMF loans to stabilize sterling and the Healey/Jenkins/Crosland era of Labour politics. The aims, then, are not new, but they have been embraced with all possible enthusiasm by the two Thatcher administrations. In docklands, in particular, the consensual interventionary approach which had lasted for more than three decades was to be replaced by 'the single-minded discipline of the market place'. The UDCs are not just an element in government policy. They are, in a real sense, the economic and philosophic flagships of the new right. So much of the government's credibility has been nailed to the UDC mast that any reversion to the previous local participatory, public sector led, approach would strike a serious blow at the government's prestige in a number of other policy areas. It is necessary to keep this ideological dimension in mind when analysing events.

From the beginning, the London Docklands Development Corporation (LDDC) saw docklands' housing problem as a tenure problem – only 4 per cent of the housing was owner-occupied. This lack of private housing had, argued the LDDC, inhibited industrial investment (Wolmar, 1982). The obvious implication was that the area did not have enough of the 'right' kind of people. A shift of emphasis was therefore needed: 'Housing is part of our regeneration task whereas the Docklands Joint Committee looked at housing solely in terms of need' (R. Ward, Chief Executive, LDDC). Usable housing land was now available as a result of the previous efforts of the boroughs. By 1982 Newham had drained and cleared land in Beckton for 7500 houses and Tower Hamlets had prepared 100 acres (Wolmar, 1982). Much of this was scheduled for sheltered, or low-rent family housing. The LDDC rapidly used their newly legislated powers to 'vest' (or compulsorily acquire) over 600 acres of publicly owned land. This was then sold off to volume housebuilders who expressed themselves as well satisfied. Barratt's spoke of 'the fine deal' by which they acquired land from the Docklands Board for '£30,000 per acre compared with a market value of perhaps twice that'. Certainly this led to the production of houses at 'loss leader' prices but they were built to standards far inferior to similarly priced houses built for sale by Newham

Council. In addition to these moves towards privatization, the LDDC allowed and actively encouraged the conversion of riverside warehouses into luxury flats thus accelerating the process of job loss as adjacent owners of working warehouses saw the financial possibilities.

The corporation has continued to pursue a market-oriented, 'demand-led' strategy. The 1983/4 *Annual Report* highlights, in its review of the year, the visits of various royals and ministers and the helicopter viewing days for property investors. It refers to 1.35 million sq. ft of business space under construction in the Isle of Dogs Enterprise Zone and another potential 2.0 million on Hays Wharf. The most important growth sectors are seen as telecommunications, media activities and high-technology industry. There are also two new Asda superstores and various mixed developments such as Heron Quays with offices, studios, flats and shops. All this is part of 'the new spirit of regeneration, growth and change'. A total of 3850 new jobs are claimed since July 1981. This figure is strongly contested by local groups and has to be offset against the

Figure 8.2 *New private housing in Rotherhithe of the type generally known as 'Heseltine hutches'. There is little room to hang curtains so Austrian blinds are used instead. Burglar alarms abound. Prices on original sale were partly controlled (at £33,000 to £55,000) but have soared since, giving good capital gains to speculative first purchasers.*
(© Peter Ambrose 1986)

considerable, but unspecified, losses due to plant closures – some of them directly attributable to LDDC activities.

In the field of housing, the corporation claims around 4000 units completed or under construction, with a continuing production rate of about 2000 per year. The vast majority of these are for owner-occupancy and prices (in mid 1984) ranged from around £28,000 to £80,000 or more per unit. It concedes that only a low percentage of the houses have been bought by local people, (see Figure 8.2). It refers to the expenditure committed to environmental regeneration and considers that it 'would be helpful' if the local housing authorities would also draw up ten-year plans for housing regeneration. This implied criticism of local authority housing policies has a cynical air and must be seen in the light of the earlier 'vesting' by the LDDC of land which the boroughs had for some time been preparing for their own housing programmes. It also chooses to ignore the savage government cuts in local authority funding which has meant that the boroughs could not possibly afford to buy back land they had lost on the terms and conditions the LDDC were offering.

Developments in docklands infrastructure have included the light railway running from Tower Hill in the City to the southern end of the Isle of Dogs. This is capable of carrying 2500 people per hour on the ten-minute journey and will no doubt produce a premium on house prices in this area by reducing the journey to work time for City workers. Another large project, geared to the needs of business travellers from the City to various continental cities, is the Short Take-off and Landing Airport (Stolport) in the former Royal Docks. This was subject to long and acrimonious dispute at a Public Inquiry in 1983; the *Annual Report* notes severely that while inquiries are 'an essential part of the democratic process', they do cost money and sap the efforts of key executives thus delaying development and regeneration. They should not be allowed to 'drag out beyond the time needed to allow the inspector to understand all points of view'.

The LDDC can be seen as a prime example of the blurring of the distinction between 'public' and 'private' sector agencies. Although a public corporation and heavily state-funded, its two chairmen so far have been private sector property magnates. One can hardly believe that conflicts of interest do not arise. The corporation sees itself primarily as a pump-primer whose main aim is to attract

228 Whatever Happened to Planning?

private sector investment. Its claim (in the 1983/4 *Annual Report*) that £80 million of public investment has provided the conditions in which more than £485 million of private investment has been attracted into the area is a revealing statement of its redevelopment philosophy. So is the remark that 'On the whole, higher land values are helpful'. The 1980 Local Government, Planning and Land Act laid upon the UDCs a duty to secure the regeneration of their areas and to ensure that 'housing and social facilities are available to encourage people to live and work in the area'. It did not say which people. The LDDC has no doubts. At a conference discussion on 16 October 1982 it was pointed out that the Corporation receives direct instructions from the Department of the Environment to 'short circuit the planning procedure'. The problem is seen as 'a surplus capacity of people'. Broakes, the first chairman, stressed that there was no statutory duty to take account of local feeling: 'we are not a welfare association but a property based organisation offering good value' (*Docklands News*, no.11).

Land owners' interests

The land ownership pattern in docklands is very different from that of the greenfield arena, and different from almost anywhere else in Britain. The legislation of the early 1980s required the drawing up of a land register listing all sites in public ownership which were surplus to operational requirements. The intention was to increase the information available to potential private sector purchasers. In an analysis of inner London carried out in 1983 (Goodchild and Munton, 1985) four main categories of land owner were identified; the boroughs, British Gas, British Rail and the LDDC–PLA. Each owned about one-fifth of the total with the GLC owning a further 10 per cent. Thus the land is, nominally, almost all owned by the state in the guise of a number of public sector authorities and corporations. This public ownership pattern has had little inhibiting effect on the 'market-led' direction that development has taken, especially in docklands, since 1979. This is a corrective to the view that to take land into public ownership is the main precondition for more enlightened patterns of development. All this land already *is* in the hands of public agencies. Each of these organizations, however, has its own financial aims and the achievement of these aims depends heavily, in present circumstances, on private sector development capabilities.

British Gas, in 1976, owned over 600 acres in docklands. The bulk of this was in two major gasworks sites, Beckton and East Greenwich. Because of the uses to which it had been put, much of this land is heavily polluted and will require considerable reclamation expenditure. British Gas, as the provider of a key utility, have their own long-term plans for the land. Some of it is still required for the storage and manufacture of gas. In addition, the corporation has to be prepared for the future exhaustion of North Sea gas and the consequent need to revert to coal- or oil-based production. By 1982, therefore, their only major disposal was for the development of the Asda superstore in Newham. Subsequently various smaller sites have been sold to the LDDC, all of which remain unused, and other small sites have been purchased. The situation was changed in May 1985 when British Gas acquired a site in the Isle of Grain further downstream for a future coal-based gas plant. It is now necessary to retain only a small site in Greenwich for a smaller oil-fired plant. It is likely, therefore, that the corporation will have considerable amounts of land to sell over the next five years and they are currently considering their marketing strategy. It seems unlikely that they will enter the field of development, except in relation to gas production.

The Port of London Authority (PLA) owned 1495 acres in docklands in 1976. Several major docks were then in use and the assumption in the Greater London Strategic Plan was that Millwall Docks at least would remain operational until 1990 and the Royals much longer. But by the mid-1970s the PLA was already more interested in the deepwater possibilities downstream and resistant to proposals that the upstream docks should be protected or regenerated. The Authority was much more concerned with realizing the land value of its large holdings. As a result, there was virtually no dock activity left by the end of 1984 and the point was made at the Stolport inquiry in 1983 that the Authority 'had no brief to consider the wider interests of the community' which is, of course, strictly correct. By the end of 1984 the PLA's land disposal policy was well advanced. Two-thirds of their land had been sold, 311 acres to local authorities and 659 acres to the LDDC, representing 52 per cent of all land acquired at that date by the corporation. Their intentions for the land they have retained

Figure 8.3   *A brisk trade in development land has generated good business for estate agents and others in what was previously characterized as a 'no-go' area for the development industry.*
Source: Estates Gazette, *11 January 1986 (advertisement)*

(nearly 500 acres) are rather more entrepreneurial than those of British Gas. In Tower Hamlets, in and around the Enterprise Zone, they have promoted a number of private sector schemes for activities such as fish marketing, bottling and small-scale manufacturing. An Asda superstore has been built and a mixed scheme of 155,000 sq. ft of offices plus 75 residential units is under construction. Most of this development is not in accord with the 1976 London Docklands Strategic Plan, which envisaged more housing and open space. In Newham the major PLA initiative is Stolport on a 90-acre site in the Royal Docks. This received ministerial approval in May 1985 following nearly four years of local and national debate. This development will partially negate previous statutory plan intentions for housing and open space on the site.

The LDDC itself has now become the major land owning interest in docklands. It acquired 625 acres when first set up in 1981, and by late 1984 had added another 650 acres or so. The main areas of

acquisition were the Isle of Dogs, Surrey Docks, Silvertown and
Beckton. By 1984 15 per cent of this land had been developed and a
further 18 per cent was committed for development (Greater
London Council, 1985), although this does not mean that construction on these sites is imminent. A rather larger amount, about 41
per cent of the land, was lying unused and with no plans for use. The
rate of development in the period 1981–4 was about 65 acres per
year, so that it would take, at this rate, twenty years or more for
redevelopment to be completed, even if no further land acquisitions
were sought.

In its development pattern the LDDC has paid virtually no regard
to the 1976 London Docklands Strategic Plan or the various
statutory local plans since prepared by the boroughs. There has
been a heavy concentration of housing development in Beckton but
with, as we have seen, an emphasis on speculative private sector
housing which is quite out of line with planning intentions. Open
space has not been adequately linked through to the river and there
are few riverside walkways with public access. The concept of
phasing residential, shopping, community and social facilities, and
particularly the provision of services accessible on foot, has been
abandoned and local centres envisaged in previous plans have not
been built. Commercial development, amounting to over 800,000
sq. ft has been concentrated almost entirely in the Isle of Dogs and
Poplar areas where it is not easily accessible to the housing built in
Beckton.

The LDDC is actively seeking to acquire much more land before
the anticipated land price rises occur. They seek to 'capture the
subsequent development value' and 'recycle it back' into docklands.
The pattern of benefit resulting will depend on the way it is
recycled. If the 1981–5 policies are continued, the benefit will go
mainly to private developers and housebuilders in the form of
cheap, serviced land. The LDDC's plan is to acquire a further 1000
acres by 1988/9 (LDDC, *Corporate Plan*). This intention may well
be optimistic. Most of the pool they originally acquired, much of
which had been prepared for development at public expense, has
now been released for development. Relatively little land has been
prepared for development by the LDDC since 1981, and to maintain
the past flow of land release considerable money will have to be
spent. It may be beyond the intentions of even a friendly Treasury
to allow sufficient funds for all the activities the LDDC have in

mind, especially since so small a proportion of land already owned by the corporation has been developed.

The corporation, as a land owner, also appears to have been driving some pretty soft bargains with the development industry. It is prepared to adopt a 'flexible approach' to land disposals and to offer leases of up to 200 years, apparently at low ground rents and without rent reviews. It is clearly aware of, and in fact advertises, rapid rises in land values but seems content not to benefit from these value increases by periodic rent reviews or by negotiating an ownership or rental share in developments. Similarly, volume housebuilders in Beckton were able to specify their own construction cost and profit projections and the land was sold to them at a price derived by subtracting these estimates from the selling value of the houses. The builder was then able to defer payment for the land until the houses were built and sold, thus avoiding financing costs in a way not possible in normal development situations. No doubt the corporation would argue that an approach of this sort was necessary to attract private investors to the area. It is, however, clear that the public purse has lost out to a very considerable extent as a result of the LDDC's favourable attitude to the property industry.

Commercial development interests

> In the inner cities, we expect the Urban Development Corporations, both in Docklands and in Merseyside, to become the vehicles for releasing joint venture capital on a large scale, bringing together the land assets held by the UDCs and the substantial finance that is potentially available from institutions and developers. The potential of such schemes for releasing additional construction activity in the 1980s is enormous. (John Stanley, Minister for Housing and Construction, March 1982)

This ministerial statement clearly sums up the various elements of the Thatcher government's inner city strategy. 'Joint venture capital' is the salvation, although it must be 'released' by a combination of inducements – most notably a flow of land on advantageous terms via the urban development corporations (UDCs). So long as this is the dominant strategy it is important to understand what the private sector is looking for and how they assess the inner city from the investment point of view (Cadman,

1979). Commercial developers are involved in promoting building projects for rental income and asset growth. As we saw in Chapter 6, this is a quite different activity from speculative housebuilding, although the same company or group may be engaged in both. The finance is largely from large institutions, many of which have a trustee status (because they are investing contributors' or depositors' money). This normally lends caution to their activities, although as we saw in Chapter 4, this caution has on occasion been thrown to the winds. What positive aspects of the dockland situation might encourage the private investment that the government is seeking? And what negative factors might lead to hesitation?

To consider the negative aspects first, derelict docks and industrial land on this scale are unfamiliar territory to developers and financiers. They are more used to the smaller-scale, piecemeal opportunities offered on the fringes of the central business districts. In these areas late-nineteenth-century housing is falling into decay, for whatever reason, and new commercial floorspace can be promoted adjacent to similar existing uses. Land on the south bank of the Thames, opposite the City, can be regarded as a safe area to 'colonize' with office and retail developments. Land several miles further downstream, in Newham, is a different matter entirely. There are at least three reasons for caution regarding the sites downstream of, say, St Katherine's Dock, and they apply, although with varying force, to all forms of rental development. These reasons are to do, firstly with assessments of demand in different locations; secondly with rates; and thirdly with the perceived social nature of dockland areas.

The product of commercial developers is floorspace to let to tenants involved in office, retail, industrial and warehousing activities. The first two of these (which we can lump together as 'commercial') have the greatest social and financial significance, in that they generate both more jobs and more rent per unit area of space. The office boom of the early 1970s saw a considerable overproduction of commercial space in central London. One result was a drastic slump in rentals, and thus profitability, in the mid-1970s. A gradual recovery of demand and rent levels occurred towards the end of the decade as the trend continued for national and international corporations to seek a London headquarters. But in the longer term there must be doubt about the effect of new computer and communications technology on the total demand for

Estates Gazette, 6.7.85

£110m SCHEME FOR WEST INDIA DOCKS

The London Docklands Development Corporation has announced a major regeneration scheme for North Quay, West India Docks, Isle of Dogs. The new complex will be serviced by the Docklands Light Railway, which will have a station on North Quay.

The scheme will be handled in two halves, each side of the station, and the LDDC has selected the Allied Entertainment Group for the western portion of the scheme. Negotiations are well in hand with the Port of London Authority, backed by a Singapore syndicate for the eastern portion.

Allied's scheme, designed by Fitch & Co and costing about £110m, includes a 400-bedroomed hotel, museum, international food hall, exhibition centre, shops and leisure pavilions. The developers have a 16-week period in which to finalise their plans and to confirm financing. The overall project will also include residential space, offices and a re-creation of old Chinese Limehouse — on the eastern side of the development. Eventually it is planned that the scheme will extend further to incorporate Poplar Dock and a centre for square-mast sailing ships.

Meanwhile the consortium of Credit Suisse First Boston, Morgan Stanley International and First Boston Real Estate, which has £1.5bn plans to develop at Canary Wharf, Isle of Dogs, is considering funding an extension of the Docklands Light Railway.

The extension would link Canary Wharf, through Tower Hill where the rail line currently starts, to Bank in the heart of the City.

The transportation advisers to the consortium, Steer Davies & Gleave, have made a report which will be considered in New York as we go to press, with a decision expected in two to three weeks. The consortium has already stated that "a key factor will be the provision of good physical communications with the City".

Figure 8.4   *The property industry press is full of reports of new schemes in docklands. Many of the schemes are for mixed uses and are backed by capital from overseas.*

specially designed office and retail buildings. Futurists have a clear vision of the growth of home-based activities in both these fields. Given these presumed long-term tendencies, and the ongoing and proposed construction of something like 10 million sq. ft of commercial floorspace along the south bank of the Thames in easy reach of the City, the level of interest by commercial developers in areas further east is not spontaneously high – although it does seem to be growing slowly.

Levels of demand depend, among other things, on price – in this case occupancy costs. Occupiers face two cost elements: rent and rates. The three dockland boroughs most involved – Tower Hamlets, Newham and Southwark – all face chronic and deep-seated social and financial problems. As a result, they have sought to increase, or at least maintain, their rate income in real terms so as to protect their residents from the hardship of declining service provision. Given the reduction in central government funding since the mid-1970s, this has meant a more than doubling of rates in real terms over the past decade (see Hillman, 1983). Over the same period commercial rents have fallen in real terms and the effect has been a sharp increase in the ratio of rate to rent payment by occupiers. Rents can be fixed for five years or more by the letting agreement but rates can increase annually leading to a greater uncertainty in operational costs for tenants. In the particular case of International House on St Katherine's Dock a rise of £600,000 in the rates bill in April 1981 reduced the asking rent from £16 per square foot to £11. This obviously confounded the original viability calculations for the whole project and reduced the asset value of the building. The 'new right' administration of the post-1979 period is aiming to reduce the power of local authorities to bring about such uncertainties in the property environment and thus to reduce inhibitions to private investment. This helps to explain both Mrs Thatcher's own obsessive opposition to rates as a form of revenue-gathering and the general unease of her government with the whole idea of local government – and especially with certain Labour-controlled authorities which, in their view, 'cannot be trusted'. Certainly these attitudes find an echo in the market. One developer remarked, 'Why go to docklands if the costs are the same, or more, than those in more accepted places?'

The reference to 'acceptability' reveals the third negative characteristic of docklands in the eyes of developers. Unlike housebuilders, who are in and out of an area with a freehold sale in a year or two, developers or purchasers of rental premises have a long-term interest in the social complexion of the area. They like to hold land on a freehold, or very long leasehold (125 years or more), so as to allow the possibility of future redevelopment as market circumstances change. They, therefore, need to be assured about what might be termed the future political stability of the area. Various articles in, for example, the *Estates Gazette* during the early

1980s made it clear that there were doubts on this score. Docklands was seen as an area of neglect, vandalism and failing law and order. Its economy was seen as uncertain, its land ownership pattern as fragmented, its indigenous industry as damaging to the environment and its residents as poor and unskilled. In fact in some ways the concept of 'outcast London', so brilliantly elaborated by Stedman Jones (1971) lives on in the minds of the property industry. The more personal aspects of this dismal catalogue of defects are hopefully based on ignorance rather than an intention to insult. But certainly the critique has made a mark with the LDDC whose policies towards land, housing mix and the squeezing out of industrial jobs can only be seen as a calculated answer to the various points of concern listed by investors. In particular, the massive promotion of owner-occupancy is very explicitly a drive to attract the right kind of residents so as to reduce the risk of damage to property and thus to help 'stabilize' the area as an arena for commercial investment.

Turning to the positive characteristics of docklands, as seen by property investors, one is the sheer amount of land available and the other is the set of government policies that have reduced the price and increased the attractiveness of this land. The latest LDDC *Annual Report* refers to 282 acres of industrial or commercial land either available or being prepared. Studies have referred to 2000 acres of derelict land in inner London of which about 500 are in Tower Hamlets. To the developer, to whom site acquisition is often the most troublesome aspect of development, this is potentially manna from heaven. But now more than ever the terms have to be right. A whole series of government incentives has tried to make them right.

Spending on the urban prgramme as a whole has increased from £30 million in 1976/7 to £348 million in 1983/4. This uncharacteristic increase in public expenditure would hardly have occurred unless the underlying intention had been to benefit private sector investors. The LDDC has been increasingly well funded and has spent £12 million on new roads and infrastructure in the Isle of Dogs alone. The 1978 Inner Areas Act encouraged local authorities in partnership with central government to initiate programmes of environmental improvement. But this was nothing compared to the post-1979 handouts. The Enterprise Zones offer exemptions to all rate charges on industrial and commercial property, 100 per cent tax allowances on capital spending, exemption from Development Land Tax (which anyway was abolished in 1985) for ten years and simplified planning control procedures. Derelict Land Grants are on offer to cover 50 per cent of the cost of reclaiming derelict land. Urban Development Grants for joint private–public schemes cover 75 per cent of the public cost in order to get schemes initiated by 'levering in' private capital. Without them the public input to the initiation of new partnership development is often limited to the product of a 2p rate.

How have these various schemes appealed to the property industry? Healey and Baker, as estate agents monitoring docklands, consider that there has been a growth of interest by developers and institutions in the Isle of Dogs as a result especially of the ten-year rates exemption and the offer of 200-year leases at peppercorn rents. In one development, Indescon Court, rates would have been about £1.75 per square foot per year. Rents for similar premises just outside the Enterprise Zone are around £2.50, which together with rates bring the cost to users to about £4.25. But inside the zone, with no rates, a rent of £3.35 has been fixed for five years. Thus the benefit has been split roughly equally between developer and user. This concession has helped to produce a high enquiry rate from developers with, as at 1984, a use breakdown as follows: workshop/industrial 41 per cent, storage 33 per cent, offices/studios 18 per cent and high-technology 8 per cent. Although there is, at present, a low ratio of enquiries to actual lettings, various notable tenants including Limehouse Productions TV studios have already taken space.

The input of local authority money under the Urban Development Grant (UDG) scheme, which can apply to most categories of use, has in many areas raised the commercial viability of a scheme above the threshold necessary to induce private investment. The basis of each public–private partnership is subject to separate negotiation but it is accepted that there is very limited scope for the public sector to 'claw back' future profits. Mallinson and Gilbert (1983) refer to the 'levering in' of a total of £239 million of private investment for the expediture of £63 million of public grant, a leverage ratio of 4:1. In one particular scheme (in Nottingham) a grant of £197,600 stimulated a development costing £1,078,000, a ratio of 5.46:1. One developer remarked that the UDG scheme 'enabled the company to make a reasonable return from a site we could not otherwise have looked at'.

Grants and concessions on this scale can, of course, be cancelled under future governments with different political philosophies. The development industry has, over the years, grown used to rapid changes in 'the rules of the game' with swings in government policy. It does seem, however, that by the time any government of the left is elected the amount of investment that will have flowed into dockland areas under the current extremely generous set of arrangements will be very large. It may be so great that any large-scale reduction in the expensive concessions that are currently 'buying' it will be difficult to achieve. It also follows that if a big reduction *is* achieved, there may well be serious destabilizing effects both on docklands itself and on the financial position of investors. Since much of this investment is coming from 'trustee' institutions, which have been very much under the protection of government in recent decades, a significant reversal of policy may be very difficult to achieve.

Volume housebuilders' interests

The volume housebuilder is engaged in making a product which is normally for freehold sale. In addition, he may be involved in carrying out construction contracts for some other promotion agency such as a housing association. In neither case is there a long-term financial involvement in the area. As a result, the housebuilder's requirements of an unfamiliar area such as dock-lands are more straightforward than those of commercial developers – although there is, of course, some overlap. In 1980 Tom Baron, one of Britain's most influential volume builders, listed four precon-ditions for his industry's interest in the inner city:

1 demand must be identified and quantified;
2 meeting the demand must produce an adequate profit;
3 sites must be available at less than the cost of opportunities forgone;
4 the builder must judge that better opportunities do not exist in alternative possible arenas.

In short, the industry is not in the business of giving anything away and very special conditions are necessary to attract the volume builders to the inner city. Such conditions might be a plentiful and cheap flow of suitable building land plus restrictive policies in the 'greenfield' arena as discussed in Chapter 7.

A study carried out in Nottingham (Nicholls *et al.*, 1982) confirmed these points. A large sample of builders were asked how they approached inner urban possibilities and, in particular, to list in order the obstacles they perceived to profitable activity there. The rank order of obstacles for those with experience of building in the inner areas was as follows:

1 local authorities asking too much for land;
2 private owners asking too much for land;
3 planning conditions too stringent;
4 too many clearance problems;
5 lack of demand;
6 public authorities un-cooperative.

In addition, many builders stressed that large sites were needed so that 'large estates can create their own social environment'. Small sites in and among derelict or industrial land were not attractive. Builders have elsewhere made the point that while the 'pioneer' speculative houses may be offered for first sale at low prices, as more and more private development is carried out on adjacent sites there is a build up of possible asking prices by a 'contagion' effect. Thus the expectation of rapid capital gain is offered as part of the inducement to the early buyers. But the sites have to be carefully chosen. Many builders have made the point that it is misleading to talk generally of 'inner city possibilities' since prices achievable are very specific to particular areas and sites. In the docklands, for example, housing near the City or along the river-front sites will fetch much more than similar housing in less desirable areas.

The LDDC's housing inducement policy (it is not strictly speaking a promotion policy because the corporation does not itself build) is an exact reflection of the industry's checklist of needs. This is hardly surprising in view of the very close informal links, including frequent regular meetings, between the volume builders group and senior ministers. The LDDC has, in effect, expropriated land in large parcels and sold it on to builders at submarket prices. It has cleared, drained and prepared the sites, it has taken development control into its own hands and it has built up demand with a glossy and aggressive sales drive. The builders have responded. The

1983/4 LDDC *Annual Report* shows that in the short period since 1981 Broseley had built over 600 housing units, Barratt and Comben about 500 each, Wimpey over 400 and Countryside and Lovell over 200 each. In the same period local councils had found the land and money to build only about 200 units in the area.

By September 1984 Broakes (the LDDC chairman) was claiming in the *Housebuilder* that: 'We have made Docklands part of the London property scene where previously it was a no-go area.' (Although presumably the many people who already lived there went there.) Housebuilders were busy 'unlocking' land by direct negotiation with the Port of London Authority and the Central Electricity Generating Board. Wates were offering flats at £50,000 and four-bedroom houses at £110,000. For two-bedroom houses at £40,000 or more there was 'terrific demand . . . from local people'. There were good chances for first purchasers to trade up later at a considerable profit. In the *Housebuilder* for December–January 1985 it was noted that the 'revival' of the cities was faltering – except for London's Docklands. But in order for the housebuilders to keep things moving, the government must continue to provide the necessary conditions. The demands were familiar ones; 'land

Figure 8.5   *Old warehouses and other industrial premises have been converted into riverside apartments available at luxury prices. In this Barratt conversion at Gun Place, Wapping, very small one-bedroom flats were costing £115,000 in 1986. Penthouses will range up to £350,000. Riverside apartments which sold originally for £70,000 are now changing hands for £135,000. (© Peter Ambrose 1986)*

prices must come down', 'more government grants', 'larger sites needed', and so on. If the GLCs policies can be seen, as they often are, as a blueprint for those of a future Labour government it is quite likely that the LDDC's housing inducement policies could be more widely adopted as an aid to privatization by present and future rightist governments.

Local residents' interests

In an area with a large and diverse population, and more than its fair share of individualists, it would be foolish to assert that all local residents want the same outcome from the redevelopment process. Docklands politics are extremely complex. There are old-style 'labourist' party faithfuls, younger and more militant left-wingers on the councils, strong women's representation, church-based and ethnic pressure groups and a continuing presence of organized labour rooted in the traditional industries of the area. On many issues the diversity of views is as broad as it could possibly be. Stolport, for example, split local opinion into mutually antagonistic camps. Despite this, there are a number of issues on which a very high proportion of local people are agreed, and on most of them the local opinion is diametrically opposed to the strategies of the LDDC (see Figure 8.6). Innumerable documents outlining local

Figure 8.6   *Local opinion is often diametrically opposed to the strategies of the LDDC.*
Source: The Guardian, *25 January 1986.*

needs and preferences have been produced since the early 1970s. This characterization of local interests will be based on three of them.

In March 1982 the Joint Docklands Action Group (JDAG) produced a paper called 'The 2nd East End Blitz'. It drew attention to the severe housing problems of Newham borough which stemmed partly from the failure of the 1960s tower blocks to provide suitable, or even safe, accommodation. It recalled that the Greater London Development Plan and the London Docklands Strategic Plan (both 1976) had specified that the overriding priority was for local authority rented housing with gardens. The rents would need to be geared to take account of 'the broad distribution of incomes' in the area. By 1981, however, the borough's housing programme was well behind schedule as a direct result of reductions in central government funding. Despite this, a start had been made with the proposed scheme for the redevelopment of the Cyprus area. A total of 1631 units were scheduled, some for special needs groups such as the elderly. Of these, 56 per cent were to be public rented units. The land had been cleared and prepared for this scheme by the borough, and some service facilities were already provided.

The LDDC housing strategy is, as has been shown, sharply different. Very quickly the remainder of the Cyprus site was 'vested' by the corporation and made available to volume housebuilders including Barratt's and Wimpey. Planning consents for speculative housing were granted within 20 days following only token consultation with Newham Borough (which has statutory responsibility, as a housing authority, to provide for the housing needs of residents). The borough made it clear that this rapid switch towards private housing constituted 'a critical hazard to the Council's housing strategy'. This was, if anything, to put it mildly since this particular vesting operation, and others that followed, have in fact almost totally sabotaged the authority's building programme. As a result of various central government policies, they are left with little land and little money with which to build.

The question of access to the new housing is crucial because a change in promotion methods would be of little consequence if prices to the users remained the same. The familiar claims were made by the LDDC that the houses being built were 'low cost', 'a good bargain' and 'readily accessible to local people in terms of price'. The JDAG paper simply refutes the latter point. Given the price levels and the current mortgage interest rates, households would need to have annual incomes of between £10,000 and £14,000 to buy even the cheapest houses on offer (which were, in any event, *very* small and referred to locally as 'Heseltine's hutches'). But the 1981 New Earnings Survey shows that fewer than 10 per cent of Newham residents actually have incomes of this level. It is reasonable to conclude that the other 90 per cent of local residents, and especially those in poor housing who would have been rehoused by Newham's Cyprus scheme, have interests that are totally opposed to those of the LDDC and the volume housebuilders.

A second relevant document on which to base an assessment of residents' interests is the 'The People's Charter for Docklands', drawn up in April 1984 and carried up-river to Westminster by an armada of boats (see Figure 8.7). This was produced following consultation in all the dockland boroughs with a total of 123 local groups. On this basis it can safely be regarded as expressing the opinions of a wide cross-section of residents. The Charter makes five main points. It calls for a return to participatory democracy with a reversion of power from the LDDC to the elected councils. It also urges more public expenditure on housing, especially low-rental council houses with gardens; more government support for *existing* industry and retraining schemes; more public transport facilities to connect the various parts of docklands with each other (rather than just the new housing to the City); and the restoration of acceptable levels of health, education and social service provision. Other requirements are for better local shopping facilities, which are not always met by the large superstores, more all-day childcare facilities and better recreational and open-space provision. The Charter is absolutely clear that among developments *not* wanted are more offices, tourist 'gimmicks', luxury housing, private hospitals and Stolport. The contrast with the intentions of the LDDC is again striking.

The third document is 'The People's Plan for the Royal Docks', produced in 1983 for the Stolport Inquiry. The plan makes clear that Stolport and its safety zone 'will neutralise much land and prevent alternatives'. Newham residents do not want to be 'porters and lavatory attendants for passing businessmen'. In several detailed sections the plan calls for the regeneration of dock activities such as boat construction and repair, and for investment in facilities to handle certain kinds of freight (for example, commodities not

The People's Charter for Docklands

Throughout Docklands there is a growing sense of frustration. Local people know what they need for their areas, but no-one will listen.

To make the decision-makers listen, community groups throughout Docklands decided that a People's Charter should be drawn up by the local community themselves. The Charter would then be taken on an armada of boats from docklands up the river to Westminster and presented to Docklands MP's and to the Prime Minister.

The People's Armada took place on Tuesday April 17, 1984, and this is the Charter it carried. It sets out what local people want and need. These demands must be met. Only if they are will Docklands have a _real_ future, one that benefits the people already living there.

APRIL 1984

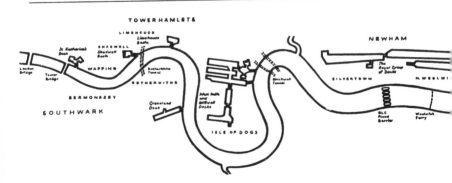

Figure 8.7   *The People's Charter was drawn up following consultation with 123 local community groups. It calls for a return to local democracy and increased spending on local housing and transport facilities.*

normally containerized such as scrap metal and building materials). It points out that there are actually seventy companies carrying out dock-related activities and that half of these have been attracted in the last five years. There is provision for better local shopping facilities since a combination of low car ownership rates, an ageing population and poor public transport means that superstore provision does not meet all needs. Other sections of the plan call for better recreational and sports facilities (for example, by using the enormous Shed 4 on the Victoria Dock), better linkages between the scattered communities especially in south Newham, better childcare facilities, a garden centre and a zone for co-operative production enterprises. The plan is carefully related to the pattern of land available in the Royal Docks area.

Political difficulties aside, the key problem is of course funding, as those who prepared the plan well recognize. It would be futile to look for private sector investment for many of these activities because, in this area and at this time, they would not provide a competitive return on funds invested. Three possible sources of funds were identified: the Greater London Enterprise Board (which in its present form is hardly likely to survive the GLC), the EEC Social Fund and the government. The last idea is clearly at present an ironic joke although, as the Plan points out, the Treasury is willing enough to provide £58 million (in the year in question) to the LDDC to attract and promote a whole series of developments which most people expressly do *not* want. The problem for the Plan, and for the docklands as a whole, is how to achieve, if not socialism, then at least some semblance of local participatory democracy as a small island in an increasingly centralist and capitalist sea.

Local planning interests

The local planning authorities, in this case the GLC and the five boroughs most concerned with docklands, have statutory responsibility for preparing plans for the area. As we have seen, the conflicting interests they must seek to reconcile and the economic and land reclamation problems they face would have made the task an extremely difficult one even given goodwill and financial support from central government. In fact both these have been virtually withdrawn and a central agency has been imposed with all the alien characteristics set out earlier in the chapter. Specifically, the LDDC is empowered to draw up its own 'planning frameworks' (described by local planners as simply development briefs) which do not require public consultation. It has acquired development control powers. It has also expropriated most of the landbank of several of the boroughs. In these circumstances the time and energy devoted by local planners to the preparation of statutory plans may well have little effect in terms of outcomes. Nevertheless, it is important to note the intentions of the statutory plan-makers in order to grasp the full dimensions of the conflict.

There has been a long series of plans for docklands. The idealistic intentions of the Abercrombie era were reviewed earlier in the chapter. By 1976, when the full nature of the problems and opportunities had become apparent, the Docklands Joint Committee had prepared the London Docklands Strategic Plan which, although outside the legal planning framework, had been drawn up after 'searching analysis and criticism by people and organizations throughout Docklands and beyond'. The aim was to provide a 'clear, guiding framework' for subsequent local statutory plans. The basic philosophy of the plan was 'to redress the housing, social, employment/economic and communications deficiencies of the Docklands area'. It was, therefore, specifically about local needs and aspirations.

It aimed, among much else, to arrest and reverse the population loss, to promote non-containerized dock activity and associated industry, to provide better local services and to build upon and link up existing communities. Given that much of the housing was nearly obsolete, and that some of the more recent additions were in a unacceptable form, a large-scale housing drive was envisaged. A move towards more variety in tenure was recognized as locally desirable but because of land preparation costs and high interest rates it was clearly seen that private housing was for the moment 'beyond the financial grasp of all but a minority'. (It was pointed out that in 1974 15 per cent of the docklands population claimed welfare benefits compared to the Greater London average of 5 per cent). The emphasis, therefore, should be on local authority plus a variety of 'mid-tenure' housing – housing associations, equity sharing, co-ownership schemes, and so on.

The implementation of the Plan was envisaged by the early 1990s. Over the intervening period it was expected that a total public expenditure of £1138 million would be required (at 1975 prices) and that this could be achieved by a switch of only 2 per cent in national local authority expenditure. An additional investment of £600 million from private sources was also anticipated, so that the overall public–private balance would be of the order of 2:1. This is radically different from current philosophies which envisage 'leverage ratios' of 4:1 or 5:1 with the minimum possible public expenditure as the 'pump-primer' to attract private funds. The inability of the local authorities concerned to keep to the LDSP development programme over the ensuing five years up to the initiation of the LDDC in 1981 has been widely held to be a 'failure'. In this context it is crucially important to recognize the savage government cuts, and the sharply falling rate income, which severely curtailed the capacity of the boroughs to carry out housing and development programmes.

In the planning framework provided by the LDSP Newham produced the Beckton District Plan early in 1980. This dealt with the area north of the Royal Docks where the land was owned primarily by the borough and by several utilities including the British Gas Corporation. There was still some optimism about because the introduction claimed that 'Beckton now stands ready to relieve this inner city area of many of its problems'. The Plan 'seeks to regenerate Newham's docks, industries, commerce and communities'. In stark contrast to subsequent LDDC policy 'existing residents have a high priority'. On the reasonable assumption that the land it owned and had proposed for building would actually be retained, the borough envisaged a massive housing programme with 50 per cent for public renting (all low rise with access to gardens), 30 per cent 'mid-tenure', and the rest private. Five new communities of 4000–6000 people were planned on design principles that envisaged a hierarchy of groups, clusters, neighbourhoods and communities, each with carefully matched recreational and local services. Open space was envisaged at the rate of 1.8 hectares per 1000 residents – well in line with established planning standards. The economic emphasis was to be on manufacturing industry with specific assistance for local firms. An extension of the Jubilee Line, which had the backing of the GLC, was to provide better access to central London. The implementation of the Plan was expected to take thirteen years and to cost a total of £214 million (at 1977 prices). The source of this was expected to be £146 million public and £68 million private, a ratio of over 2:1 in favour of public investment. The Plan made reference to the public consultation procedures that had been carried out and added that it was import to recognize 'a background of rising expectations on the part of the public to be consulted and involved in planning decisions'.

It would be wearisome to detail the provisions, and the unease, of the other statutory local plans that have appeared since 1980. For example, the Tower Hamlets Borough Plan of 1983 disagrees with much that was by then emerging as LDDC policy and, in particular, was opposed to the Enterprise Zone strategy, as managed by the corporation. The local planners believed that the effect was to divert attention and resources to this particular area without any account being taken of their plans for the borough as a whole. The neighbouring boroughs certainly share this view in relation to docklands as a whole. (See Figure 8.9.) The 1985 South Docklands Local Plan, produced by Newham following the usual extensive consultation with local groups and people, contains a number of proposals for filling part of the Victoria Dock so as to allow new housing to help link up with those living south of the Royals. It is ironic that Newham is now having to envisage major expenditure on site preparation having lost much of the housing land it had previously prepared as a result of 'vesting' operations by the LDDC. The housing intentions are for at least 60 per cent local authority housing in several of the proposed developments with over 70 per cent of the properties to have gardens. Other intentions include better public transport, pedestrian and cycle routes, a regular review of provision for groups with special needs such as the disabled, a wide range of environmental protection policies and recreational facilities 'to meet the needs of Newham's residents'. The point about local needs was well made with a clear message to the LDDC in the 'Preface' to the 1984 *Report of Survey* of the plan:

> There is a danger here that in the rush to promote and encourage large scale developments, the needs and aspirations of local people are set aside, 'for the time being', as having a less immediate or substantial claim on the future. History has shown that once set aside, local interests tend to be kept in the background.

The exasperation of many local planners and others was strongly expressed in a joint memorandum from the Docklands Consultative Committee to the Environment Secretary in August 1985

Estates Gazette, 21.9.85

DOCKLANDS ADVERSARIES IN HOUSING DEAL

BY ALEX CATALANO

The London Docklands Development Corporation and Southwark council have concluded an unprecedented profit-sharing agreement to redevelop and refurbish seven 1930s housing estates in the "Downtown area" of Rotherhithe, SE17.

Relations between the two have been strained since a change within the Labour administration in 1982, when the new council adoped a policy of non-co-operation with the LDDC.

Now, however, Southwark has agreed to sell seven estates to the LDDC containing about 500 flats, many of which are empty. The council will lease back five of these — the Amos Estate, 406-438 Rotherhithe Street, Acorn Walk, Bryan House and Silver Walk — and rehouse the residents. As the estates are vacated, they will be handed over to the LDDC.

The LDDC intends to sell some of the estates to developers or housing associations for refurbishment. Those that are in a very bad state will be demolished and the land sold for new housing. The net profits from the LDDC's sales will be split equally between it and Southwark.

The exact price that Southwark will get for the estates is yet to be agreed, but it will be at least £3m. Southwark will use these funds to refurbish 250 flats on the Redriff Estate in Downtown and neighbouring parts of Barnards Wharf, Commercial Pier Wharf and Greenland Wharf.

An earlier agreement between Southwark and the LDDC was rescinded by the council in 1982. According to this deal, Southwark would have sold the seven estates to the LDDC along with the Redriff Estate and purchased 550 homes in Surrey Docks from the corporation.

These were earmarked for tenants of the Downtown estates. For its part, the LDDC intended to demolish and redevelop the Southwark estates.

A High Court case, initiated by the LDDC, was due to begin earlier this year, but after negotiations, Southwark and the LDDC agreed the new formula.

Figure 8.8   *The docklands boroughs, beset with many social problems and hampered by lack of central funding, have sometimes needed to adopt a philosophy of 'if you can't beat them, join them'.*

(Docklands Consultative Committee, 1985). This pointed out that the LDDC was, in effect, carrying out an alternative, non-statutory planning process based on very limited and selective consultation with local people. The corporation's policies were in clear conflict with local planning intentions. There was an evident drive to attract almost any form of private investment, especially large-scale office schemes which bore little relation to the needs of local unemployed people. As part of this drive, local industry and people were being squeezed out by increases in the price of local land and housing. The LDDC's approach was 'secretive and speculative'. Meetings of the board were closed to the public and no agenda or minutes were available. The corporation was therefore not subject to proper public scrutiny and, unlike local authorities, it could complete deals with developers before members of the public had any chance to put an opinion. As an example of the cynical approach to local boroughs, reference was made to a particular site which Southwark had originally bought for £653,000 which was 'vested' (for an unknown sum) by the LDDC and then offered back to the borough (one of the poorest in London) for £2.8 million. As a final criticism the memorandum referred to the very high administrative, publicity and management costs of the LDDC (scheduled to rise to 24 per cent of total budget).

The GLC planners, predictably, have very little in common with

---

Construction News, 3.10.85

DOCKLAND SNUB TO DELEGATION

The London Docklands Development Corporation snubbed the body representing the five Docklands boroughs which tried to present a detailed memorandum last week.

The Docklands Consultative Committee, along with Docklands MPs Nigel Spearing, Ian Mikardo, Peter Shore and Simon Hughes arrived at the LDDC offices to present the document, which calls for reforms in the way the corporation works, but there was no member or senior officer of the LDDC to receive them.

The deputation said it had informed the LDDC exactly when it would be arriving. George Nicholson, who chairs the Docklands Consultative Committee, said the committee would be sending the corporation a strongly worded letter of protest.

"This attitude by the LDDC plus their callous disregard for local plans and needs are the key issues in the memorandum," he said.

Figure 8.9   *The LDDC has been less than welcoming to democratically elected representatives seeking to present views widely held in the area.*

the LDDC. Papers given at their conference on 'The Future of London' in mid-1985 spelled out a totally different 'needs-led' philosophy of planning. The revised Greater London Development Plan of 1984 brought new dimensions to plan-making by stressing the need to develop policies specifically geared to furthering equal opportunities, ecological protection and community development. It considered at length the need to reconcile private property rights with the achievement of social goals, and it argued that this must involve public sector agencies as developers. To achieve this it would set up Planning Action Zones where all land would be registered and there would be a public right to buy at existing use values. Taxation would occur not just at the point of development or value realization, but during the life of existing buildings and at a rate reflecting the highest permitted use of that site. The proposals stressed the need for local control of the planning process, for example, in the declaration of Planning Action Zones, and a needs-related planning strategy that necessarily considered the requirements of particular groups such as women and the elderly. The overall intention was to produce a land development regulation system that was open, democratically accountable, efficient at revenue-raising and capable of influencing to some extent the evolution of the employment profile in local areas. Whether these aims can be achieved, even given the strongest central government support, in an era of the growing internationalization of capital is very much open to question.

There is no real need, at the end of this chapter, to present specific case studies in order to demonstrate that the post-1947 planning system has been effectively bypassed in docklands since 1981. The area has been 'taken into care' by central government because its natural parents, the local boroughs, were too leftish, too committed to local needs and too sensitive to local feelings to carry out the kind of private sector led redevelopment strategy the Thatcher government had in mind. The pattern of redevelopment, the opportunistic philosophy and the divergence from democratically produced plans in almost every important respect has been demonstrated. However well or badly the crude rate of development between 1981 and 1985 may compare to the rate that would have occurred without the LDDC (and this is not knowable), there is no doubt at all that the *content* of development does not suit the generality of local housing and employment needs. There is no doubt either that the corporation has engineered a huge public sector subsidy to the private development industry. The link has been virtually cut between a powerful planning agency and the local people who have a vital and legitimate interest in the workings of that agency. When the chance exists that a proposal for a 10-million sq. ft mixed commercial development in the Isle of Dogs with three 850-ft skyscrapers can be approved after a two-week public consultation period, then 'democratic planning' has been reduced to a charade.

This situation does not reflect a failure of public planning, because local authority planners would no doubt be united against this scheme unless proper planning criteria concerning visual intrusion and balanced growth were observed – which at present they are clearly not. Neither is it, strictly speaking, a failure of democracy because the LDDC can reasonably argue that they are an arm of a government democratically elected in 1979 and re-elected in 1983. The crux of the matter lies in the mismatch between clearly and democratically expressed *local* needs and the 'new right' government's perception of *national* needs. There is no simple answer to this dilemma and those committed to achieving

better living standards for lower-income people living in docklands can only work for a change in the total configuration of forces at work in the area.

PART IV
Taking stock

Achievements, shortcomings and the future

Town and Country Planning formed a part of the 'welfare' offer made during a period of grave national crises in the early 1940s. Necessarily it held out the morale-boosting vision of better things to come after the war – better housing, schools and factories, more open space, an end to the slums, and so on. But the war was, in the end, as much about the defence of British capitalism as anything else and it would be unrealistic to expect that any fundamental changes would have resulted from it (although as Chapter 2 shows, observers as acute as Nicolson and Macmillan expected changes of this magnitude).

The critical social theorist Claus Offe, in a short but perceptive paper (Offe, 1972), has set out a number of crucial points about welfare offers in advanced capitalist systems and they help to structure the analysis of the impact of land use planning over the past four decades. They include the following:

1 The welfare state bears no resemblance to what Marxist theorists would call a revolutionary process, that is, basic structural change.

In terms of benefit to the public at large, the achievements of planning have been limited and tactical. To adopt the famous Titanic analogy, the effect has been to produce a pleasing rearrangement of the deckchairs rather than to save the ship. More order has been brought to the visual and functional pattern of land development (see Hall et al., 1973). This is no mean achievement. If we can visualize the continuance of the unregulated growth pattern of the 1930s through the ensuing half-century to the present day, the benefits become apparent. Cities would have expanded in a piecemeal fashion at their peripheries, neutralizing vast amounts of agricultural and amenity land by 'ribbon' development. The arrangement of uses within cities, in the absence of zoning to separate out mutually conflicting activities, would have produced unpleasant and dangerously polluted environments for far more people than currently suffer these conditions. The South Downs would be covered to their smoothly moulded summits in bungaloid growth and the Yorkshire Dales would be filled with a series of linear weekend cottage developments. Historic urban settings would be hemmed in with Manhattan-type tower blocks (as the Mansion House recently very nearly was) and the St Paul's site might have been redeveloped, without benefit of a Public Inquiry, as a new commercial/retailing complex. The avoidance of all these has been a general gain in terms of environmental protection.

But this may be where the general benefits end and the sectional benefits begin. Offe continues:

2. Although the term 'welfare' connotes a paternalistic solicitude by the state on behalf of the lower classes, corporate business enterprises derive far greater proportionate benefits.

This argument could be followed through in terms of food subsidy policies (Body, 1982), health service expenditure or indeed housing subsidies. But for the present the focus is on planning. The planning system serves the interests it seeks to regulate in a number of ways. First, and probably most irritatingly to planners, it acts as a scapegoat. If tower blocks collapse or a new city centre shopping mall gets vandalized or the housing waiting-list lengthens or the reduction of transport services isolates an estate, the blame is often laid at the planners' door. If some vast white elephant such as the Brighton Marina fails to make a return on investment, this too is somehow the planners' fault. There is, in short, a great confusion in the minds of the public and media commentators (many of whom should know better) about what professional planners actually *do* and the limits of their capability to affect events. Very often a large scheme, with its own powerful commercially based momentum, has gone ahead with local council approval despite the best efforts of the authority's planning staff to warn against it. This has not prevented local residents from blaming 'the planners'. This tendency is not merely irritating; it reflects a belief that local authority planners have decisive power (which many of them probably wish they had) when dealing with promoters of large developments. Since the developers of many big schemes are multinational in scope, and have the backing of powerful financial interests, often protected by the state, this belief is wide of the mark. (See Figure 9.1.) It is also politically disabling, in that community opposition may be wrongly targeted.

The planning system also serves the interests of the development industry by collating information in a way that has commercial value. Planning officers spend a lot of time assessing, for example, the retail shopping floorspace requirements to serve the needs of proposed residential developments of given size. The retail and service centres to serve these needs are rarely carried out by public sector initiative. Instead the information is incorporated in statutory plans and an area of land is zoned in some suitably accessible location. The field is then clear for developers to prepare a scheme of appropriate size, working to the local authority's brief, and to seek planning consent. They can feel confident that the authority will not allow two competing (and expensive) schemes to go ahead if all the planning calculations show that the spending power in the locality will support only one profitable scheme. In other words, the optimism that led mid-nineteenth-century railway entrepreneurs to build several competing lines, all but one of which were doomed to fail, is guarded against and the 'self-destruct' tendencies endemic in speculative activities such as land development are averted.

This information-centralizing role works also at a broader scale. One of the main aims of structure planning and national transport planning is to identify those areas best suited for such developments as the M25 motorway around London. These planning intentions reflect a careful analysis of transport, employment, amenity and infrastructural constraints and opportunities. Once a preferred development or motorway pattern has been worked out, it can be (or it used to be) assumed that future planning decisions will be consistent with it. Therefore, those who have earliest access to this conveniently centralized and reliable information, and those who see its implications most fully, will be those best placed to benefit in various ways, for example, by negotiating options to purchase land likely to be favoured for development. Structure Plans may not arouse much general interest, but they are usually carefully examined by land investors and developers.

Figure 9.1 (above and right)   *In the optimistic days of the 1950s and 1960s, planning was still able to present itself as a force for enlightened change (above). By 1985 (right), the advice was to seek to influence events by moving to the private sector. Some senior planners have concluded, perhaps belatedly, that real power rests with multinational private capital.*
Source: Network, June 1985

The current state of the art

The experience of over half a century of planning debate has produced a vast, if uneven, body of literature. A large number of ideas has been developed and tested, and a lot of people are now dedicated to the general idea of some enlightened regulation of land development. No matter what governments of the right may try to do, this experience, commitment and set of ideas will not go away. Virtually every advanced capitalist country has some kind of system for regulating land development, often based on the British experience. Any serious attempt to remove development control (which in itself must depend on prior plan-making) would be met by solid resistance from an alliance ranging from socialists on the left to the Tory squirarchy on the right. Moreover, the land development industry, for the reasons suggested, would probably not favour much more deregulation either. Certainly interests who have invested heavily in specific sites for their 'hope value' would not be happy to see most of this value evaporate following a widespread relaxation of development control.

But the analysis of power relationships in much of the planning literature is seriously deficient. The dynamic imperatives of capital

---

Network, June 1985

GO PRIVATE CALL TO POWERLESS PLANNERS

Planners are becoming increasingly powerless to deal with the problems of the inner cities and declining regions like Greater Manchester, a gathering of planners was told.

Leading planners, Ray Green and David Hall were speaking at a joint meeting of the North-West Branch of the Royal Town Planning Institute and the North-West Planning Forum of the Town and Country Planning Association, at County Hall, Piccadilly, Manchester.

Ray Green of the RTPI, said that real power lay increasingly with those in commerce and industry who made decisions about investment. Their interests were predominantly global or continental. They were not concerned with the problem of inner cities or mining communities.

Mr Green, who is City Planning Officer for Exeter, said: 'If planners are to have any influence, it may be necessary for more of them to find work in private industry. At present 85 per cent of professional planners work in local government where they're not having much effect.'

accumulation, which stem from the private ownership or control of land, finance and construction resources are often seriously undervalued or left unrelated to the analysis. Yet some of these private interests are under the close protection of government and in an emergency may be given far more state help than the planning system that seeks to regulate them. For example, the banking system was helped out of difficulties caused by its own over-impetuous behaviour in 1973–4 and the housebuilding industry is heavily favoured over the planning system at the moment (see Chapters 7 and 8) because it is the delivery agent for higher rates of owner-occupancy – a paramount priority of government. Similarly, in view of the central role the financial institutions have gained in post-retirement welfare provision, the vast sums they invest in property can hardly be regarded as risk capital. If it looked as if some dramatic change in market conditions were about to lead to major losses of institutional funds, steps would be taken to adjust these market conditions (probably by fiscal concession) to limit the risk. Planning, therefore, cannot properly be regarded as some isolated, Olympian force. It needs to be seen as part of a constellation of forces, and its regulatory power assessed in this context.

A second failure of analysis stems partly from the particular historic tradition from which modern British planning emerged. Those who sought to improve urban conditions in the late nineteenth century had at the top of their agenda issues of aesthetics, environmental conditions and the dreaming up of land use layouts calculated to achieve more comfortable lifestyles. Certainly the seminal work of Ebenezer Howard and Patrick Geddes was of this nature and led to the very significant notions of garden cities and green belts. But the founding fathers could well have been motivated instead by some other aims, for example, to maximize national economic performance and industrial efficiency. Certainly these latter concerns were at least as important as aesthetics to Salt, Cadbury, Lever and the other 'philanthropic' town-makers of the late nineteenth century. The point is that had the originating concern of planning been with production process rather than built form, with economic efficiency rather than neat environment, then the legal and administrative planning system that emerged in 1947 might have avoided one of its main shortcomings – it might have focused more centrally on seeking to regulate the land development accumulation process itself rather than trying to control events by specifying a preferred land use output. The tail, in other words, would not have been expected to wag the dog.

The vital difference between these two strategies became very apparent in the early 1950s. Uthwatt and the postwar Labour government had thought in terms of taking land speculation out of the development process, using the public sector as the main initiator of development and controlling, by a licensing system, the total amount and mix of construction in any given year. Thus the development industry would stand in a largely contractual relationship to the state and would take its profit solely in construction activity. The key role of development promotion, and the control of resources, would remain with the state. But this was too rapid a move from the historic norm to be tolerated by private interests, except temporarily and in a situation of national crises. By the early 1950s most of the inhibitions to the resumption of speculative dealing in land, and all the constraints on the way input materials could be used, were removed. The private sector rapidly regained its role as the main promoter of development. Planning, the regulatory force, was left with little more than a limited power, via plan-making, to indicate what it would like to see happening and with one main weapon to achieve its preferred pattern: the power to say no to development proposals which were not in line with planning intentions. The subsequent provision under section 52 of the 1971 Town and Country Planning Act to negotiate some 'planning gain' out of the developer (see Loughlin, 1981) has hardly changed the basic balance of power.

The planning education literature has not, until quite recently, seen the full implications of this enforced retreat from the control of promotion and resources to the control only of use. One implication is the limitation of the agenda. As Cooke (1983) has pointed out, planning emphasizes technical expertise and rationality. The constant process of negotiation between planner and developer is normally carried out on the safe, technically complicated, terrain provided by current, use-dominated, planning legislation. This suits the developer very well. He cannot be asked at a public inquiry such simple, but crucial, questions as 'whose money are you using?' or 'how much profit do you expect to make?' These would normally be held to be 'not relevant planning matters'. Yet they are matters of legitimate concern to the planners and

---

The Observer, 9.2.86

TRAFALGAR ON MEPC's TRAIL

EXCLUSIVE
BY MELVYN MARCKUS, CITY EDITOR

Trafalgar House, the £1.07 billion industrial conglomerate led by Sir Nigel Broackes, is reliably understood to be considering a near £1 billion take-over bid for MEPC, Britain's second largest property company.

Trafalgar's directors have no intention of launching a hostile take-over bid for MEPC, but the possibility of achieving an agreed deal has been under consideration for several weeks.

Speculative activity on the London Stock Exchange on Friday raised MEPC's share price by 10p to 298p at which price the company is capitalised at some £717 million.

Eric Parker, chief executive of Trafalgar House, said yesterday: 'I would rather not comment.'

MEPC's managing director, Christopher Benson, succeeded Broackes as chairman of the London Docklands Development Corporation in 1984.

Trafalgar has been poised to launch a major expansion move ever since its abortive attempt to take-over P&O in 1984.

Trafalgar's interests in property and construction would blend with MEPC's property portfolio which is extensive in the US and Australia.

Benson is credited with spearheading MEPC's recovery in the wake of the 1973-74 secondary banking and property crash. The ultimate accolade came recently when Standard & Poors awarded the company an 'A' rating.

Broackes, for his part, created Trafalgar via a series of shrewd acquisitions — Trollope & Colls and Cunard and The Ritz and Beaverbrook Newspapers — and his refusal to resume the battle for P & O, despite a Monopolies Commission clearance, bears witness to his caution.

By its predatory nature Trafalgar is understood to be considering several takeover options but MEPC is clearly high on the list.

Trafalgar's pre-tax profits for the year to end-September last rose from £113 million to £142 million on turnover up from £1.6 billion to close on £2 billion. MEPC's profits for 1984-85 were struck at £51.6 million — up from £45.2 million.

Figure 9.2 *Britain's largest conglomerate considers a takeover bid for Britain's second largest property company – a striking example of capitalist concentration of power. Broackes was the first Chairman of the London Docklands Development Corporation and Benson the second. Neither is likely to miss opportunities arising from massive government investment in the regeneration of docklands.*

residents of the area in which the developer is working. Without open discussion of these issues it is impossible to make a realistic assessment of the distribution of benefits and costs arising from a development or to insist on possible alternative schemes. The discussion, in other words, is safely confined to matters technical rather than political.

The planning system's lack of power to affect events stems only partly from the particular circumstances of its emergence. Probably more important are several fundamental changes that have occurred in the organization and operation of capitalist production since 1945. The multinationals have emerged as a dominant force in the capitalist world, capturing an ever increasing share of total production (see Figure 9.2). A land use regulation system that has remained at the scale of the city or county can hardly hope to 'control', or even meaningfully negotiate with, an industrial corporation capable of dividing its activities between areas according to its assessment of labour costs and tax structures (see Morgan and Sayer, 1983). The production strategy of large corporations, especially in highly technical fields, may now require research and long-term planning to be located in a 'heartland' area such as 'Silicon Valley' in California. Divisional management and more skilled production processes might occur in areas such as Singapore with its compliant labourforce partly disciplined by, and cheaply reproduced by, a heavily state-organized housing system. The less skilled, more labour-intensive production may be located in an area with excess labour, low wages and stable politics such as South Korea.

This new global production economy is light-years away from the industrial process of the 1930s when there were very few multinationals. Yet the 1947 system was a product of that prewar world. It may still be fighting a battle in prewar terms, hoping that simply to provide land for 'hi-tech' industrial estates will somehow attract lucrative 'front-end' electronic activity and jobs with a wide range of skill requirements. This is overoptimistic. By 1983 it was reported (*Guardian*, 5 January 1983) that between thirty and forty local authorities were setting up 'science parks' in the hope of becoming silicon valleys. But there is far too little investment of this kind to go round. When Japanese or American firms do consider locations in Britain for high-technology activities, they are often thinking far more of convenience of access to the EEC market than of the zoning policies set out in local authority plans. Fiscal incentives or well-developed infrastructure may interest them but not the general statements of good intent often made in Structure

Plans. The evolving configuration of industrial activity is also affected by decisions made by public authorities about the placing of defence contracts, the location of major airports, the alignment of motorways and the forward capital investment programmes of the water, gas and electricity utilities. The Structure Plan team may have little decisive power over these agencies and in some cases no prior knowledge of their decisions.

The way forward

It may seem hardly appropriate at present even to think about ways forward. Currently much of the planning profession's energy is devoted to survival. Given the aggressively market-orientated stance of governments on both sides of the Atlantic, and the moves towards the deregulation of land development evident from Chapters 7 and 8, the planning system is not in a strong position to be pressing demands. It would, therefore, be totally unrealistic to advocate elaborate theoretical ways of achieving some egalitarian millennium via land development reforms. Instead it looks much more likely, should rightist government continue, that the LDDC-type, market-led solution may be applied to situations elsewhere – although probably not with the same level of central funding.

Political philosophies do, however, come and go and one credible scenario is that a future government of the centre or left will wish to return to the interventionary stance of most British governments since the war. This may be because the effects of deregulation are judged to be economically counter-productive and socially divisive, which is often clearly true, or because too much environmental damage is being done. It is very unlikely that there will be a crisis on the scale of 1940–2 to trigger off any Uthwatt-type prescription. In fact the trustee nature of the institutional finance now so closely bound up with property investment profitability makes such moves unthinkable. Constructive proposals can, however, be made both for planning education and for the broad strategies that might be adopted by any future government with planning as a serious item on its agenda.

In terms of education there needs to be far more inducement in the formal secondary and further education syllabus to encourage young people to think critically about the political economy of the built environment. This environment is a direct visual manifestation of the power relations that produced it. Commerce-dominated city centres, car-dominated movement and shopping, market-determined segregation of different ethnic and income groups, and appalling dereliction of much of the urban fabric, have become the hallmarks of capitalist land development. In total contrast, mixed-use city centres combining housing, recreation and work space, efficient and energy-conserving public transport, greater intermixing of higher- and lower-status housing and a high priority for investment in the condition of the stock is a product of socialist city management. These connections between invisible forces and visible outcomes are easily made by direct observation and could be opened up much more for analysis and discussion were it not for the inhibitions imposed for curricular inertia, disciplinary boundaries outdated by events, and strict control of the political content in the educational agenda. In other words, these varied development characteristics, and the structural reasons for the differences, are hardly likely to feature on a Geography A-level syllabus. But everybody has to live in an environment fashioned by the land development industry so it seems reasonable to make the workings of this industry a high-priority issue in the general education syllabus rather than to tolerate the reproduction, generation by generation, of the same old menu of established, uncritical 'subjects', none of which have land development as a central concern.

There are ways, too, in which professional training for planners can be strengthened. Planning, and the present piecemeal removal of it in the interests of powerful minority groups, is a wealth-redistributive mechanism. Structure Plans and Local Plans create new maps of land value, producing vast extra wealth for some landowners and none for others:

> The first impact of a planning system on the price of land for development is to increase the value of the land that has received permission. (Department of the Environment, 1976)

Particular transport strategies confer patterns of advantage and disadvantage. The spatial configuration of retail provision reduces prices (including travel costs) for some and increases them for others. In the greenfield arena those who own or have speculated in land with consent for housing development can become million-aires overnight. This windfall gain is generated for them partly out of the lifetime earnings of those who purchase the housing and partly from general taxation, via the tax concession to purchasers which serves to elevate house prices:

> Fiscal policies which should have been designed to minimise price increases in fact encouraged them. In areas of high demand the benefits of all the unnecessary fiscal incentives to owner-occupation were passed straight on to the landowners. (Britton, 1965)

There they join another set of unnecessary fiscal incentives – farming subsidies under the Common Agricultural Policy – which have enormously elevated the value of farmland. In the docklands arena the redistributive effects are more easily visualized. Most of the 40,000 local residents, especially those on low incomes, have lost out grievously by the demolition of the boroughs' low-cost rental housing programmes and the squeezing out of pre-existing jobs. The volume housebuilders have achieved profitable sales on land obtained at publicly subsidized prices and first purchasers of the housing, very few of them local people, have the confident expectation of personal capital gains.

There has been very little systematic assessment, even at professional level, of the redistributive consequences of planning (although see Radical Institute Group, 1976), largely because the measurement of the wealth shifts is extremely difficult. But it seems reasonable to assert that everyone is affected, to some degree, by their effects. In fact the redistributive consequences of planning might be as weighty and pervasive as the effects stemming from taxation of all kinds. But whereas most people can comprehend the significance of direct and indirect taxation, the impact of public intervention in land development is difficult to grasp. The suspicion must be, no matter what the founding fathers intended, that the distributive effects are consistently regressive. This is clearly a matter of legitimate concern to everyone and especially to practising planners. It is therefore vital that it is systematically dealt with on the planning curriculum, so that the serious assessment of redistributive effects can become a statutorily required part of the handling of any development application.

Analysis of distributive effects depends upon a clear understanding of capital accumulation processes and especially of the differences, on which planning law is silent, between the three main avenues of accumulation dealt with earlier in this book.

These are investment development, speculative housebuilding and contracting. Ideally all planners should have a good working knowledge of the way an entrepreneur's mind assesses opportunities in each of these fields, which financial interests are involved, how schemes are promoted and roughly what rate of profit is to be expected. The planner can then make a reasonable assessment of the commercial value of the development consent the entrepreneur is seeking, which at present often amounts to a licence to print money, and can enter into a realistic debate about the distribution of future benefits and profits. For example, it might make sense to ensure that a proportion of the development profits is fed back to the authority granting the consent and earmarked to cover the cost of rehousing those currently living on the site. The negotiation between the public agency and the developer should, in other words, have a strong financial and social content as well as a concern for such established 'planning' criteria as traffic generation and visual intrusion. The preconditions for this shift might have more to do with planning education than changes in planning law, although some new statutes would be required.

It follows from the analysis of Offe (1972) and other critical theorists that a future government of the centre or left, if seriously seeking an enlightened regeneration of planning, could not realistically seek to implement policies that were seen to be, or actually were, threatening to rates of capital accumulation. But this does not mean that nothing useful can be done. To reach this conclusion would be to ignore the experience of other European social democratic states (see Ambrose and Barlow, 1986). The British arrangements have two glaring defects — arguably for capitalist entrepreneur and planners alike: firstly, speculation in land occurs *before* it becomes an input to the construction process (see, for example, Davidson, 1975), and secondly, the amount of construction promoted each year fluctuates considerably and, because it is affected by many factors, unpredictably. A political party setting out to eradicate these defects would start with an important advantage. Very few electors, and not many people in the development industry, would defend either of these characteristics because the first benefits only a small handful of interests and the second benefits nobody.

These defects do not exist, certainly not to the same extent, in some states with a broadly similar political structure, perhaps most notably Sweden (Dickens *et al.*, 1985). Visitors from such countries, and from socialist states, regard the British system as perplexing – even bizarre. Expensive subsidies to house purchasers serve only to elevate house prices and then work through to elevate the bids made for development land. The housing consumers through whose pockets they pass believe *they* are the ultimate beneficiaries and this belief underpins a solid electoral force against reform. Simultaneously, tight zoning restrictions (now being relaxed but in an opportunist fashion) serve partly to further overheat the land market, make developable sites into speculative commodities and confer capricious patterns of benefit – now largely untaxed. The construction industry, faced with a notoriously unpredictable pattern of future demand, is understandably averse to the kind of investment in new materials and processes that would ensure better long-term profitability and more efficient production. It reacts instead with *ad hoc* innovations, sometimes inadequately researched and tested, and labour practices that are exploitative and short-sighted.

A set of policy proposals can be identified which might please critic and industry alike. They would need to be developed to meet the conditions of the 1980s and 1990s and not, as are the present arrangements, as a crisis response to the conditions of the 1930s. Late-twentieth-century capitalism is powerful and internationally organized but it faces apparently ever-deepening crises of demand instability. To ensure that construction capital produces the socially appropriate amount and mix of development – and produces it at access prices that suit the needs of all income levels – the state must either expropriate the whole sector, which is a totally unrealistic prospect, or generate the conditions in which the socially required output is privately produced with an attractive return on the funds invested. To maintain, on theoretical grounds, that this is impossible is to throw out the baby with the bathwater.

The key issues are land flow and effective demand for the finished product. The land-release problem could be solved in an efficient and equitable fashion by some variant of the Swedish practice (see Figure 9.3). All land for development should be acquired by elected public agencies at existing use value and then released to the building industry at a slightly higher price and with a substantial subsidy towards the cost of the construction on the site. If builders acquired land by other means, they would not

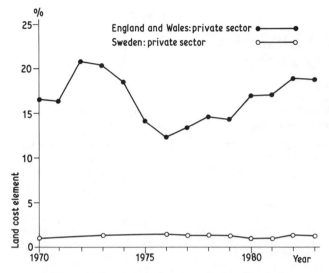

Figure 9.3 *The land cost element of private sector housing: Britain and Sweden, 1970–83. Swedish land regulation arrangements do not allow high and fluctuating prices for housing land, so the land price element in total housing production cost is minimal and speculation in land prior to construction is virtually impossible.*
Source: *Duncan (1986)*

receive the construction subsidy. The agencies, which would operate at some scale larger than the county, should also have planning powers and be responsible for ensuring an appropriate flow of land to meet rationally assessed future demand in the area. The planners would have much more direct control over the evolution of development and the land market would be firmly regulated because a self-financing public authority would control the price at which land is both acquired and released for construction. There would thus be no possibility of a speculative trade in sites prior to construction.

In the owner-occupied housing field, this policy should be complemented by the phased removal of the enormously expensive tax concession to the purchaser. In the British context 85 per cent or so of purchases are of second-hand houses. Subsidizing the price

GOVERNMENT SNUB FOR CANARY CRITICS

BY ROGER MILNE

The Government has rebuffed calls for a public inquiry into the £1.5bn plan to develop a financial centre at Canary Wharf in London's Docklands.

Faced with increasing pressure to call in the scheme, Environment Secretary Kenneth Baker told MPs on Tuesday that: "It would not be right to intervene."

The announcement was welcomed in public and in private by the London Docklands Development Corporation and the American consortium, fronted by affiliates of First Boston Inc and G Ware Travelstead.

Both parties hope to complete negotiations on a master building agreement by Christmas, with work on the first phase of the 10m-sq ft development starting in the spring.

But the scheme is not out of the woods yet. Objectors to the proposal, including a clutch of London councils, community organisations and amenity groups, are considering a legal challenge.

The consortium is insisting on firm commitments from the Government and the LDDC over crucial improvements to the transport infrastructure in Docklands before it will proceed with the project.

Not all these commitments have been settled yet and the consortium has made no secret of its intention to shift the project out of the UK, possibly to Frankfurt, if additional planning hurdles emerge.

Most of the 70-acre development is inside the Isle of Dogs Enterprise Zone and does not need conventional planning permission. The corporation gave its approval to the consortium's master plan this month.

This week's Government decision not to call in the scheme came after mounting pressure for a public inquiry. The calls had come from a spread of interests including the Royal Town Planning Institute, English Heritage, the Victorian Society and the Greater London Council.

The Royal Fine Art Commission was meeting, as Estates Gazette went to press, to consider the visual impact of the scheme — which includes provision for three office blocks each taller than London's Nat West Tower.

The developers have indicated that the height of the towers will depend on the decision of the occupiers. However, the height of the development may well have to be trimmed to safeguard flightpaths in and out of the Docklands' Stol-Port and to answer critics concerned over the visual impact of buildings across the Thames at Greenwich — the Royal Naval College, the National Maritime Museum and the Royal Observatory.

Figure 9.4 *The final nail in the coffin of participatory planning in Britain? 'It would not be right to intervene' – despite mounting pressure on all sides. The ultimate power relationships are revealed in the paragraph about possibly shifting the project to Frankfurt.*

of these existing properties is pointless and of no direct benefit either to the housebuilding industry or to purchasers. Part or all of the revenue gained by the phased removal of the concession should be used to finance the construction subsidy so as to stimulate new housebuilding, although it would be important to control the initial sale price. (The combined effect of these measures would be to reduce house prices substantially.) Similar land flow, subsidy and rent control procedures should apply to properties developed for investment. In this case the public agencies controlling planning and land supply should be technically equipped to negotiate leasing or sale agreements that provide a realistic return to the public purse, especially in relation to the future profits based on inflation in rent levels.

Instability in demand for the product is the other major problem. The situation is close to anarchic. The year-by-year fluctuation in effective demand for new houses reflects unpredictable variation in such factors as interest rates, the level of fiscal concession and the market share of savings (itself a variable quantity) cornered by the building societies. Similarly, no one knows from year to year how much construction business will be generated by public capital expenditure programmes in ensuing years. In current times, when a high proportion of construction capability is internationally owned and organized, the industry may well require longer-term assurances about the flow of future business in Britain before it invests more funds in the capital intensification programmes that are the prerequisites for greater efficiency. In the 1980s, as opposed to the 1930s, many firms are now capable of seeking overseas contracts (see Chapter 6) if fluctuating demand makes Britain an unattractive arena.

One solution is to work towards policies that produce a more assured flow of future business for the industry. Public capital expenditure needs both to be increased and to be worked out in five-year spending programmes to which high priority is given and on the basis of which longer-term construction agreements could be made between government and industry. This does imply a bi-partisan approach between the parties to the problem of environmental renewal. It is true that this is difficult to visualize in the present political climate, but it is also true that the present climate is exceptionally combative in the context of recent British history.

Some of these ideas are being implemented by the LDDC, but in a totally unacceptable way; no account is taken of the needs or views of residents, land deals are done in secret and no proper monitoring or public consultation about development preferences is possible. Any future British variant of the Swedish scheme must avoid these features. Instead the ultimate aims of the combination of policies proposed would be to achieve positive and democratically based planning, to neutralize land speculation, to end the festering conflict between central and local government, to ensure a predictable and investment-inducing flow of business for the construction industry, to promote better labour relations, and to regulate the prices and rents that govern access for purchasers and tenants. Although the negotiation about the 'deal' would no doubt be long and complex, there should in the end be some benefits here for almost all producers, planners and users of the built environment. There might also be the tools necessary to achieve some such answer as 'It recovered' to the question posed on the cover of this book.

References

Ambrose, P.J. (1976) *The Land Market and the Housing System*, Urban and Regional Studies Working Paper No. 3, University of Sussex.

Ambrose, P.J. and Barlow, J. (1986) *Housing Provision and Housebuilding in Western Europe: Increasing Expenditure, Decreasing Output*, Urban and Regional Studies Working Paper No. 50, University of Sussex.

Ambrose, P.J. and Colenutt, B. (1975) *The Property Machine*, Harmondsworth, Penguin.

Ashworth, W. (1954) *The Genesis of Modern British Town Planning*, London, Routledge & Kegan Paul.

Atkinson, A.B. (1974) *Unequal Shares*, rev. edn, London, Allen Lane.

Backwell, J. and Dickens, P. (1978) *Town Planning, Mass Loyalty and the Restructuring of Capital: The Origins of the 1947 Planning Legislation Revisited*, Urban and Regional Studies Working Paper No. 11, University of Sussex.

Bailey, R. (1985) *The Abolition of the Metropolitan Counties, a Denial of Civil Liberties*, London, Planning Aid Service.

Balchin, P.N. and Kieve, J.L. (1977) *Urban Land Economics*, London, Macmillan.

Ball, M. (1983) *Housing Policy and Economic Power*, London, Methuen.

Ball, M. and Cullen, A. (1980) *Mergers and Accumulation in the British Construction Industry*, Economics Discussion Paper 73, Birkbeck College, London.

Bank of England (1978) *The Lifeboat Operation*, F1 (78)55.

Banwell, H. (1964) *Placing and Management of Contracts for Building and Civil Engineering Work*, London, Ministry of Public Building and Works.

Barlow, J. (1985) *Landowners, Property Ownership and the Rural Locality*, Urban and Regional Studies Working Paper No. 41, University of Sussex.

Barlow, M. (1940) *Report of the Royal Commission on the Distribution of Industrial Population*, Cmd 6153, London, HMSO.

Barnett, J. (1982) *Inside the Treasury*, London, Deutsch.

Barrett, S., Boddy, M. and Stewart, M. (1979) *Implementation of the Community Land Scheme*, Occasional Paper 3, School of Advanced Urban Studies, University of Bristol.

Barrett, S. and Healey, P. (1985) *Land Policy: Problems and Alternatives*, Aldershot, Gower.

Barrett, S., Stewart, M. and Underwood, J. (1978) *The Land Market and Development Process: A Review of Research and Policy*, Occasional Paper 2, School of Advanced Urban Studies, University of Bristol.

Barrett, S. and Whitting, G. (1983) *Local Authorities and Land Supply*, Occasional Paper 10, School of Advanced Urban Studies, University of Bristol.

Bellman, H. (1928) *The Silent Revolution*, London, Methuen.

Bennett, R.J. (1982) *Central Grants to Local Government*, Cambridge, Cambridge University Press.

Blowers, A. (1980) *The Limits of Power: The Politics of Local Planning Policy*, Oxford, Pergamon.

Boddy, M. (1978) 'Community land scheme is dying of neglect', *Roof*, May.

Boddy, M. (1979) *Land, Property and Finance*, Working Paper 2, School of Advanced Urban Studies, University of Bristol.

Boddy, M. (1980) *The Building Societies*, London, Macmillan.

Boddy, M. and Fudge, C. (1981) *The Local State: Theory and Practice*, Working Paper 20, School of Advanced Urban Studies, University of Bristol.

Body, R. (1982) *Agriculture – the Triumph and the Shame*, London, Temple Smith.

Body, R. (1984) *Farming in the Clouds*, London, Temple Smith.

Briggs, A. (1963) *Victorian Cities*, London, Odhams.

Brittain, V. (1981) *England's Hour*, London, Futura.

Britton, W. (1965) *Public Control of Land Use*, Reading, College of Estate Management.

Bruton, M. and Gore, A. (1981) 'Vacant urban land', *The Planner*, 67/2, 34–5.

Burnett, J. (1978) *A Social History of Housing 1815–1970*, Newton Abbot, David & Charles.

Cadman, D. (1979) 'Private capital and the inner city', *Estates Gazette*, 249.

Cadman, D. (1984) 'Property finance in the UK in the post-war period', *Land Development Studies*, 1(2), 61–8.

Cadman, D. and Austin-Crowe, L. (1978), *Property Development*, London, Spon.

Calder, A. (1971) *The People's War*, London, Panther.

Cannadine, D. (1980) *Lords and Landlords: The Aristocracy and the Towns 1774–1967*, Leicester, Leicester University Press.

Castells, M. (1978) *City, Class and Power*, London, Macmillan.

'Cato' (1940) *Guilty Men*, London, Gollancz.

Cawson, A. (1982) *Corporatism and Welfare*, London, Heinemann.

Cherry, G.E. (1974) *The Evolution of British Town Planning*, London, Leonard Hill.

Churchill, W.S. (1951) *The Second World War. Vol. IV, The Hinge of Fate*, London. Cassell.

Clark, G. and Dear, M. (1981) 'The state in capitalism and the capitalist state', in Dear, M. and Scott, A.J. (eds), *Urbanization and Urban Planning in Capitalist Society*, London, Methuen.

Clarke, L. (1981) 'Subcontracting in the building industry', *Proceedings of 1980 Bartlett Summer School*, University College London.

Coakley, J. and Harris, L. (1983) *The City of Capital*, Oxford, Basil Blackwell.

Cockburn, C. (1977) *The Local State*, London, Pluto.

Cooke, C. (1957) *The Life of Richard Stafford Cripps*, London, Hodder & Stoughton.

Cooke, P. (1983) *Theories of Planning and Spatial Development*, London, Hutchinson.

Council for the Protection of Rural England (1981) *Planning – Friend or Foe?*, London, CPRE.

Counter Information Services (1973) *The Recurrent Crisis of London*, London, CIS.

Cox, A. (1980) 'The limits of central government intervention in the land and development market: the case of the Land Commission', *Policy and Politics*, 8(3).

Cuddy, M. and Hollingsworth, M. (1985) 'The review process in land availability studies; bargaining positions for builders and planners', in Barrett, S. and Healey, P. (eds) *Land Policy: Problems and Alternatives*, Aldershot, Gower.

Cullen, A. (1982) 'Speculative housebuilding in Britain. Some notes on the switch to the timberframe production method', *Proceedings of the 1981 Bartlett Summer School*, University College London.

Cullingworth, J.B. (1975) *Environmental Planning. Vol. 1, Reconstruction and Land Use Planning 1939–1947*, London, HMSO.

Cullingworth, J.B. (1982) *Town and Country Planning in Britain*, 8th edn, London, Allen & Unwin.

Davidson, B. (1975) 'The effects of land speculation on the supply of housing in England and Wales', *Urban Studies*, 12, 91–9.

Davies, H. and Healey, P. (1983) *British Planning Practice and Planning Education in the 1970s and 1980s*, Working Paper 70, Town Planning Department, Oxford Polytechnic.

Dear, M. and Scott, A. (1981) *Urbanization and Urban Planning in a Capitalist Society*, London, Methuen.

Dearlove, J. (1979) *The Reorganisation of British Local Government: Old Orthodoxies and a Political Perspective*, Cambridge, Cambridge University Press.

Department of the Environment (1976) *The Recent Course of Land and Property Prices and the Factors Underlying It*, London, HMSO.

Department of the Environment (1979) *Study of the Availability of Private House-Building Land in Greater Manchester*, London, HMSO.

Dickens, P., Duncan, S.S., Goodwin, M. and Gray, F. (1985) *Housing, States and Localities*, London, Methuen.

Direct Labour Collective (1978) *Building with Direct Labour*, London, DLC.

Docklands Consultative Committee (1985) *A Memorandum on the London Docklands Development Corporation*, London, DCC.

Docklands Joint Committee (1976) *London Docklands Strategic Plan*, London, DJC.

Duncan, S. (1986) 'House building, profits and social efficiency in Sweden and Britain', *Housing Studies*, 1(1), 11–33.

Duncan, S. and Goodwin, M. (1985a) 'The local state and local economic policy: why the fuss', *Policy and Politics*, 13-3, 227–53.

Duncan, S. and Goodwin, M. (1985b) *Central Control versus Local Autonomy: The Local Government Crisis in Britain 1979–84*, Geography Discussion Papers 13–15, Graduate School of Geography, London School of Economics.

Dunleavy, P. (1980) *Urban Political Analysis*, London, Macmillan.

Evans, A.W. (1983) 'The determination of the price of land', *Urban Studies*, 20, 119–29.

Eversley, D. (1975) *The Re-Development of London Docklands*, London, Regional Studies Association.

Fielding, N. (1982) 'The volume housebuilders', *Roof*, 7.6.

Fleming, S. (1984) *Housebuilders in an Area of Growth: Negotiating the Built Environment in Central Berkshire*, Geographical Papers 84, University of Reading.

Flemming, J.S. and Little, I.M.D. (1975) *Why We Need a Wealth Tax*, London, Methuen.

Foot, M. (1975) *Aneurin Bevan*, London, Granada.

Forshaw, J.H. and Abercrombie, P. (1944) *County of London Plan*, London, Macmillan.

Fothergill, S. and Gudgin, G. (1982) *Unequal Growth – Urban and Regional Employment Change in the UK*, London, Heinemann.

Friedman, M. (1962) *Capitalism and Freedom*, Chicago, University of Chicago Press.

Friedman, M. and Friedman, R. (1980) *Free to Choose*, Harmondsworth, Penguin.

Glasgow University Media Group (1982) *Really Bad News*, London, Writers & Readers.

Goldsmith, M. (1980) *Politics, Planning and the City*, London, Hutchinson.

Goodchild, R. and Munton, R. (1985) *Development and the Landowner*, London, Allen & Unwin.

Gough, I. (1979) *The Political Economy of the Welfare State*, London, Macmillan.

Greater London Council (1976) *Greater London Development Plan*, London, GLC.

Greater London Council (1985a) *The London Industrial Strategy*, London, GLC.

Greater London Council (1985b) 'Monitoring the London Docklands Strategic Plan 1976: land availability', unpublished report, Docks 354.

Habermas, J. (1976) *Legitimation Crisis*, London, Heinemann.

Hall, D. (1983) *The Cuts Machine*, London, Pluto.

Hall, P. (1974) *Urban and Regional Planning*, Harmondsworth, Penguin.

Hall, P. *et al.* (1973) *The Containment of Urban England*, London, Allen & Unwin.

Hambleton, R. (1978) *Policy Planning and Local Government*, London, Hutchinson.

Hamer, M. (1975) *Wheels within Wheels*, London, Friends of the Earth.

Hardy, D. (1983) *Making Sense of the London Docklands: Processes of Change*, Papers in Geography and Planning, Middlesex Polytechnic.

Hardy, D. and Ward, C. (1984) *Arcadia for All: The Legacy of a Makeshift Landscape*, London, Mansell.

Harloe, M. (1977) *Captive Cities*, Chichester, Wiley.

Hartley, J. (1982) *Understanding News*, London, Methuen.

Harvey, D. (1982) *The Limits to Capital*, Oxford, Basil Blackwell.

Healey, P. (1985) *Local Plans in British Land Use Planning*, Oxford, Pergamon.

Healey, P., Davis, J., Wood, M. and Elson, M. (1982) *The Implementation of Development Plans*, Department of Town Planning, Oxford Polytechnic.

Held, D. (ed.) (1983) *States and Societies*, London, Martin Robertson.

Henney, A. (1984) *Inside Local Government*, London, Sinclair Browne.

Hepworth, N. (1980) *The Finance of Local Government*, 6th edn, London, Allen & Unwin.

Hillman, J. (1983) 'High rates – a deterrent to developers', *Estates Gazette*, 265.

Hooper, A. (1982) 'Land availability in south east England', *Journal of Planning and Environmental Law*, 555–60.

Howells, C. (1983) 'The politics of local authority finance', *Critical Social Policy*, 2(2), 73–9.

Ive, G. (1980) 'Fixed capital in the British building industry', *Proceedings of the 1979 Bartlett Summer School*, University College London.

Jackson, A.A. (1973) *Semi-detached London*, London, Allen & Unwin.

Jefferys, J.B. (1954) *Retail Trading in Britain 1850–1950*, Cambridge, Cambridge University Press.

Jenkins, S. (1975) *Landlords to London*, London, Constable.

Joint Land Requirements Committee (1983) *Housing and Land 1984-1991: 1992-2000*, Housing Research Foundation, London, JLRC.

Jowell, J. (1977) 'Bargaining in development control', *Journal of Planning and Environment Law*, 414-33.

Keays, S. (1985) *A Question of Judgment*, London, Quintessential Press.

Kincaid, J. (1973) *Poverty and Equality in Britain*, Harmondsworth, Penguin.

Kirk, G. (1980) *Urban Planning in a Capitalist Society*, London, Croom Helm.

Labour Research Department (1944) *Land and Land Owners*, London, LRD.

Lawless, P. (1981) *Britain's Inner Cities*, London, Harper & Row.

Leopold, E. (1983) 'The costs of accidents in the British construction industry', *Proceedings of the Bartlett Summer School, London 1982*, University College London.

Loughlin, M. (1981) 'Planning gain: law, policy and practice', *Oxford Journal of Legal Studies*, 1, 61-97.

McRae, H. and Cairncross, F. (1973) *Capital City*, London, Eyre Methuen.

Mallinson, H. and Gilbert, M. (1983) 'The urban development grant scheme', *Estates Gazette*, 268.

Marriott, O. (1967) *The Property Boom*, London, Hamish Hamilton.

Massey, D.B. and Catalano, A. (1978) *Capital and Land: Landownership by Capital in Great Britain*, London, Edward Arnold.

Mead, G. (1983) 'The hut and the machine in a Brighton suburb', undergraduate dissertation, University of Sussex.

Miliband, R. (1973) *The State in Capitalist Society*, London, Quartet.

Minns, R. (1980) *Pension Funds and British Capitalism*, London, Heinemann.

Minns, R. (1982) *Take Over the City: The Case for Public Ownership of Financial Institutions*, London, Pluto.

Moor, N. (1983) *The Planner and the Market*, London, Godwin.

Morgan, K. and Sayer, A. (1983) *The International Electronics Industry and Regional Development in Britain*, Urban and Regional Studies Working Paper No. 34, University of Sussex.

Mowat, C.L. (1955) *Britain Between the Wars*, London, Methuen.

Munton, R. (1983) *London's Green Belt: Containment in Practice*, London, Allen & Unwin.

National Federation of Women's Institutes (1940) *Town Children through Country Eyes*, Dorking, NFWI.

Newham Borough Council (1985) *South Docklands Local Plan*.

Newham Dockland Forum (1983) *The People's Plan for the Royal Docks*.

Newton, K. and Karran, T.J. (1985) *The Politics of Local Expenditure*, London, Macmillan.

Nicholls, D.C., Turner, D.M., Kirby-Smith, R. and Cullen, J.D. (1982) 'The risk business - housebuilding in the inner city', *Urban Studies*, 19, 331-41.

Nicolson, H. (1967) *Diaries and Letters 1939-45*, London, Collins.

Nicolson, N. (1973) *Portrait of a Marriage*, London, Weidenfeld & Nicolson.

Northfield Committee (1979) *Inquiry into the Acquisition and Occupancy of Agricultural Land*, Cmnd 7599, London, HMSO.

O'Connor, J. (1973) *The Fiscal Crisis of the State*, New York, St Martin's Press.

Offe, C. (1972) 'Advanced capitalism and the welfare state', *Politics and Society*, 2.4, 479-88.

Orwell, G. (1941) *The Lion and the Unicorn*, London, Secker & Warberg.

Paris, C. (1982) *Critical Readings in Planning Theory*, Oxford, Pergamon.

Parker, H.R. (1985) 'From Uthwatt to DLT - the end of the road?', *The Planner*, April.

Pearce, B.J., Curry, N.R. and Goodchild, R.N. (1978) *Land, Planning and the Market*, Occasional Paper 9, Department of Land Economy, University of Cambridge.

Pickvance, C. (1982) 'Physical planning and market forces in urban development', in Paris, C. (ed.), *Critical Readings in Planning Theory*, Oxford, Pergamon.

Pilcher, D. (1975) *Commercial Property Development*, London, HMSO.

Pliatzky, L. (1982) *Getting and Spending*, Oxford, Basil Blackwell.

Poulantzas, N. (1973) *Political Power and Social Classes*, London, New Left Books.

Priestley, J.B. (1934) *English Journey*, London, Heinemann.

Property Advisory Group (1980) *Structure and Activity of the Development Industry Report*, London, HMSO.

Radical Institute Group (1976) *The Distributional Consequences of Town Planning*, London, RIG.

Ratcliffe, J. (1976) *Land Policy*, London, Hutchinson.

Ratcliffe, J. (1981) *An Introduction to Town and Country Planning*, 2nd edn. London, Hutchinson.

Reith, J. (1949) *Into the Wind*, London, Hodder & Stoughton.

Richardson, K. (1972) *Twentieth Century Coventry*, London, Macmillan.

Roberts, N.A. (1976) *The Reform of Planning Law*, London, Macmillan.

Rodgers, W. (1982) *The Politics of Change*, London, Secker & Warberg.

Rose, J. (1985) *The Dynamics of Urban Property Development*, London, Spon.

Rose, R. and Page, E. (1982) *Fiscal Stress in Cities*, Cambridge, Cambridge University Press.

Roweis, S.T. (1975) *Urban Planning in Early and Late Capitalist Societies*, Department of Urban and Regional Planning, University of Toronto.

Rydin, Y. (1983) *Housebuilders as an Interest Group*, Discussion Paper, n.s., 6, Graduate School of Geography, London School of Economics.

282   Whatever Happened to Planning?

Sampson, A. (1982) *The Money Lenders*, London, Coronet.

Saunders, P. (1979) *Urban Politics: A Sociological Interpretation*, London, Hutchinson.

Saunders, P. (1981) *Social Theory and the Urban Question*, London, Hutchinson.

Saunders P. (1982) 'Why study central/local relations', *Local Government Studies*, March–April.

Scott, A.J. (1980) *The Urban Land Nexus and the State*, London, Pion.

Scott, L. (1942) *Land Utilisation in Rural Areas*, Cmd 6378, London, HMSO.

Sharpe, L.J. (1981) *The Local Fiscal Crisis in Western Europe*, Beverly Hills, Calif., Sage.

Shepley, C. (1982) 'Talking to the housebuilders', *Planner News*, 9.

Shoard, M. (1981) *The Theft of the Countryside*, London, Temple Smith.

Short, J. (1982) *Housing in Britain*, London, Methuen.

Skinner, D. and Langdon, J. (1974) *The Story of Clay Cross*, Nottingham, Spokesman Books.

Smyth, H. (1984) *Land Supply, Housebuilders and Government Policy*, Working Paper 43, School of Advanced Urban Studies, University of Bristol.

Smyth, H. (1985) *Property Companies and the Construction Industry in Britain*, Cambridge, Cambridge University Press.

Solomon, M. (1980) *Beethoven*, St Albans, Granada.

Spence, N. *et al.* (1982) *British Cities: An Analysis of Urban Change*, Oxford, Pergamon.

Stedman Jones, G. (1971) *Outcast London*, London, Oxford University Press.

Sutcliffe, A. (1981) *Towards the Planned City*, Oxford, Blackwell.

Tower Hamlets Borough Council (1983) *1983 Borough Plan*.

Uthwatt, A. (1941) *Expert Committee on Compensation and Betterment – Interim Report*, Cmd 6291, London, HMSO.

Uthwatt, A. (1942) *Expert Committee on Compensation and Betterment – Final Report*, Cmd 6386, London, HMSO.

Wilson, H. (1980) *Report of the Committee to Review the Functioning of Financial Institutions*, Cmnd 7937, London, HMSO.

Wolmar, C. (1982) 'Sold down the river', *Roof*, July–August.

Young, K. and Garside, P.L. (1982) *Metropolitan London*, London, Edward Arnold.

Index